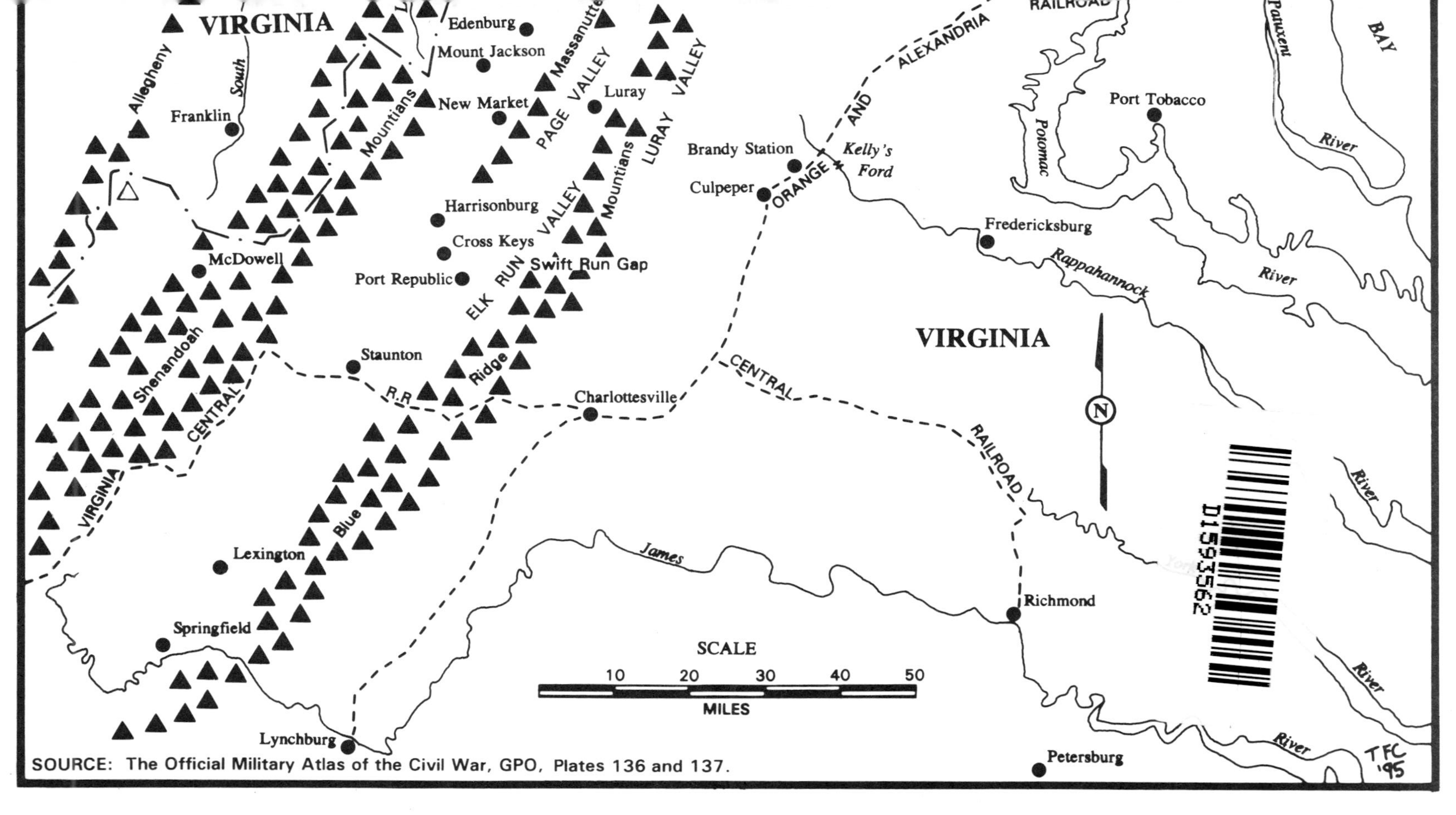

SOURCE: The Official Military Atlas of the Civil War, GPO, Plates 136 and 137.

SABRES AND PISTOLS

The Civil War Career of Colonel Harry Gilmor, C.S.A.

Sabres and Pistols

~~~~~~~~~

"Whenever the vandal cometh,
    Press home to his heart with your steel,
And when at his bosom you cannot,
    Like a serpent, go strike at his heel.
Through thicket and wood go hunt him,
    Creep up to his camp fireside,
And let ten of his corpses blacken,
    Where one of our brothers hath died.

~~~~~~~~~

(An excerpt from *The Guerrillas: A Southern War Song*, by S. Teacle Wallis.)

TO

WILFRED YOUNG,

who first sparked my passion for the study of the past.

SABRES AND PISTOLS

The Civil War Career of Colonel Harry Gilmor, C.S.A.

Timothy R. Ackinclose

Stan Clark Military Books
Gettysburg, Pennsylvania

FIRST EDITION

Published in 1997 by:
STAN CLARK MILITARY BOOKS
915 Fairview Avenue
Gettysburg, Pennsylvania 17325
(717) 337-1728

Cover photo: Barry Pipino Collection

ISBN: 1-879664-30-5

Printed and bound in the United States of America

Contents

List of Illustrations

Acknowledgements

During my work on this project, several people offered a helping hand. First and foremost, I extend my gratitude to David Dixon, Associate Professor of History at Slippery Rock University of Pennsylvania. Professor Dixon devoted entire evenings to studying my manuscript and thereby affording me key insights. Indeed, for his contribution to the following project, as well as my education in general, I will be forever indebted.

In addition, Daniel Toomey was kind enough to write an introduction to my narrative and also meticulously proofread my manuscript. His comments and suggestions, all of which demonstrated a thorough knowledge of Maryland's role in the conflict, enhanced my own work. Another historian familiar with Maryland and the Civil War, Daniel D. Hartzler, significantly facilitated both my research and the preparation of my manuscript. Although I didn't collaborate with Hartzler, his book *Marylanders in the Confederacy* enabled me to get off to a very good start on my research. Any person attempting to write a biography on a Marylander who fought for the South in the War Between the States must consult his work first. Also, Ted Alexander gave me a strong insight into the Burning of Chambersburg. His level of expertise was greatly appreciated.

I am also very grateful for the assistance that I received

when researching information pertaining to Harry Gilmor. First, the staff at the Maryland Historical Society was extremely professional. They made my hours of research in Baltimore very worthwhile. In particular, Jennifer A. Bryan, Curator of Manuscripts, took considerable time to answer any queries along the way. Also, P. James Kurapka, former Commander of the Colonel Harry W. Gilmor Camp # 1388, Sons of Confederate Veterans, kindly sent me information from the Baltimore County Historical Society. He too, offered me significant advise that improved my narrative. His generosity and encouragement was most welcome. Allow me to also extend my debt of gratitude to the Baltimore County Historical Society for information that added to my narrative.

Many others made indispensable contributions. Thomas Clemens and Brian Pohanka provided me with some important contacts. Todd Colosimo lent his professional cartography skills. His maps, which significantly enhanced the text, turned out far better than expected. Leslie Volaric worked diligently to turn my manuscript into a form suitable for publication. Her work was invaluable to my project. Finally, I am also grateful to Craig Horn and Barry Pipino who loaned photographs to enhance this study. Their excitement and encouragement spurred my efforts.

Lastly, friends and family members contributed to this project by lending support and encouragement. In particular, Brad Pflugh acted as a liaison between my advisor and the publisher. His support and strong friendship enhanced both my work and my attitude toward scholarship in a positive manner.

Introduction

The American Civil War has often been referred to as the last romantic war. The conflict began with organizations like Rush's Lancers and Cobb's Legion waging a "civilized" war that for the most part respected private property. It has also been called the first modern war. One with its aerial reconnaissance, land mines, and rapid fire weapons, that made the leap from Napoleonic tactics to the darkest side of humanity - total war!

Few participants of this war represented the evolution of military thought and action more than Harry Gilmor. Born in the upper strata of Maryland society, Gilmor was no vagabond turned criminal when the war presented an opportunity to break the law. His father was a Harvard graduate with international business connections. Harry was privately educated at his home in Baltimore County and trained in business before his independent nature led him out West to try homesteading.

Gilmor's participation in this sectional conflict is a reflection of what many young Maryland men did at the time. He returned home during the winter of 1860 and enlisted in The Towson Horse Guards, one of the many militia companies being raised in both the North and the South at this time. Following the Pratt Street Riot in April of 1861 the Horse Guards were called into service along with every other Maryland militia company during this brief period of "armed neutrality." When Baltimore City was occupied by General Benjamin F. Butler the following month, thousands of Marylanders made their way across the Potomac River to fight for the Southern Cause. Some sought to form Maryland commands while others were content to enlist in the first unit they came across.

Harry Gilmor's career from start to finish was associated with the lower Shenandoah Valley of Virginia. He first enlisted in the Seventh Virginia Cavalry, under the command of Turner Ashby. His ability to ride, shoot, and gather information led to his promotion as Sergeant Major, and later to Captain of Company F in the Twelfth Virginia Cavalry. During the Valley Campaign of 1862 Gilmor often acted on instructions directly from General Thomas "Stonewall" Jackson and the case can be made that he filled the void for Jackson after Turner Ashby's death at Harrisonburg in June of 1862.

In May of 1863 Gilmor was promoted to Major and authorized to raise an independent battalion of cavalry, assigned to General Richard Ewell's Second Army Corps; he temporarily commanded the First Maryland Cavalry Battalion during the opening stages of the Gettysburg Campaign. He was present at Gettysburg, the Chambersburg Raid, and all the major battles in the Shenandoah Valley during the war.

The gentleman's war of 1861 gave way to total war in 1864. Gilmor's battalion was active in the Shenandoah Valley and helped to siphon off a considerable amount of material and manpower from the Union armies that penetrated deeper into the Valley with each successive thrust. As the Confederate defense force withered away Gilmor was pushed to the forefront on more than one occasion. When ordered to attack the Baltimore and Ohio Railroad and disrupt the flow of Federal supplies he captured and burned a train. During the raid some of his men began to rob the passengers. Gilmor was vilified by the Northern press but it is highly unlikely that his prewar life of wealth and privilege would have allowed him to ever consider personal gains of that nature.

Gilmor and General Bradley T. Johnson brought the war to many parts of their native state during a raid around Baltimore in the summer of 1864. While exciting, Gilmor accomplished little due to the diminutive size of his strike force. Their trip to Chambersburg, Pennsylvania, a few weeks later would be a different story. Gilmor would receive orders to burn the town in retaliation for the wanton destruction of private property in the Shenandoah Valley. Bradley Johnson would personally find the order impossible to carry out.

By the end of the war Gilmor was considered a hero by the people of the Shenandoah Valley and many pro-Southerners back home. His association with such Confederate leaders as Ashby, Jackson, Stuart, Fitzhugh Lee, Breckinridge, and Early bear witness to his many accomplishments. For this he paid a terrible price. Gilmor was imprisoned three times during the war and wounded four.

When the war ended, Gilmor, like Bradley T. Johnson and many other Marylanders, did not return home immediately. He lived for awhile in New Orleans. When he did return to Baltimore County he became an officer in the Maryland National Guard and a police commissioner of Baltimore City. Visits to his grave site are still a part of that police department folklore. Gilmor was also a successful businessman until the cumulative effects of his wounds brought about a premature and agonizing death.

In 1866 *Four Years in the Saddle* was published. Written in collaboration with Colonel Francis H. Smith, the book has drawn criticism from both his contemporaries and modern historians. While his very presence during an engagement would have been credit enough, Gilmor's account tends to overplay his part in the outcome. It would be instructive to know how much of this was the work of his ghost writer. Regardless of the error factor, it cannot be denied that *Four Years in the Saddle* was one of the first Civil War memoirs ever published and Harry Gilmor was one of the South's most successful partisan rangers.

Daniel Carroll Toomey
Linthicum, Maryland

Preface

In 1866, Harper and Brothers published *Four Years in the Saddle*, the war memoirs of Colonel Harry Gilmor. Gilmor, raised in the tidewater region of the border state of Maryland, went south a few months after the opening salvos of the Civil War in order to cast his lot with the Confederacy. Using surprise and savvy, Gilmor's Second Maryland Cavalry Battalion struck fear into the hearts of his Union adversaries in the Shenandoah Valley. As with many Civil War participants, Gilmor kept notes of his activities, and his memoirs, published only one year after the guns fell silent, provide the historian with a fresh insight into the role played by partisan fighters in the Valley.

In the latter half of the twentieth century, Civil War scholars have been quick to criticize Gilmor's memoirs. In *Gray Ghosts and Rebel Raiders*, Virgil Carrington Jones labeled the Marylander an "extrovert" and a "pistol shooting egotist." Jones's work remains the classic, comprehensive study of Civil War partisan warfare, and his unflattering convictions concerning Gilmor have remained relatively intact. Two decades later, James I. Robertson, Jr., another brilliant student of the period, called *Four Years in the Saddle* into question. Robertson concluded that the book was "unreliable" and "abounds in errors." Lastly, Robertson took issue with the memoirs because they were ghost written.[1] With such renowned names expressing reservations with the Marylander's accounts, it is not surprising that many are skeptical when first reading *Four Years in the Saddle*.

The original objective of the following study *was not* to prove the veracity of *Four Years in the Saddle*. The goal was, however, to create an objective, meaningful biography of Harry Gilmor. By reading *Sabres and Pistols: The Civil War Career of Colonel Harry Gilmor, C.S.A.*, the reader will hopefully have a better understanding of partisan warfare in the Shenandoah Valley and the impact irregulars had upon Union strategy and tactics in the region. Also, *Sabres and Pistols: The Civil War Career of Colonel Harry Gilmor, C.S.A.* sheds light on both phases of the conflict: the gentlemen's war and total war. Gilmor was at the very heart of the transition between both phases of the conflict.

In order to maintain objectivity, the narrative is a synthesis of primary accounts, archival material, and secondary sources. Since Gilmor is the subject of this biography, the narrative detailing his war experience is of necessity centered around *Four Years in the Saddle*. When possible, accounts from other participants are incorporated into the story. However, in a few cases, due to vast differences in accounts of actual participants in an event, a neat synthesis was impossible. In cases such as these information was placed in explanatory notes, thereby not disturbing the flow of the narrative.

Irrefutably, Gilmor's memoirs contain errors, both in factual and chronological nature. Despite these shortcomings, there is a strong basis of truth in his accounts, as demonstrated by a careful evaluation of primary documentation from participants on both sides of the conflict. Rarely can a person in a large historical drama remember events with perfect precision. Gilmor was no exception. However, his errors in detail and dates are not enough to erode his overall credibility. Jones was correct in his description of Gilmor as an "extrovert" and "egotist." Gilmor's personality was one of strong, defiant independence and keen daring. These characteristics are extremely pronounced in his memoirs. Confidence, recklessness, and daring are all common traits of a bold partisan commander. Indeed, these same terms can easily be used to describe the Cause for which he fought, and others died.

1

"The Yankees Are Coming!"

On a busy, foggy harbor front in Scotland a handsome twenty-one year old Robert Gilmor was carefully observing workers cautiously load valuable merchandise into his cargo ship. Gilmor, who began his career with his father's counting business, was preparing to embark on a venture to the Chesapeake region, where American colonists anxiously awaited the arrival of the precious goods. This was his second journey to the colonies in as many years. However, this time, in 1769, the young Scottish merchant would decide to remain in America, settling in St. Mary's County, Maryland. Thus, the seed of the Gilmor family was planted in the tidewater region along the Chesapeake. The Gilmors would not only sparkle in Maryland's social and political limelight, but they would also leave an indelible mark on the history of the United States.[1]

After the Continental Congress formally declared independence from Great Britain, Gilmor joined the St. Mary's County militia. In 1778 Gilmor's military service ended and he moved to Baltimore, where the patriotic merchant entered into partnership with two other successful mercantilists from Philadelphia. One year prior to the official conclusion of the American War for Independence, Gilmor traveled to Amsterdam, Holland, where he represented a firm that boasted, among other prestigious Americans, the renowned financier Robert Morris. Morris's firm wanted Gilmor to establish a business network in the Dutch city that would enable them to export staple products to western European markets from Virginia and Maryland. Gilmor's efforts in Holland were successful and he eventually entered into partnership with the firm. The Baltimorean then decided to reside in Amsterdam for a short period of time, where he could be in close proximity to the center of his business interests. Gilmor's partnership with Morris, financial connections with the Baring Brothers, bankers in England, as well as a keen knowledge of mercantilism, particularly the tobacco trade, propelled him up the social and economic ladder among European and American elite.[2]

Returning permanently to Baltimore just prior to the turn of the century, Robert Gilmor allowed his two sons, William and Robert, to form a partnership with him. Robert Gilmor and Sons would prove a sound business venture. While keeping a close eye on the ledgers belonging to Gilmor and Sons, Robert, along with other representatives of Maryland's elite, was involved with the creation of the Bank of Maryland, the construction of Fort McHenry, and the collection of books for the Baltimore Library. Gilmor was also extremely instrumental in forming trade connections with Calcutta, China, and Russia. Lastly, Gilmor and other prominent Baltimoreans raised money to aid 1,500 refugees from St. Domingo (present day Haiti) who arrived at their city's doorstep after fleeing the French island colony in wake of a bloody slave uprising.[3]

During the first decade of the nineteenth century, with European trading vessels driven from the oceans due to the war in Europe, wealthy United States merchants, such as Gilmor, prospered under an almost complete American monopoly of world trade. However, soon the British began to seize American vessels and impress United States seamen, leading Gilmor and other prominent Baltimore merchants to sign a memorial requesting that the national government redress the impressment controversy. By the end of the first decade of the new century American trade policy began to hinder commerce, and the War of 1812 had a further detrimental impact upon American tradesmen. For example, "Baltimore merchants Robert Oliver and Gilmor together were sitting on three million pounds of warehoused tobacco in 1814."[4]

The Gilmor family was able to weather the storm of financial distress stemming from events of the period, and by the time of his death in 1822, Robert Gilmor's sons were well prepared to continue the financial legacy that he created. The second Robert, in addition to boasting a reputation as a keen merchant, was a gentleman who freely passed through the esteemed intellectual and philosophical circles of western Europe and the United States. He also served proudly as the president of the Maryland Academy of Science and Literature. As a proud patron of the arts, the second Robert eventually boasted a large, much admired collection. Gilmor's art collection was almost equaled by his fabulous wine cellar, which he encouraged guests to exploit judiciously, saying "Fill what you please, but drink what you fill."[5] As with his father, the gifted painter Gilbert Stuart made a portrait of Robert; a portrait by such an esteemed artist served to highlight his standing in the Maryland culture.[6]

Robert Gilmor's brother, William, like his predecessors, boasted a prestigious, affluent background characteristic of the Gilmor clan. In 1799, he married Marianne (Smith) Drysdale, who was widowed from the late Dr. Drysdale of Northampton County, Virginia. All told, their union produced eleven offspring, including a son, Robert, in 1808. Robert III graduated from the prestigious Harvard College in 1828 and during the next several years served the United States as an attache in Paris, France. As with his grandfather, the young Robert interacted with the political and economic elite in both America and Europe. He was the guest of the great Scottish poet and novelist Sir Walter Scott at his Abbotsford estate near Edinburgh, Scotland. Gilmor was so impressed with the beauty of Abbotsford that his own estate, "Glen Ellen," was based upon a similar design. In particular, "the sunken gardens and terrace" situated on Gilmor's estate were modeled after those seen on the Scottish writer's holdings. The mansion overlooking the plantation was equally lavish. The Gilmor castle "contained twenty-five or more bedrooms, a large library, [and] a circular ballroom, chief glory of Glen Ellen." The ballroom was adorned with "stately bay windows mullioned with colored glass ... [and] its walls were handsomely ornamented with plaster moldings of fruits, flowers, and conventional designs." Finally, "a gallery running around the ballroom provided a place for spectators and musicians." Glen Ellen was named after Ellen Ward, a native of Baltimore, who Robert married after his return from western Europe. The union would produce nine sons and two daughters.[7]

One son, Harry, was born January 24, 1838. Harry Gilmor, as indicated by his family heritage, was born into a caste of privilege, rank, and honor. Gilmor was educated by a private tutor from Harvard at his father's Glen Ellen estate. The future partisan ranger also served a machinist apprenticeship with the Vulcan Iron Works and later worked as a clerk with William Fisher and Sons. It appeared as if Harry was almost predestined to follow in his forefathers' established footsteps, and his handsome, well endowed six-foot tall stout frame seemed to indicate that even nature tended to bless the Marylander. A tan complexion, high forehead, and a properly groomed mustache touched off facial features that were sought after by not a few Southern belles during the war years. However, Gilmor made his way westward to Wisconsin and Nebraska, where he made an attempt at homesteading.[8] Perhaps a dispute with his father turned Gilmor toward the independence of the western frontier, a marked antithesis to his elite social standing in Maryland. Or, maybe it was Gilmor's penchant for ruggedness and adventure, so obvious during his service to the Confederacy, that drew the rambunctious young man westward.

Gilmor would eventually return to Maryland, where he would continue farming, this time applying the plow to his father's soil. Gilmor made his return to Maryland just as the state's internal divisiveness was being inflamed by the larger political uncertainty in the United States during the late 1850s and early 1860s.[9] Indeed, with the Confederate bombardment of the Federal force stationed at Fort Sumter in April 1861, the Old Line State, situated at the crossroads between the pro-Union North and the states of the Deep South who were seeking their independence, clung to a precarious neutrality. Maryland would watch her youth answer the calls of both President Lincoln in Washington as well as the blossoming number of Southern regiments that were augmenting their ranks in northern Virginia that summer and fall. The secession of the Upper South, namely Virginia, North Carolina, Tennessee, and Arkansas only served to heighten Maryland's strategic importance to both sections while simultaneously highlighting her own internal political division.

The eastern and southern parts of the state, with its tidewater culture that had as its major underpinnings large tobacco plantations, associated more with the agricultural South than the industrially oriented North. Furthermore, Maryland's mercantilists, inextricably tied to the tobacco economy, were pushed further into the Southern camp every time Northern officials offered demands to Congress for higher tariffs to protect their neophyte industries. Conversely, the rugged topography of western Maryland housed a populace who demonstrated a pro-Union, antislavery attitude. Thus, when in April 1861 the Maryland legislature formally rebuked secession, it was a fine veneer over the internal heated debate between the Unionists and "the Sesesh." "The Sesesh" referred to those wealthy tobacco plantation owners, mercantilists, and other Marylanders who favored secession. The Gilmor family figured prominently on the side of the secessionists, as the terrible spring of 1861 was about to set upon Baltimore.[10]

As the sound of the guns at Fort Sumter echoed throughout the divided nation, President Lincoln became concerned for the safety of Washington; if the Upper South bolted from the Union and the border state of Maryland followed suit, the Federal capital would be hazardously situated like an island in a sea of secession. Soon the Sixth Massachusetts Regiment was ordered dispatched to the beleaguered capital. The Sixth Massachusetts, under the charge of Colonel Edward F. Jones, would have to travel through Baltimore, which, with its railroad and geopolitical location, was considered by the Washington government as the main artery for the defense of the Northern capital. On April 19, the New Englanders were rudely welcomed by a group of Baltimoreans, who resisted the Massachusetts regiment by pelting them with bricks, stones, and even occasional pistol shots as they passed through the Maryland city. The militia defended themselves, firing randomly into the hostile crowds. The melee would result in extensive damage, but more importantly, twelve Baltimoreans were killed and an untold number were wounded. Maryland blood was now spilled. All told, Jones counted four killed and thirty-nine wounded as a result of the fracas.[11]

In the nucleus of the tempest during that misty, overcast day, was Harry Gilmor. Gilmor was a corporal with the Baltimore County Horse Guard, one of the many paramilitary volunteer organizations that were formed in that turbulent winter and spring of 1861. The future Confederate cavalier was temporarily detached from the Horse Guard, which was preparing to assemble in Towsontown the following afternoon.[12] Always wanting to be in the center of the action, a penchant so very pronounced during his service to the

Confederacy, Gilmor took charge of the efforts to defend the armory of the Fifth Regular Maryland Guard. A mob of rioters, thus far armed with mostly bricks and a few other weapons, eyed the nine-hundred Springfield Rifles situated in the Fifth Maryland Guard's armory. Gilmor and a small command of about fifteen men of the Fifth Maryland Guard forced their way through the crowd and into the armory building. Once inside the arsenal, the Marylander ordered ten men to go up a flight of stairs into the armory proper. There, they were to fix bayonets and prepare to charge. Another group, composed of only five men armed with broken chair legs, were assembled on the steps inside the arsenal. They were the first line of defense between the reckless mob and the Springfields. While he was hastily organizing the men, the ferocious mob began breaking the large doors to the arsenal, which finally gave way to the sheer weight of the bodies pushing against them. Second Sergeant Edward Ayrault Robinson, of Company A, Fifth Maryland Guard, was with the group on the steps. He would later commit his observations to paper:

> All at once the doors gave way and on they came like an avalanch [sic], but they were met by our clubs and fists and feet. We soon had the steps blocked with fellows we had knocked down, and felt relieved when we heard the tramp, tramp of the men coming down the steps. We retreated behind them, and the sight of cold steel being too much for the mob they retired to the sidewalk to curse and howl.[13]

Quite early Gilmor demonstrated a penchant to lead men into the thick of the action.

As the city began to settle, Marshal of the Baltimore Police George Kane hurried a message off to Bradley T. Johnson, warning his fellow Marylander that "Fresh hordes [Northern invaders] will be down on us to-morrow [sic]." Kane desperately concluded that "We will fight them and whip them or die." Johnson, an influential Maryland Democrat, was busy attempting to coordinate the efforts of several volunteer companies in the state that were preparing for an anticipated large-scale Union invasion. On the following day several of these companies shuffled into Baltimore in response to Kane's telegraph and the wild rumors of a possible Yankee invasion that were spreading like wild fire through Maryland. One company arrived from Frederick, and soon two cavalry troops from Baltimore County appeared in the city. Soon, Baltimore's defense was bolstered by light artillery, the Patapsco Light Dragoons, Garrison Forest Rangers, Howard County Dragoons, Independent Grays, and the Maryland Guard (six companies), among others. Maryland Governor Thomas H. Hicks ordered the bridges north of the city destroyed in order to slow the movement of Northern forces into Baltimore. He would later deny giving the order.[14]

One of the two cavalry forces that arrived in Baltimore immediately following the riot was the Baltimore County Horse Guard. More likely than not, Gilmor rejoined his comrades in the Horse Guard in time for their march into Baltimore. The Horse Guard Company was conceived on January 15, 1861, in Towsontown, situated just outside of Baltimore. Here, a number of Baltimore County Southern sympathizers gathered, and undoubtedly fearing Northern retaliation against the portions of their state that favored states' rights, urged the formation of a cavalry company. The next week would see the official organization of the Horse Guard, along with the election of its officers. The Horse Guard numbered fifty-three men, and they wore "a blue frock coat bearing Maryland state seal buttons, gray pants, and black slouch or 'army' hat."[15]

During the following month the Horse Guard was armed with "weapons consisting of fifty sets of .36 caliber Whitney 'navy' revolvers, Ames cavalry sabres, belts, cartridge boxes and holsters." The Horse Guard "was [also] attached to the First Regiment of Cavalry, Maryland Militia." Not unlike similar military units that were forming throughout eastern and southern Maryland during this period, the Horse Guard met once a week to drill and discuss tactics as well as other concerns of the outfit. In April they were mustered in Towsontown, their native town, and then proceeded to make their way toward Baltimore, to defend the city and the Old Line State.[16]

On April 21 a young Baltimorean by the name of Gist Cockey, along with a companion, rode into Baltimore screaming "The Yankees are coming, the Yankees are coming!" They promptly rode to Colonel Kane's office with the news that five thousand Pennsylvania soldiers (the actual number being twenty-four hundred) were stationed in the vicinity of Cockeysville, north of Baltimore. The Northerners choose to encamp there due to the burned bridges that prevented their movement south. Corporal Gilmor and the Horse Guards were ordered back to Towsontown, in order to patrol the countryside near the Federal encampment. However, to avoid a confrontation, President Lincoln consulted with Mayor Brown of Baltimore and Governor Hicks and ordered the Pennsylvania force back to Harrisburg. Also, he agreed that no additional Northern soldiers would be sent through Baltimore on their way to Washington. As the Federal force headed northward to their destination, a handful of Horse Guard men followed and destroyed several rail bridges along the route. Such a move was intended to insure the safety of Baltimore against another Northern movement on their soil.[17]

The issue with Maryland was far from settled. On April 27 President Lincoln suspended the writ of habeas corpus in an area that stretched from Philadelphia to Washington.[18] The embattled President simply could not risk the supply of troops and armaments to the Federal capital. The ultimate defense of the Union, with its inherent liberty and equality, paradoxically demanded extra-Constitutional measures. In the hearts of many Baltimoreans sprang the contention that the only way to preserve their liberty and way of life was to flee and fight against the government that nominally guaranteed such political amenities. In essence, they believed they were choosing "Liberty without Union," rather than "Union without Liberty."

The events in Maryland during late April only worsened the already heated tension and divisiveness within the Old-Line State. According to one witness, "the people were divided politically and socially, life long friends passing each other without speaking." The debate between loyalists to the Union and the Sesesh even made its appearance in families, where "men and their wives quarrelled [sic] over the question of the day." One man, an ardent advocate of the Union, stated sadly that "I was cut in the street evry [sic] day by my lady friends, and cursed by the men." The Union man also commented upon the changing nature of many of the religious people of Baltimore. For instance, one elderly woman who was considered to be one of the most religious representatives of the community, "turned into a very demon, and among other of her kind the Christian remarks made about unionists, and Yankees, was that every Yankee ought to have his heart cut out with a butcher knife."[19] Indeed, it appeared that both the Constitution as well as Christianity could not heal the bleeding sores of a nation tearing asunder.

On May 13, without official authorization, Major General Benjamin Butler sent Federal forces into Baltimore and occupied Federal Hill, a strategic location that afforded an advantageous view of the city. Immediately after occupation, Butler ordered a halt to all supply shipments to the South (from Baltimore) and outlawed the formation of military organizations. In addition, all existing militia units were disbanded. These units, such as the Horse Guards, showed too much steadfastness toward their cause during the April disorder, and the new Federal occupiers thought their elimination a must. Not surprisingly, many who served in such outfits found their way to the Southern rank-and-file during the War of the Rebellion. Furthermore, the display of any secession flag, such as the "Stars and Bars," was outlawed. The day after his move into Baltimore, Butler was recalled, but the tactical position on Federal Hill was bolstered by artillery. The Union guns located on Federal Hill and at Fort McHenry (which served as a Federal prison) were meticulously placed so as to prevent a possible pro-Confederate attempt to retake the hill. In addition, the guns overlooked most of south Baltimore, with its lucrative shipping harbor.[20]

With their city under Federal occupation and civil rights denied, many Baltimoreans found themselves in the summer of 1861 either under strict Federal surveillance or imprisoned at Fort McHenry. The Gilmor family, due to their economic heritage and elite status, both of which blended neatly into ardent Southern sympathies, found themselves under close Federal scrutiny. Other prominent city inhabitants, such as Ross Winans, capitalist and politician, as well as police commissioner Kane, were placed in the federal stockade at Fort McHenry. During the latter weeks of August, Harry Gilmor would take his place in a cell in Fort McHenry due to Federal convictions that he was communicating with the Confederates. In a strange irony of history, the headstrong Gilmor was detained in an improvised Federal bastille that his great-grandfather, Robert, raised the needed funds to construct over a half century earlier.[21]

After detaining Gilmor for two weeks in Fort McHenry, the Federal officials decided to release the Marylander, and on August 30, 1861, he "crossed the Potomac River at the mouth of Cherry Run." After entering Virginia, the future partisan ranger managed to spend the night at a friend's house located at Bunker Hill.[22] Before retiring to bed that evening, Gilmor probably relived in his mind the last four months in Baltimore. No doubt he heard over and over again as he dosed off to sleep the sounds of Baltimoreans debating the right of secession and his orders to report to Cockeysville, where he and other Marylanders would see possible combat with the Pennsylvanians located there. Even more so, he could perhaps never forget the strict government surveillance of his family and his own confinement in Fort McHenry. At any rate, Gilmor "carried a much lighter heart, and breathed more freely," now that he was in Virginia. "That night's sleep was a sounder [sic] one than [he] had known in some time past."[23]

Thus, without the pomp and pageantry of a farewell parade such as thousands of men in both the North and South were treated, Gilmor, like many of his Maryland compatriots, slipped clandestinely across the border into Virginia. While some had a vested economic and political interest in a Confederate triumph and were socialized within an elite Baltimore culture that related more with the Southern aristocracy than the wealthy industrialists of the North, others deemed it their duty to flock to the side of their Southern brethren. "'Old Virginia needs assistance... and like the knights of old rushed into the conflict, their battle cry on their lips: A rescue! A rescue! Virginia and the South.'"[24]

Gilmor was a son of the South, imbued with the traditions of a distinct and parochial culture, where honor and personal courage were at the core of a constellation of values. He viewed the Union forces passing through his native state as an invasion. For a young hot-blooded Southerner, this was tantamount to a challenge in the tradition of the code duello. This Union challenge, combined with his own sense of adventure and Southern patriotism, propelled him to join his brethren across the Potomac. It was a decision that sparked the career of one of the South's most noted partisan rangers.

2

"If I Follow You, I Go Far Enough"

The day after Gilmor made his relatively uneventful entry into Virginia, he traveled with a friend to Charles Town. A short time later the rebellious Marylander made his way to Camp Turner, a Confederate cavalry bivouac. Gilmor walked curiously around the camp, until a group of men who were engaged in conversation captured his attention. As the future guerrilla approached the crowd he began to recognize some of the men as his comrades in "Captain Charles Ridgeley's [sic] company of [the] Baltimore County Horse Guards." However, lying upon the grass in the midst of the Marylanders was Lieutenant Colonel Turner Ashby of the Seventh Virginia Cavalry. Gilmor could make out Ashby's "gallant" features, "his sad, earnest gray eyes, jet-black hair and flowing beard." He reflected for a moment on what he saw and "said to himself, 'If I follow you, I go far enough.'"[1]

That day Gilmor decided to join Lieutenant Colonel Ashby's command and enlisted in Captain Frank Mason's Company (Company G). Mason's unit was composed exclusively of Maryland men, which obviously acted as a magnet for those Marylanders like Gilmor who fled to Virginia to take up the Cause. However, for most Southerners who had an insatiable thirst for adventure and shared those Southern cultural traits of chivalry and honor, Ashby was their commander *par excellence*. Until his death in 1862, men south of the Mason-Dixon Line would continue to flock to his command. In one incident in October 1861, hundreds of young men wished to volunteer under his command. However, since he was still a subordinate officer to Colonel Angus McDonald in the Seventh Virginia, they refused to enlist. These volunteers, like so many others who flocked to the Seventh, demanded that they take their orders only from Lieutenant Colonel Ashby - no other commander would do.[2]

Shortly after joining the Seventh Virginia, Gilmor saw his first action in his service to the Confederacy. Lieutenant Colonel Ashby managed to penetrate northward and came to a halt at Bolivar Heights. Bolivar Heights overlooked Harper's Ferry, which was nestled a mile to the east. Lieutenant Colonel Ashby asked for two volunteers to enter the "Ferry proper" and discover the numerical strength and disposition of the enemy. Gilmor and George James, a fellow Baltimorean, quickly volunteered. The two men slowly made their way down Shenandoah Street, when, suddenly, a group of Union troops armed with Enfield rifles appeared from their hiding places and greeted the curious Confederates in a most unceremonious manner. The Marylanders wheeled their horses quickly, Gilmor coming so close to being struck by a Yankee bullet "that splinters of lead lodged in his skin." However, Ashby's men, who were properly positioned on a bluff overlooking the enemy's position, managed to scatter the Northern soldiers.[3]

Skirmishes such as these provided Gilmor with an opportunity to sharpen his skill as a soldier. Whereas he was lacking experience as a fighter, the Marylander was in no way uncertain of his skill as a marksman. With his forty-four caliber Colt revolver Gilmor would pluck tin cups and apples off the heads of his equally daring, if not foolhardy, comrades. For a wager, the boastful Marylander would also gallop full speed down a roadway, filling each telegraph pole with lead as he passed. As Union and Confederate accounts would show, there was good reason to fear Gilmor's accuracy with the revolver.[4]

Also, but of no less importance, shared fighting experience provided the cast in which friendships were molded. Warner Welch and Gilmor formed a strong mutual admiration from the very beginning of the war, and when the Baltimorean formed his own company the following year he appointed Welch his first lieutenant. Another comrade, Thomas Gatch, also a resident of Towson, was a sergeant in the Baltimore County Horse Guard. Gatch, not unlike Gilmor, would be wounded during the war. Thaddeus L. Thrasher, a hot-headed firebrand, provided all of those who knew him with a great many anecdotes to share with generations after the war. Friends such as these ate together, rode alongside one another in the Shenandoah countryside, and relied upon each other during a daring cavalry raid. They were indeed the substance that held together a fighting force.[5]

During another brief skirmish with a small Yankee force in September, Gilmor and seven others captured a group of prisoners. Lieutenant Colonel Ashby ordered Gilmor to take the prisoners off to Richmond, the Confederate capital, for confinement. Upon returning, Gilmor saw his first major action of the Civil War. Ashby decided to force a Federal unit from their position on Bolivar Hill (Heights), and eventually drive the enemy out of the town. On the evening of October 15 Ashby received reinforcements, thereby bringing his force on the morning of the assault to some three hundred militiamen and 180 cavalry troopers. This included Captain Frank Mason's Company and two artillery pieces. Across the Shenandoah River, on Loudoun Heights, a Confederate force was stationed in order to prevent Federal reinforcements.[6]

On the morning of October 16 the Rebels struck at the Union strongholds. Mason's company was placed at the extreme left of the Confederate assault and was soon ordered by Lieutenant Colonel Ashby to strike at a field-piece, which the Federals had concealed among some rifle-pits and log-pens. Gilmor, in order that he might concentrate upon the enemy, placed his company flag in a fence corner. As Gilmor was blazing toward the Yankee forces with his sorrel, he quickly overcame the rest of his column. Amidst the excitement, the sound of horses galloping and the crackle of gunfire, Gilmor heard Tom Gatch yell, "Hurrah for old Baltimore County!" which encouraged the Marylander. The disgruntled Northern forces, who retreated from the Heights to Lower Bolivar (a small town half mile east of Bolivar Heights), now opened fire with a vengeance, wounding three of Mason's men as they made their way to the top of the Heights. However, during the morning's attack, no Confederate trooper lost his life.[7]

Then disaster struck. During a limited Northern counter thrust, the command in charge of the large, twenty-four pound gun panicked, and, in their haste to remove the weapon, unwittingly snapped the gun's axle-tree. The tide of battle now began to turn. Lieutenant Colonel Ashby requested five volunteers to take over the firing of the smaller rifled piece and Gilmor was promptly placed in charge of the crew. The rejuvenated Northerners, with an entire regiment, went on a massive counteroffensive, threatening to outflank the Rebel forces. Gilmor was ordered to retreat with his rifled piece in hand, but, sensing that the Yankees were too close to move back safely with the gun, he decided to get off one more shot at the advancing enemy. The force of the blast caused the wheel to strike Gilmor on the hip, sending him falling down an embankment. However, the force at the receiving end of the blast proved far more devastating to the Northerners, who suffered eleven men killed and wounded as a result of the explosion.[8]

The Confederate position was no longer tenable, and after four hours they retreated back to their enemy's original picket line, counting one killed and nine wounded. Lieutenant

Colonel Ashby, despite the operation's failure, offered an official commendation to his officers and men for "their gallant bearing during the whole fight," especially in light of their inexperience and "bad arms." On the other side, Moses O'Brien, First Lieutenant of Company C, Third Wisconsin Volunteers, also complimented his men for their gallant behavior and "great bravery and coolness under galling fire."[9]

As early as the middle of October, 1861, reports trickled into official headquarters on both sides of the conflict concerning the war's increasing brutality. In one case a frantic writer told Confederate President Jefferson Davis about the pillaging and ravaging of Virginian holdings south of Harper's Ferry by Union soldiers. He also warned that the enemy would attempt to destroy woolen factories and flour mills located along the Shenandoah River. Also, in an official report detailing the recent fighting at Bolivar Heights, Colonel John Geary of the Twenty-eighth Pennsylvania Volunteers described how several Southern cavalrymen desecrated and mutilated the bodies of four Union soldiers who were killed in action. Geary expressed his conviction that such inhuman treatment could spark retaliatory acts on the part of disgruntled Union troops. Incidents such as these were microcosms of what was to come in 1864 and 1865, as the conflict mutated into a "total war." Gilmor, as he rested after his first fighting at Bolivar Heights, could not have known that his military career would transverse both phases of the War Between the States.[10]

Since September of 1861, the Confederate military leadership was concerned with damaging the Chesapeake and Ohio Canal, which was built alongside the Potomac River. Damage to the canal could disrupt a major supply route for the Federal garrison located in the vicinity of the Northern capital. Unable to do direct material damage to the canal, during that month Gilmor and a group of Southern sharpshooters would clandestinely sneak down to the edge of the canal just before the break of daylight and conceal themselves. Then, during the day, the Rebels would pop at the Federal soldiers and boats as they passed. Union efforts to discover the concealed Confederates became as futile as the Rebel attempt to permanently disable the canal. However, by the middle of December the Rebels attempted to destroy two dams, Dams Number Four and Five, situated on the Potomac northwest of Harper's Ferry. Damage here could consequently render the canal useless.[11]

On December 17, shortly after Colonel Ashby appointed him sergeant major of his command, Gilmor took part in the Southern attempt to destroy dam Number Five. A Confederate force containing two rifled pieces were tactically placed over a bluff which looked down upon the Yankee positions, but had to be vacated after Union soldiers opened "a very hot fire of musketry." In addition to the guns, a lieutenant and sergeant, in their haste to get out of range of the Yankee fire, vacated their horses in the vicinity of the guns. Colonel Ashby soon galloped up and explained to a subordinate officer that the guns and horses had to be brought to safety, but not a man in the force volunteered for the hazardous mission. Gilmor turned to his faithful comrade, Welch, and suggested that they should bring away the Confederate property. Gilmor and Welsh made their way toward the horses and rifled pieces by crawling, and, when they were within approximately two hundred yards of their objective, the enemy from the canal opened up. The Confederate duo then sprinted toward the horses, unfastened them, leaped upon their backs, and placed their bodies snug to the horses' necks, in order to lessen the target they provided the enemy. When back at camp, Gilmor and Welch returned the horses to their owners and admonished them by saying, "Gentlemen, here are your horses. Don't get them into such a tight place again." It would not be until December 21 that a breach was made in the dam.[12]

After such a breathtaking mission, Gilmor decided to take

a short respite at the base of a knoll, when Colonel Ashby approached the tired Marylander and informed him that a "Captain Moore, of the Second Virginia Infantry, was in a very precarious position in a large mill." Ashby concluded by telling Gilmor that he wanted him to carry an important message to the embattled Moore. Gilmor would undertake the mission alone and on foot. He managed to reach the mill safely, using the cover of a number of rocks and trees, which afforded him protection from the deadly Federal fire. After delivering his dispatch, Gilmor returned to camp fearing that he might receive a grapeshot in the back along the way - "a soldier's dread," since his back was exposed to the enemy. For the Civil War soldier, to be wounded in the back would make him appear cowardly, thereby irreversibly damaging his reputation among his comrades at the front and family and friends back home.[13]

During this last month of 1861 Major General Thomas "Stonewall" Jackson reviewed the last details of his ambitious plan to capture the Federal garrison at Romney, western Virginia. By surprising the Union garrison at Romney, Jackson assumed that such a move would lead General George McClellan, commander of the Army of the Potomac, to the hasty conclusion that General Joseph Johnston's army was significantly weakened in the vicinity of Centerville. According to "Stonewall," McClellan would then order an attack in that area. After the initial Federal assault, Jackson's force, supplemented by General William Loring's, who was charged with the task of seizing and later occupying, Romney, would together march to central Virginia and deliver a defeat to the unsuspecting McClellan. Afterwards, Loring would march westward and reoccupy northwestern Virginia.[14] Gilmor would find himself in the center of the tactical operations of what would become known as the infamous "Bath and Romney expedition."

As the first step in his plan, Jackson ordered that the Union garrison at Romney, under the command of General Benjamin Kelley, be isolated by dispersing Federal forces located at Bath and Hancock. In addition, key telegraph lines situated in the mountainous region would be cut. Jackson realized that marching through this region was difficult under the best conditions. However, the first heavy snowfall of 1862 only exacerbated the already treacherous mountain trails. Conditions notwithstanding, General Jackson believed that his men "[would] be prepared to make the sacrifice when animated by the prospects of important results to our cause, and distinction to themselves."[15]

As the Confederate forces that were earmarked to carry out Jackson's plan awaited the order to move out from their headquarters in the northern Shenandoah Valley, a severe winter storm howled through the countryside. Reverend James B. Averitt, Chaplain of the Seventh Virginia, was with Gilmor and his comrades during that awful month. Averitt was, according to an officer, an ardent follower of the Lord and wholly devoted to the Cause, and his presence in this regiment was a "good [influence] upon the popular mind" of the men. However, facing the harshness of the brutal cold, the chaplain may have excused some of his spiritual convictions in order to face the immediate reality. It appears that the Episcopalian carried "a flagon of whisky" to warm his "inner being." Gilmor, upon discovering that the reverent Averitt had alcohol on his person, "stole it from his ambulance and distributed it among the field officers, claiming that he "did not believe in parsons drinking spirits." Undoubtedly, Gilmor's desire for the parson's "spirits" emanated more from his own desire for fortitude against the cold than it did from his need to be the chaplain's moral steward. Needless to say, Averitt was furious when he discovered his loss.[16]

On January 1, 1862, Jackson's command set off from Winchester on their trek that would eventually take them to Romney. Colonel Ashby's cavalry, along with Gilmor, formed the vanguard of Jackson's operation, which started under bright, clear skies that served as a welcome reprieve from the usual bitter weather. By the second day additional forces were added to Jackson's offensive, bringing the total number of men to approximately 8,500. In the meantime, a force under Colonel Ashby broke away from Jackson's main command with the objective of enlarging the breach made in Dam Number Five the previous month.[17]

Late on the third day of the campaign, darkness began to cover the countryside, just as Jackson's men were forcing Federal skirmishers back towards Bath. Jackson thus decided to rest his men until morning. The brightness of the first day of the campaign gave way to horrific weather, as winter came back with a vengeance. The demands of the campaign tested the fortitude of all of Jackson's men. Some who made the appalling trek did so without shoes, while many others retired hungry at night without a campfire or even blankets for warmth. Rebels who went to sleep at night often awoke covered by several inches of snow. As each man arose it appeared as if he was rising from a grave, leading one jocular Southerner to exclaim, "Great Jehosophat! The Resurrection!" Even the teetotaler "Stonewall" Jackson succumbed to the hardship of the bitter cold. It appears that the general drank large gulps of what he thought was wine, but was instead whisky. Soon Jackson was sweating and complaining of being warm, despite the precipitous drop in temperature. He unbuckled his overcoat and several buttons on his uniform, and he began to discuss several diverse topics. Paradoxically, the terrible weather and infamous campaign provided a backdrop in which many humorous anecdotes were born.[18]

On January 4 Jackson was finally able to enter Bath, which was so hastily vacated by the Federals that they left behind a large amount of supplies for their attackers. Gilmor, one of the first to enter the town, advanced with his fellow Confederate horsemen and proceeded to "cut down" or capture all Yankees who retreated from Bath. The Southerners gave chase to the Union troops as far as the bluffs of the Potomac, beyond which lay Hancock. Suddenly, the Southern horsemen ran into an ambush. Posted along both sides of the road outside Bath, Federal infantry were concealed, awaiting the unsuspecting horsemen. The Confederates found it extremely difficult to wheel their horses on the icy, hazardous roads. In many instances their horse's legs gave out from under them, causing both man and beast to tumble to the ground. A Lieutenant Lontz had both his arms snapped by musket balls, one of which entered his body. The lieutenant's horse, panicked by the yelling Confederate officers, sound of cracking rifles, and the general confusion, threw Lontz to the ground. Gilmor aided a handful of men as they managed to carry off the soldier's broken body.[19]

By the morning of the sixth, General Jackson considered Hancock too heavily fortified to attempt its seizure without a tremendous loss of life. However, admitting that he could not take the town, Jackson still wanted to cut the telegraph wires above and below the quaint, Maryland town. This would considerably reduce communication between General Banks in Frederick, Maryland, and his counterpart, General Rosecrans in western Virginia. During the prior evening, Jackson and Colonel Ashby, who had rejoined Stonewall on the fourth after his operations against the dam, summoned Gilmor and asked him if he could cut the telegraph lines to the north and south of Hancock, as well as take out a water-tank that was located in the area. Gilmor thought about the query, and then, in a rare moment of self-doubt, replied that he did not know if he could accomplish the mission. Jackson then stated, "'Why, Colonel Ashby says that you can. Well, general, if Colonel Ashby says so, then I can do it,' Gilmor replied." With the issue now settled, the General remarked coolly, "Then, sir, go and do it as quickly as possible."[20]

Gilmor took two of his comrades, a Jim Buck and William

Kemp. Buck had invaluable knowledge of the surrounding area. The trio slipped out of camp that night and finally made their way to the telegraph poles. Harry climbed atop one of the poles and began chopping at the wire. He soon attracted the attention of Union pickets, who greeted him with inaccurate fire. After completing the destruction of the telegraph wires, the men became disappointed as they approached the water-tank; the Confederates would be unable to burn the water-tank due to its stone composition. Gilmor reported the results of the mission to "Stonewall." Jackson, after hearing the results replied by simply saying "'Good,' bade Gilmor a good night, and turned over in his blanket and went to sleep."[21]

Just one day after Gilmor, Kemp, and Buck cut the wires above and below Hancock, Colonel Ashby ordered Gilmor to take about fifteen to twenty men and raid the Alpine Depot, on the Baltimore and Ohio Railroad. The depot itself was situated "opposite of Hancock, on the Virginia side of the [Potomac] river."[22] In addition to the Yankee force stationed there, "a long train of cars, filled with army supplies," was in the depot.[23] As the clandestine Rebels slipped quietly into the depot with their wagons, Gilmor stood awestruck by the large amount of supplies and other materiel.

> Such quantities of stores at one view I had never before seen. There was case after case loaded with shoes, and clothing of all kinds; sugar, coffee, whisky, molasses, and stores of every description, besides haversacks, knapsacks, canteens, and two cases of Enfield rifles - the aggregate value not less than half a million dollars.[24]

Gilmor and his entourage made their way back to camp; some of the men, with the wagons full of the seized Yankee goods, carried what they could on their backs. Back at camp Gilmor informed a captain, whose men were lacking many of the essentials for warfare, of the discovery. Soon the officer and many of his men, with Gilmor as their guide, made their way to the Alpine Depot, where they plundered the Yankee depot. What could not be carried away as booty, Colonel Ashby ordered destroyed by fire.[25]

Jackson's command managed to reach Romney during the middle of the month, only to discover that the enemy vacated it earlier. He ordered General Loring's forces to take up position in Romney. Loring's extreme left brushed the Allegheny Mountains to the south, while his right stretched out along the South Branch to the Potomac River. His command protected the fertile Moorefield Valley as well as three major roadways providing access to the Shenandoah Valley. With his losses counted at four killed and twenty eight wounded, Jackson no doubt concluded that the winter campaign was at a successful conclusion.[26]

Almost immediately after Loring was ordered into winter quarters at Romney, several of his officers, spurred by his approval, petitioned Richmond for their withdrawal. Loring and his command were against Jackson's "winter campaign" from the very beginning, and now it appeared as if they would be isolated in the frigid confines of Romney. The pleas from Romney had their desired effect, and the Richmond government ordered Loring's force be moved closer to Winchester. Jackson complied with the order, but at the same time forwarded his conditional resignation to War Secretary Judah Benjamin.[27] For Jackson, the fruits of victory that were gleaned during the recent expedition now became the agony of defeat due to the intervention of the Confederate government.

Jackson's tender of resignation was officially withdrawn. Furthermore, the incident did nothing to tarnish his growing reputation among the Southerners who followed his commands. However, it would be during the spring of 1862, during that famous campaign that would later bear his name, that he reached the apex of his career in the Confederate Army and became forever endeared to the Southern people. Gilmor provided invaluable tactical support for Jackson's Bath and Romney expedition, and during the famous Spring campaign of the following year, he will serve as a scout for the indomitable Jackson. According to one Southern officer, Jackson "never forgot him nor his fidelity. After the death of Ashby (June 6, 1862) Gilmor in a measure took his place in the Army of the Valley."[28]

3

"They Must All Rally On Myself"

As demonstrated by the ten months following Fort Sumter, the Northern forces were not going to be able to hand "Johnny Reb" a quick drumming. However, as the sun dawned upon the spring days of 1862, the military situation for the South was no less precarious. Marching toward Richmond was General George McClellan's Army of the Potomac, which boasted over 100,000 well-equipped and well-disciplined Union soldiers. Meanwhile, stationed at Fredericksburg was General Irvin McDowell's force. McDowell's command was to be bolstered by General Nathaniel Banks's army which was then serving in the Shenandoah Valley. Union officials designed a plan by which the McClellan and McDowell-Banks combined force would march upon the Confederate capital and thus bring the rebellion to a conclusion.[1]

In addition to the movement of Federal forces in northern Virginia, the Southern government became increasingly concerned with the growing number of guerrilla bands that were plaguing the Shenandoah Valley. Some of these bands were composed of men who despised discipline and were motivated more by plunder and brutality than allegiance to either side. These forces tarnished the reputation of the Confederacy. Other partisan forces in the region openly sided with the Southern war effort. For example, in the mountainous landscape of western Virginia, Union authorities were frequently harassed by pro-Confederate guerrillas who attacked Federal pickets and burned property belonging to those who fought for the North. Back in the Valley, one Union colonel warned his superior officer to keep a close vigilance upon the rear of his army as he moved through the Shenandoah due to the number of guerrilla units in the area that sought vengeance for "rapes and other crimes committed by Union men."[2]

In another case, Brigadier General Robert Schenck, who was encamped near Franklin, reported that a small group of Federal scouts were ambushed by a party of "bushwhackers," who managed to "beat out the brains" of a Union soldier that was captured.[3] Union Assistant Secretary of War Peter H. Watson summarized his feelings concerning guerrilla bands in a blunt telegram to Major General McDowell:

> Like pirates and buccaneers they [irregulars] are the common enemies of mankind, and should be hunted and shot without challenge wherever found. Such treatment would soon put a stop to the formation of guerrilla bands and to the assassination of sentinels and other barbarities practiced by those who engage in irregular warfare.[4]

Official reports such as these often found their way into Northern newspapers, which crystallized public opinion against the South. These "bushwhackers" were an embarrassment to the Confederacy, and more important, detrimental to their war effort.

While the snow melted on the peaks of the Blue Ridge Mountains and the ice disappeared from atop the crystal clear streams of the Shenandoah Valley in March of 1862, Harry Gilmor contemplated raising his own cavalry command. After receiving Colonel Ashby's permission, Gilmor did indeed begin to form a company. He was awarded a commission in late March and on April 10 the future partisan ranger was officially appointed a captain. Gilmor's close friend, Warner Welch, became the first lieutenant of this company, which was composed of men exclusively from the Old-Line State. Gilmor's company would not remain in the Seventh Virginia Cavalry, for in June of the same year it was attached to the Twelfth Virginia Cavalry, under Colonel Arthur Harman's command.[5]

In late March, after Gilmor's company was organized, the Marylander reported with twenty of his men to General Jackson. The general ordered Gilmor's command to be equipped "with Mississippi and Derringer rifles" and sent them off to "Lieutenant Colonel J.R. Jones, who was the provost marshal of Harrisonburg."[6] Gilmor was about to receive his first test as a company commander.

Jones ordered Gilmor's force, which was supplemented by a militia company, to dissolve by force of arms a group of irregulars whose area of operations were the Blue Ridge Mountains in the vicinity of Swift Run Gap, located approximately twenty miles southeast of Harrisonburg. This guerrilla force, under the command of a man named Gillespie, was composed of somewhere between two hundred to five hundred men, all of whom resisted service in the Confederate Army. As Gillespie's band illustrates, not all Southerners favored the new Confederate government. When Gilmor's command arrived at the base of the Blue Ridge Mountains, the militiamen refused to give chase to the band through the scenic mountains and their hazardous passes. After three days of charging the elusive band into the base of the mountains with just his own unit, Gilmor, who showed little results for his efforts, reported the failure to General Jackson. Jackson then commanded Jones to lead the entire operation against Gillespie, and he further ordered artillery and "four companies of sharpshooters" in a renewed attempt to break up the band. This time the Confederates were successful, pushing the irregulars out of the mountains and capturing forty eight men, all of whom Gilmor marched to captivity in Harrisonburg.[7]

Thus Gilmor, who would later gain a reputation as a ferocious partisan commander in the Shenandoah Valley, saw his first action as a company commander against irregular forces. Here, he no doubt learned something about the effectiveness of partisan operations. It was irregulars such as Gillespie's unit, and to a much larger extent Champ Ferguson and William Quantrill's bands, that would somewhat tarnish the reputation of all partisan forces, Gilmor's not excluded. For many officials on both sides of the struggle, all partisan forces, regardless of their affiliation with the Confederacy, were nothing more than "bushwhackers."

In early March, General Banks marched his 38,000 man army upon Winchester. A short time earlier, President Lincoln had ordered this handsome, stately political general to rid the Shenandoah Valley of Jackson's force, then move eastward to aid in McClellan's operations against Richmond. On March 11, as a result of Banks's movement, Jackson left his winter quarters at Winchester and hustled his small command of 4,600 men southward. Some ten days later, Confederate officials learned that a portion of General Banks's army (General James Shields's division) was preparing to leave the Valley and join McDowell in the combined Union efforts against Richmond. Jackson quickly moved his force "down the Valley" or, from the South's perspective, northward, back towards Winchester. At Kernstown, just outside of Winchester, Jackson gave battle to a Northern force that turned out to be much larger than what he expected, with the result that "Old Stonewall" was soundly beaten and had to retreat back up (southward) the Valley. However, Jackson's defeat was actually a strategic victory for the Confederacy. President Lincoln began to fear that the South was preparing a march on Washington. Thus, he ordered McDowell to take up the defense of Washington and General Banks to remain in the lower Shenandoah.[8]

Jackson's situation in the northern Shenandoah was still poor. Out of the west, General Robert Milroy was moving toward the southern half of the Valley and threatened to form a junction at Harrisonburg with the victorious Banks. Fearing that these two armies would march together upon Staunton, in early May, General Jackson's army left the Shenandoah. The stealthy Jackson disposed segments of his force in order to protect the rear of what appeared to be his retreating force. However, Jackson used the Virginia Central Railroad to quickly return his hardy command to Staunton. Here it was joined by General Edward Johnson's Brigade as well as eight hundred of Ashby's cavalrymen (Gilmor's company included).[9] This new enlarged army of nearly nine thousand men marched westward, where they struck Union General Milroy's force at McDowell on May 8, 1862.[10]

The Confederates attacked with a vengeance, forcing their way through McDowell one day after opening the assault. General Milroy's force, which was augmented by General Schenck's command, were both thrown into a hasty retreat northward toward Franklin. At Franklin, the battered Union forces awaited the arrival of reinforcements from Petersburg, located approximately thirty miles to the north. The Confederates followed up their victory at McDowell by pursuing the retreating Yankees, eventually encountering heavy Union resistance at Trout Rock, situated on the South Branch of the Potomac. Mountains to the left of Trout Rock provided splendid opportunities for sharpshooters to plug away at the road below, whereas the mountain to the right was buffeted by the South Branch itself. The hills in this area were sprinkled with Federal sharpshooters, who were determined to prevent the thus far unchecked Confederates from moving to the north. Jackson, realizing that Milroy and Schenck's commands were still dazed, ordered that the offensive continue, thus, Trout Rock would have to be cleared of Yankee forces. However, three consecutive assaults upon this "natural" Federal fortress only resulted in failure.[11]

Captain John Q. Winfield, temporary commander of the Seventh Virginia, perhaps disgruntled by Jackson's growing impatience over their failure to take Trout Rock, rode up and asked Gilmor to take ten men and see if he might succeed where the others had failed. Gilmor selected the first ten men who were standing next to him, and after they galloped a short distance, he told the force that when he gave the signal, "they must all rally [upon him]." The Federal fire lessened, and Gilmor gave the signal to his men to rally. The Confederates charged with a "Rebel yell" that "was echoed by [the entire regiment] that was standing in full view of the affair." Upon making their way through the horrid defile, the ten Confederates moved "to the right," where they observed the entire Federal line. Leaving his ten man party under the command of Lieutenant Hurst, Gilmor made his way alone to Jackson and reported his findings. After another report, Jackson ordered the Federal lines shelled, thereby forcing the Yankees to within a short distance from Franklin.[12]

Sometime during his company's scouting operations for Jackson in the vicinity of Franklin, Gilmor was sitting near the general when suddenly a shell blasted a large oak tree that was only a few feet away. Fortunately for Jackson, the mighty oak fell in the opposite direction. Upon witnessing Jackson's good fortune, Gilmor briskly walked up to the general, exclaiming, "My gracious! general, you have made a narrow escape." Jackson did not hear the startled captain the first time, but when Gilmor informed "Stonewall" about the recent incident he simply replied, "Ah! you think so, sir - you think so." Jackson remained where he was and, turning to Gilmor, warned the Marylander to seek some shelter for his troops. Gilmor concluded that "fear had no lodgment in that man's breast;" his conviction was a consensus among all who followed or interacted with the general.[13]

A few days after the fighting at Trout Rock, Jackson's

army held a religious service in order to render thanks to God for the blessings that He had bestowed upon their victorious legions in the recent fighting at McDowell. The "divine service" was held in close vicinity to the front, and as Jackson's adjutant Robert L. Dabney gave a sermon to the men the crackle of shots could be heard in the distance. Gilmor and the rest of the Confederate soldiers carefully inspected the reticence of the reverent Jackson, as "not a muscle changed during the whole service."[14] Jackson, with his blend of "iron will" and strong religious convictions, became a demigod to Southern people everywhere, as news of his impressive victories in the Shenandoah that spring began to seep into every crevasse of the Confederacy.

As the Confederate guns were pounding away at Trout Rock, General John C. Fremont moved a poorly supplied division of his army off to Franklin. Later, on May 14, the remnants of Fremont's army reached Franklin. "The Pathfinder," upon observing the Confederate screen that Jackson established in front of Franklin, incorrectly assumed that the Confederate general decided to retreat. As history would show, Jackson was not on the retreat, but actually on the offensive. Stonewall "was returning to the open country of the Shenandoah Valley, hoping, through the blessing of Providence, to defeat Banks." For just one day prior to his decision to disengage the Union force at Franklin, he received an urgent message from General Robert E. Lee, telling him to move his "foot cavalry" back into the Valley and prevent "Banks from going either to Fredericksburg or the Peninsula."[15]

The "thin curtain" of Confederate forces Fremont spoke of in front of his army at Franklin was actually two companies, one of which was Gilmor's. Gilmor's company, however, was soon replaced by Captain Thomas Sturgis Davis's Company G. The future partisan was asked to take his company and scout Fremont's movements west of the

Shenandoah Mountains, while Jackson moved his army back into the Valley. Jackson depended upon Gilmor for precise reports concerning Fremont's activities, especially important being details pertaining to any possible move by the Union general eastward, which could threaten "Stonewall's" left or rear as he made his way down the Valley.[16]

Once in the Valley, Jackson moved his force northward toward Banks, whose army was situated at Strasburg. Banks was totally unaware of Jackson's movement and released Shields's division to join General McDowell at Fredericksburg, leaving his own army with only seven thousand men. Jackson, with his own force augmented to eighteen thousand with the addition of General Richard Ewell's men, moved to Front Royal. At Front Royal Jackson wished to be in position to prevent Shields's movement eastward and possibly cut off Banks's retreat route to the north. Banks decided to retreat, Jackson giving chase all the way to Harper's Ferry, with the result that Shields was ordered to retrace his steps back to the Valley. Thus, once again Jackson, by his triumphs in the Shenandoah, was having a detrimental impact upon Northern operations in eastern Virginia.[17]

Gilmor was still closely monitoring Fremont's movements west of the Shenandoah Mountains. As Gilmor observed Fremont turn his army onto the Wardensville Road to begin its trek eastward, the scout correctly assumed that the Union politician-general was attempting to block Jackson's retreat path up the Valley. Gilmor ordered "a trusty courier" to inform Jackson, whose Army of the Valley was near Charles Town, of his observations. On the evening of May 31 another scout warned Jackson that Shields was at Front Royal and Fremont had just passed Wardensville; thus, Jackson realized that if these two forces were to meet in the center of the Valley, his path of escape would be "hermetically sealed." Fortunately for Jackson, the two Federal generals were moving their forces at a leisurely pace toward Strasburg. Jackson quickly raced his "foot cavalry" through the impending Union vice and halted his march along the upper South Fork of the Shenandoah River, all the while being sluggishly pursued by the two Federal forces. However, his exhausted soldiers had enough fortitude for two more battles. On June 8 he defeated Fremont at Cross Keys, and on the following day, Shields at Port Republic.[18]

While the Southerners mourned the death of Turner Ashby, who perished protecting the rear of Jackson's main force as it moved up the southern end of the Valley, they stood amazed and elated by Jackson's triumphs.[19] Jackson's Spring Campaign of 1862 would be recorded in the annals of military history as one of the most daring operations of the war. General Jackson defeated four Federal armies, but more importantly, he interrupted Union plans around Richmond. General Lee called Stonewall's campaign "the cause of the liveliest joy in this army as well as in the country."[20] Gilmor, even as a scout, was invaluable to Jackson's success, keeping him aware of Fremont's movements west of the Valley.

During the Shenandoah Campaign, many of Jackson's "foot cavalrymen" suffered from blistered, sore feet, aching legs, and utter exhaustion. As they passed over the dusty Valley trails, many complained about what they perceived as the leisurely, carefree existence of the Southern cavalryman. However, for those who served with Gilmor west of the Shenandoah during Jackson's spring campaign, there was little time for carefree activities. For example, Gilmor and the scouts had to keep a constant vigilance on "the Pathfinder's" movements. When not scouting, the cavalrymen rode days without sleep behind enemy lines to ensure that accurate reports arrived at Jackson's headquarters. Furthermore, in addition to his uniform and equipment, the Southern cavalryman would spend at least two hours per day maintaining his mount. Also, the supply shortage in the Confederate Army was particularly acute in the ranks of the cavalry. Many cavalrymen seized equipment, weaponry, and later in the war, horses, from their Union adversaries. However, these hardships notwithstanding, most Southern horsemen had high morale and would not have traded their mounts for a pair of torn, hole-ridden, dusty infantry boots.[21]

Approximately one week after Jackson's dual victories at Cross Keys and Port Republic, the Seventh Virginia Cavalry was reorganized. It was during this time that Captain Gilmor's Company was assigned to the Twelfth Virginia Cavalry, where it would be listed as Company F. Gilmor soon reported to Brigadier General Beverly H. Robertson, who was in Harrisonburg at the time. Robertson, a strict disciplinarian, ordered Gilmor "to take command of the picket post in [the] Page Valley."[22]

Gilmor set off from Harrisonburg with command of both his own company and that of Captain Achille Murat Willis. Willis was appointed captain of his own troop in March of that year. Gilmor was quickly made permanent commander of the post, which was located near Luray, and four more companies were added to his force, making six companies, or approximately a total of 180 men under his charge. To guard against possible Yankee incursions, Captain Samuel Brown Coyner, a twenty-four-year-old lawyer by profession and boasting a six-foot one-inch frame, placed his pickets on guard outside the post. However, Coyner did not establish his picket line far enough away from the post and a large Union force was able to come in close vicinity to Gilmor's camp. The six companies under Gilmor's command had just enough time to organize their wagon supply and send it off toward White House Ford. In the meantime, Gilmor's men formed for battle within Luray proper, for the purpose of covering the retreat.[23]

The townspeople, upon discovering that their quaint Shenandoah village was about to become the center of a serious skirmish, pleaded with the Maryland captain to move his force out of the city. Gilmor obliged, forming his troops along the turnpike one hundred yards outside of the city limit. The trusted Lieutenant Welch was placed in command of Gilmor's rear guard, which was still in Luray. While retreating, Welch's command came up in a fast gallop, hotly pursued by three to four hundred Federal cavalrymen. Gilmor had his back to the wall. He had to fight it out or face losing the entire wagon train. The Marylander ordered a charge, with his own company in front; the Rebel counterattack was a success, and the Federal force split into two, along both sides of the road to Luray, thus leaving the route open to the possible recapture of the Shenandoah village. Gilmor sensed that this was a trap, for the Federals hoped that the Confederate cavalrymen would go all the way into Luray, where they could be readily surrounded. Gilmor barked, "Flank out to the right and left," while he took a seven man command with him across a lush Virginia field. The command's goal was to eventually cross a fence located at the opposite end of the clearing; however, to Gilmor's dismay, within twenty yards of the fence about six Federal soldiers made a most unwelcome appearance. One Yankee informed his commanding officer of their find, "Here they are, captain." The disgruntled Northern captain rode up to his men and curtly queried, "Why in the hell don't you fire?" Gilmor then took aim at the Federal captain, but his gun malfunctioned; he fired again, and this time his ball lodged in the captain's chest. As the wounded Federal officer fell from his horse, another Confederate placed a ball into the Union man's head. Gilmor eventually rejoined the rest of his command, and, with his own force in the rear checking the pursuing Northern troops, managed to get his whole force over the Shenandoah River to Scrabble Town.[24]

Gilmor boasted that his force of only 180 men held in check a Federal force "that had more than four hundred cavalry alone." Confederate victories against such odds bore testimony to the shared convictions of Southerners and

Northerners alike which held that "the ferocious Southern horsemen, the centaurs of the Southwest, were to trample down" their Northern adversaries, who they thought were nothing more than "greasy mechanics, small fisted farmers, and mudsills."[25] However, battles at Kelly's Ford and Brandy Station during the following year would gradually erode the belief in the superiority of the Southern cavalry. By war's end the Union cavalry would reign supreme over their adversary on the field of battle. Commenting upon the cavalry in the Army of the Potomac, one Confederate officer conceded, "but for the efficiency of this force, the War would have been indefinitely prolonged."[26]

Gilmor requested reinforcements from Brigadier General Robertson, who obliged, sending the partisan two more companies. Augmented with these additional forces, Gilmor, employing four companies, raided a main Union encampment in the vicinity of Luray, seizing prisoners, horses, and much needed supplies, before falling back to Thornton's Gap. However, Luray was still too well fortified to assault, due to both the size of the Federal force there as well as its well placed pickets. Gilmor was then ordered to report to Harrisonburg, where he met his new colonel, Arthur Harman, of the Twelfth Virginia Cavalry. After some small action with the Union enemy, Harman ordered Gilmor and a small force of Confederates to ride to Winchester "with a flag of truce to release some Federal surgeons taken at the battle of Cross Keys." While there Gilmor and his comrades were barraged, this time by neither Federal shells nor soldiers, but Southern women. The women brought encouragement to their soldiers' hearts as they shouted "God bless the gray-backs, and God bless the rebels." The Confederates were treated to refreshments, several hand shakes, and "greetings yet more tender" by their pretty Southern hostesses.[27]

In early August, Gilmor took his command out of the Shenandoah, this time eastward, into the Rapidan River Valley, where he raided local Federal forces. Suddenly, on August 9, the lull that blessed this segment of Virginia was interrupted when Union forces under the command of General Banks slammed into the Confederate flank at Cedar Mountain, almost turning it. However, the arrival of General A.P. Hill's force turned the tide of battle in favor of the South, as he pushed the Federal army back. Gilmor's command, which was off scouting near Madison Court House the day before, was hurried to the rear of the Southern force and was subsequently unable to engage in the more ferocious combat until that night. Gilmor, with Harman's consent, was permitted the opportunity to go to the front. He observed a fellow Baltimorean, a Lieutenant Featherstone, who was under a heavy Union artillery barrage. While Gilmor stood there, several Confederates fell due to the fierce Yankee shelling. Gilmor was about to leave the area when a Union shell came screaming through the trees so close to him that he felt the wind of the projectile. Then with a vengeance, it rammed into the young Featherstone, tearing apart a portion of his head before going completely through a horse and into the body of another before it finally exploded, "tearing him [the horse] to atoms." Three other Southern men lay dead; all of whom were decapitated. The Battle of Cedar Mountain, though a victory for the South, resulted in the death of Brigadier General Charles H. Winder. Winder, a Marylander who was labeled by a fellow Confederate as "handsome and attractive in person...dignified and courteous in manner," was a disciplinarian who commanded the Stonewall Brigade. His services to the Southern Cause would be sorely missed by the Confederacy.[28]

In early September 1862, General Lee, now commander of the Army of Northern Virginia, moved his force toward Maryland, desperately in search of a victory on Northern soil that would shatter the teetering Union morale and perhaps spark a French and British mediated peace that would favor the South. The Confederate Army marched into Maryland and "positioned itself at Frederick on September 7."[29] A week later, Gilmor, perhaps setting aside his better wisdom, decided to visit his friends and relatives in Baltimore, only thirty miles away. His companion for the short trek convinced him, beyond his best wishes, to visit a friend's house seven miles on the outskirts of the city. Unknown to the Confederate duo, a contingent of Union soldiers and Baltimore policemen were stationed at the residence in search of alleged contraband that was on its way to the South. Gilmor and his comrade nonchalantly galloped right into the yard, only to find themselves surrounded by the soldiers and police at gun point. The two were ordered off their mounts and then marched to Baltimore on foot, all the while being taunted by their Union captors.[30]

Gilmor, appearing very conspicuous to the Union authorities, especially in light of the large Southern force that just several days prior had entered Maryland, was charged as a "spy" by the Provost Marshal of the Union Middle Department. Labeled a spy, Gilmor would be denied the opportunity to be exchanged. Rather quickly, the captain was moved to Fort McHenry for confinement in the middle of September.[31]

Captain Gilmor was treated humanely by his Federal captors at Fort McHenry. He was afforded the privilege of having visitors, both friends and family members. He was also allowed to walk along the fort's ramparts. However, Captain Robert W. Baylor, of the Twelfth Virginia Cavalry, who was incarcerated at Fort McHenry on December 22, 1862, had a different view of conditions at the prison. Baylor describes the room (which was actually an old stable) and the sustenance that he shared with thirty other prisoners.

> This building was full of vermin, and I roosted on a roof-brace, preferring to risk my neck at this altitude

> rather than sleep in the infected quarters below. Our fare here was exceedingly hard. Black water, called coffee, and hard-tack, for breakfast and supper, and bean soup for dinner. No meat was cooked with the beans, and none was necessary, for the worms in the beans furnished the requisite grease. The coffee was made in the same camp-kettle as the soup, without rinsing, and appeared with a greasy scum on top.[32]

Whereas Baylor had a negative view of his room and food, he agreed with Gilmor concerning the amicable treatment they received from a Lieutenant William Morris. Gilmor referred to the New Yorker as a "gallant officer and [a] kind-hearted gentleman."[33]

On December 6, Gilmor was "turned over to his father" by the Federal officials in Baltimore. The captain's father, the affluent Robert Gilmor, posted a five thousand dollar bond, thereby purchasing his son's release.[34] However, his sentence was not up, for he was "ordered to report to General Dix at Fortress Monroe," which he did four days before Christmas. Gilmor was then "immediately sent to the steamer *Metamora*, which lay off the mouth of Hampton Creek, where [he] remained until January 2, 1863." On that day a tug boat pulled up along side the *Metamora*, and Gilmor, who expected to be exchanged in the next couple of days, was informed that there would be no exchange for Confederate officers held in Union stockades. This was due to Lincoln's countermeasure against President Davis's "promise to turn over captured Union officers to state governments for punishment as 'criminals engaged in inciting servile insurrection.'"[35] Lincoln ordered Confederate officers detained pending action taken by the Southern Congress. Thus Gilmor bade farewell to his fellow prisoners on the steamer and went aboard the tug boat, which took him to Fort Norfolk, where a Captain Johnston took Gilmor to his new prison, "which was located on the second floor of the old magazine." While detained here Gilmor received several lady visitors, among whom were his cousins. On February 13, 1863, just as Gilmor was making plans to escape, he was sent back to Fortress Monroe, were he was finally exchanged.[36]

The year 1862 was one of triumph and defeat for the twenty-four-year-old Baltimorean. For on one end of the spectrum, he aided "Stonewall" Jackson during his tremendous Shenandoah Campaign and was himself elected captain of his own company during the spring of that same year. However, on the other hand, for his own impetuousness and adventurism, or perhaps just a simple desire to visit loved ones and friends, Gilmor found himself captured and imprisoned by Federal forces. Such were the changing tides of war, an emotional continuum of "ups and downs" that was shared by all soldiers and officers on both sides of the conflict. Even the Confederacy itself was not excluded from the unsympathetic cycle of victory and defeat, as it would witness the miracles of 1862 overshadowed by the enormous setbacks of 1863. Gilmor, released from the Northern stockade in February 1863, was determined more than ever to stand by his Confederacy, no matter what the hands of fortune or fate chose to deal the Cause for which he fought - and others died.

4

"Marked Bravery and Cool Courage"

Eighteen hundred and sixty three proved to be a transition year for the young, dashing cavalier from Baltimore County. During this third year of the War Between the States, he continued to scout and raid as he did the previous year, and in 1863 such missions were complemented by regular fighting at Kelly's Ford and Gettysburg. However, in the midst of these major battles and raiding exploits, a partisan battalion was born, and Gilmor was commissioned a major. Following his capture and exchange, Gilmor made his way back to the Shenandoah, where he was refreshed by a renewal of old friendships. His stay in the Valley from mid-February to the middle of the following month was inactive, and after a fifteen day furlough Gilmor crossed the Blue Ridge Mountains and made his way to Culpeper, where a court-martial trial was in session. While there Gilmor first met "the twenty five year old commander of [Jeb] Stuart's horse artillery, John Pelham," who arrived a short time earlier in response to a report that a large body of Union cavalry had crossed somewhere along the upper Rappahannock. The "Boy Major," who saw his early days on a plantation in Alabama, quickly gained the respect of General Lee, who said of the young Pelham, "it is glorious to see such courage in one so young." The report that called Pelham to Culpepper was correct, and soon Yankee and Rebel guns were to blaze away at each other on St. Patrick's Day of 1863.[1]

In the early morning hours of March 17, approximately three thousand Federal cavalrymen, supplemented with an artillery battery and scores of dismounted troopers, launched an attack at Kelly's Ford and quickly grasped a foothold on the Confederate side of the Rappahannock River. The Union assault was led by Brigadier General William W. Averell, who wished "to test the new independent cavalry organization" as much as he desired to pummel his rival Brigadier General Fitzhugh Lee. Lee and Averell, former classmates at West Point, were locked in personal competition, and Lee added to the friction by challenging the Federal officer "to bring some coffee with him if the Yankee cavalry could summon the nerve to cross the [Rappahannock] river."[2] Averell responded to Lee's brazen request, but, instead of bringing "coffee," he unleashed three thousand high spirited Union troopers, who were determined to dispel the notion of the South's superiority in cavalry forces.

Gilmor was asleep during that dawn when an excited major burst into his room and informed him, in an almost nonsensical manner, of the surprise Yankee movement. Gilmor, who was "delighted [by] the thought" of serving under the reputable Stuart and Fitz Lee in a cavalry contest, wasted no time in preparing himself for battle. He soon entered the streets of Culpeper and observed the stunning cavalier Jeb Stuart with the "Boy Major" John Pelham by his side. Gilmor rode up to the duo and asked Stuart if he could accompany him into battle as a member of his personal staff; the general's reply was a hardy affirmative. The three quickly made their way out of Culpeper, as the Marylander raised his hat to Miss Bessie Shackelford, who was patriotically waving her handkerchief while she gayly cheered the gallant officers. When the horsemen "passed by the Fifth Virginia, Major John W. Puller shouted to Gilmor, 'Harry, leave me your haversack if you get killed,'" to which Gilmor replied by an affirmative nod. The three eventually reached the outskirts of town, where they followed Fitzhugh Lee's brigade (which could muster only eight hundred men for battle) toward Kelly's Ford, located ten miles east of Culpeper.[3]

Before reaching the ford, the advance halted as a body of concealed Union troopers were spotted in a small thicket known as Jamison's Woods. In response, Lee began to form his brigade along the left side of the road, while General Stuart observed the awaiting enemy. Lee exclaimed to Stuart that "I think there are only a few platoons in the woods yonder. Hadn't we better 'take the bulge' on them at once?" Stuart concurred and ordered the Third Virginia to prepare for a charge, while a squadron of sharpshooters were sent forward on foot. Gilmor, never hesitant about entering areas where some "fun" was about to occur, received permission to temporarily leave Stuart and go into battle with the sharpshooters. Captain James Bailey, who led the squadron, quickly had his horse knocked out from under him; Gilmor, noticing the troubled captain, took command of the men and ordered an attack on a stone fence that concealed a number of Union sharpshooters. The men made it to within two hundred yards of their objective, when they were pelted with tremendous Union fire. Despite Gilmor's orders, the men began to panic and retreat. Then Stuart galloped in among them and rallied the startled Confederates by warning them that "if they ran they would leave him by himself." Jeb further exclaimed, while waving his cavalry hat, "Confound it, men, Come back." Gilmor became concerned with Stuart's welfare and convinced the Southern chieftain that his men were now in good order. With the situation under control, Stuart ordered Bailey, who had found a fresh mount, to place his men behind a fence only fifty yards before the enemy's position. Gilmor stood in awe at the selfless bravery and cool composure demonstrated by Jeb Stuart and said under his breath, "I have never seen one bear himself more nobly."[4]

Later in the battle, General Fitzhugh Lee sent Gilmor with

a dispatch to Colonel Thomas Rosser, ordering him to take his regiment and sweep past the Yankee left and thereby get between them and the ford. Gilmor, after delivering Lee's message, set off with Rosser and his column toward "that [same] infernal stone fence," which extended down to the river, in search of a gate in which to pass his column. While passing through a rocky hollow about forty yards from the fence, the Union sharpshooters opened upon the flank of Rosser's column, dropping many men and horses within the ranks. Gilmor and Rosser kept moving forward despite the hot fire and observed, behind a wooded thicket near the ford proper, two brigades of Union cavalry. However, their attention was soon diverted back to the column of men, who by now were beginning to retreat in panicked confusion. In the heat of the action, Colonel Rosser yelled to Major Puller, "Why, in the name of God don't you assist me in rallying the men?" Gilmor, who himself was coming out of the hollow, slowly approached Puller from the rear and observed the major leaning over his horse's neck. The Marylander came in full view of the major who lamely lifted his head and was barely able to utter, "Colonel, I'm killed." Rosser, perhaps embarrassed by yelling at the dying Puller, changed the tone of his voice and seriously stated, "My God, old fellow, I hope not; bear up, bear up." Puller, digging deep within himself for the ideal fortitude of the Southern horseman, attempted to straighten his back, but in the process released the horse's mane; the beast, petrified by the sound of shells exploding plus the crackle of guns, hurled the weakened Puller off its back as it galloped away. Several Confederate horsemen who also had their horses shot out from under them carried the mortally wounded Puller to an ambulance, where life mercifully slipped from his limp body.[5]

After reporting his discovery of the large body of Union cavalry situated in the woods adjacent to Kelly's Ford, Gilmor made his way to the right flank of the Second Virginia, where he found Major Pelham. The Second Virginia was in the middle of a horrendous artillery barrage, and the men were growing restless, wishing to either attack the Federal line or retreat to a better position. Fitzhugh Lee approached the disgruntled Southerners and coolly suggested in a manner that was as calm as it was stern, "Keep cool, boys; these little things make a deal of fuss, but don't hurt any one [sic]." The regiment cheered him wildly, and a little later, they were allowed to move to the left in order to take a stronger position. Gilmor, sitting upon his horse, observed and cheered the men of the Second Virginia as the column slithered its way out of their exposed ground. The "Boy Major" in the meantime studied to his satisfaction the pounding of the Union position by the Confederate guns. The last few men of the column turned to their left and began to march when an enormous shell exploded near by. Gilmor was so well accustomed to the shell blasts "that he ceased to regard them" and did not even bother to turn around in order to witness the carnage caused by this latest blast. Suddenly, a soldier barked "My God, they've killed poor Pelham;" Gilmor, upon hearing the shocking news, turned quickly and saw Pelham's horse slowly move off, and then his eyes focused upon the "Boy Major," who was "lying on his back, his eyes wide open, and looking very natural, but fatally hurt."[6]

As Gilmor and two other officers lifted the severely injured Pelham upon his horse, they noticed that he was struck in the back of the head with a chunk of metal from the percussion of the blast, which caused severe hemorrhaging. Gilmor then frantically ordered the two to take the major to an ambulance and find a surgeon. Afterwards, Gilmor galloped off to General Stuart, who observed his blood soaked uniform. Gilmor told the general that it was Pelham's blood, he being killed by a Yankee shell moments earlier. The captain observed the "distress and horror" upon the general's handsome face, which was now distorted with sorrow. Upon fully grasping the sad news, the Confederate cavalier finally "bowed his head upon his horse's neck and wept, 'Our loss is irreparable!'"[7]

Stuart, regaining his senses, ordered Gilmor to go on to Culpeper and telegraph General Robert E. Lee about the day's events. In the meantime, the Confederate cavalry began a general fighting retreat to Brandy Station. On his way to Culpeper, Gilmor came upon the two men whom he had ordered to take Pelham to a nearby ambulance. He saw Pelham's lifeless body draped over the horse and halted the duo, who aided Gilmor in placing the wounded Pelham on the soft grass. Suddenly Pelham's seemingly lifeless body moved. Gilmor, who was both astonished and disgruntled at the two Confederates, who, instead of searching for an ambulance and surgeon, moved all the way toward Culpeper, carrying Pelham over four grueling miles. It was Gilmor's conviction "that had surgical aid been called to remove the compression on the brain, his life might have been saved." Pelham was taken to Culpepper where he died at one o'clock that afternoon.[8]

Meanwhile, back at Kelly's Ford, the Federal troopers continued to have their way. Then, General Averell, who heard reports that Stuart was observed along the Confederate lines, promptly ordered his victorious men to retreat to their side of the river, much to the chagrin of General Joseph Hooker, Commander of the Army of the Potomac, who realized Averell's missed opportunity to overrun Fitzhugh Lee's command. However, the Northern cavalry could claim a resounding victory over the acclaimed Southern horsemen; next to a significant boost in their morale, they tallied only seventy eight casualties compared to the 133 Southerners killed and wounded. However, and perhaps most important of all, the Southern Army was deprived of a valuable horse artillerist and "promising young officer" by the death of John Pelham. As the news of Pelham's death spread across the

Confederacy, Southerners could only grieve as they "[thought] of thy boy, 'mid princes of the sky, Among the Southern dead."[9]

The day after the action at Kelly's Ford, Gilmor succumbed to sickness caused in his own opinion by "a severe wrench received when [his] horse was plunging and rearing" after being struck by a shell. Gilmor received many prominent visitors during his confinement to bed, including Generals Stuart and Fitzhugh Lee; the latter of whom jokingly told the Marylander that he intended to report him for "running on the battlefield." Actually, both Southern cavaliers' reports commended the captain. Lee thanked Gilmor "for his marked bravery and cool courage," and Jeb Stuart reported that he was especially indebted "to Captain Harry [W.] Gilmor, Twelfth Virginia Cavalry, who accompanied [him] as a volunteer staff [officer]." During the latter half of March and most of April Gilmor and his brother, Meredith, who was expelled from Baltimore because of pro-Confederate activities, scouted in the Page Valley.[10]

In late April, Gilmor was granted approval to travel to Richmond in order to seek permission to raise his own cavalry battalion. In a note addressed to Confederate Secretary of War James Seddon, the cavalier stated that he wished to glean fellow Marylanders then in the Shenandoah Valley to fill the ranks of his proposed battalion. Furthermore, Gilmor suggested that his command should operate independently until its complete organization. Apparently, it was Gilmor's contention that his command would eventually be mustered into regular service after the few short months that he felt it would take him to raise his battalion. The War Department approved Gilmor's request on May 7, 1863. In allowing Gilmor to raise his battalion, War Secretary Seddon was acting upon the April 1862 legislation that allowed President Jefferson Davis "to commission officers as he may deem proper with authority to form bands of partisan rangers, in companies, battalions, or regiments, either as infantry or cavalry." Seddon never gave Gilmor a date by which he felt that his command should be organized. Also, despite what may have been Gilmor's early intentions, his command would remain an independent, partisan force for the duration of its existence. Even when Gilmor's "Band" was officially mustered into the regular service and designated as the Second Maryland Cavalry Battalion in May of 1864, the move was nominal at best. Gilmor's battalion remained every bit as independent, rugged, and tempestuous as its commander.[11]

After the War Department granted him approval to raise a cavalry battalion, Gilmor tendered his resignation as a Captain of Company F of the Twelfth Virginia Cavalry. The notice was officially accepted on June 13, 1863. The newly commissioned major, with General Jeb Stuart's consent, began to recruit his cavalry battalion. The formation of Gilmor's battalion was neither rapid nor without difficulty. At first, Gilmor wanted only fellow Marylanders in his command. However, after observing that most of the viable Marylanders who decided to fight for the Southern Cause were already in the regular Confederate Army, Gilmor turned to Virginians. At this point, the Confederate government intervened to prohibit Gilmor's recruitment of men from the Old Dominion who could possibly be conscripted into the Southern Army. In one instance, conscript officers disbanded one of Gilmor's companies. "The Confederate government expressly wanted only Marylanders and non-conscripts recruited from behind the enemy's lines to serve in the new unit."[12] Thus, unable to recruit from a pool of troopers who were either in a command or a potential conscript, Gilmor's battalion saw its rosters blemished with the names of deserters, men who were dishonorably expelled from service, or were criminals out for loot and adventure.[13]

In another case, during the summer of 1863 Gilmor lost perhaps half of his new command, not to Yankee forces, but to the Twelfth Virginia Cavalry. On May 22, fifty-eight Marylanders from Company F of the Twelfth Virginia requested permission from Southern authorities to follow their old commander as cavalrymen in his budding battalion. Richmond gave its consent, and Colonel Arthur Harman of the Twelfth Virginia voluntarily agreed to release the company to Gilmor's command. However, the Marylanders would remain with Gilmor for a little less than three months. Colonel Harman protested that the Maryland men were needed in his Twelfth Virginia, and they were quickly returned to his command in August. Interestingly enough, they would be returned to Gilmor's battalion in the Spring of 1864.[14]

In addition to the difficulties noted above that hindered his recruitment efforts, Gilmor also must share part of the responsibility. In some cases he selected men of questionable integrity to raise companies. Such men would raise a company, then fail to join Gilmor's overall command. In one case in particular, Gilmor appointed a George E. Shearer to aid in recruitment. Shearer's reputation was extremely tarnished. It appears that Shearer had a penchant for cruelty and thievery in the northern Shenandoah, and Virginians living in the lush countryside around Winchester expressed fear and concern over his activities.[15]

These problems notwithstanding, between May and early June, Gilmor managed to raise a company of troopers. This company would be labeled Company B. Gilmor decided to designate the men who transferred from his old command in the Twelfth Virginia as Company A, before their untimely removal in August. Soon officers were elected in Company B. Nicholas Burke, a fellow Marylander, was selected as captain. William W. McKaig, a young cadet in his early twenties who resided in Allegany County, Maryland, became the First Lieutenant. Also, Meredith Gilmor, Harry's brother, was elected to the Second Lieutenant position. Meredith, a farmer, boasted a large, six-foot frame. Undoubtedly, love for the plow and splendidly built features were shared by many of the Gilmor men. Gilmor and his newly elected fellow officers, as well as any enlisted man who joined his battalion, were, according to Confederate law, "equal to troops in the regular armies of the Confederacy and were [also] subject to the Articles of War and Army Regulations."[16]

Another hindrance to recruitment during those humid, muggy summer days of 1863 had to due with a major strategic offensive on the part of the South. During this time, all attention was placed upon General Robert E. Lee, as the commander of the Army of Northern Virginia moved his forces northward.[17] General Lee had three overall objectives in his invasion of Northern soil. One, while in the North, he could attain food, forage, and other supplies that were lacking in his own war ravaged state of Virginia. Two, a successful offensive in Union territory could remove the threat of renewed Federal operations against Richmond and could serve to draw the entire Army of the Potomac out of the South. And last, but certainly not least, a victory in the North could win the South diplomatic recognition from France and especially Britain, whose upper class espoused ardent Southern sympathies. After General Jackson's death, Lee reorganized his 75,000 man army into three corps; General James Longstreet commanded the First, General Richard Ewell the Second, and the Third would be led by General Ambrose P. Hill. On June 3, 1863, Lee, with the First and Second Corps, left Fredericksburg and marched toward the Shenandoah, in search of that thus far elusive victory on Yankee soil. Not a soul on Lee's staff or within his army knew it at the time, but this day marked the beginning of the historic Gettysburg Campaign.[18]

By the middle of June, Generals Ewell and Longstreet's Army Corps were both moving toward the Blue Ridge Mountains, wishing to pass through the scenic gaps and continue their march down the Valley. A couple of weeks earlier, Gilmor was ordered to scout in close vicinity to Winchester for "Old Baldy's" approaching Corps. Gilmor, while on his way to Winchester, stopped at Woodstock, where he found his "old acquaintance," the Confederate spy Belle Boyd. Boyd pleaded with Gilmor for permission to accompany him and the ten other men on their mission near Winchester. Gilmor excused himself from such a delicate decision by informing the anxious Southern spy that she would have to receive permission from Brigadier General Micah Jenkins, the then commander of the Valley District. Thus, Gilmor and the Southern belle made their way to Jenkins' headquarters, where the two discovered the general sitting in front of his tent. After Gilmor informed the general concerning his secret mission, Boyd stepped up to present her request. Gilmor, who "did not care to be accompanied by a woman on so perilous an enterprise," placed himself tactically behind Belle and made frantic gestures to Jenkins, attempting to nonverbally convince his superior of the hazard of allowing Boyd to go along. Jenkins followed Gilmor's lead and refused Belle, much to her chagrin.[19]

Gilmor and his scouting party managed to make their way down to the lower Valley unaccompanied by Miss Boyd. The Marylander made a continuous circle around both Winchester and Martinsburg, collecting valuable intelligence concerning the disposition and strength of the Union forces situated there. He sent a courier off to General Ewell, who was now slithering his long column through Chester's Gap, approximately seven miles southeast of Front Royal.[20]

Gilmor became ill and was bed ridden in Middletown, which was located a little over a dozen miles south of Winchester. His recovery was interrupted when he was alerted that forty Yankee troopers "dashed" into his small force in an effort to break through Ewell's outer pickets, which were posted farther south. Gilmor quickly dressed in a fancy "new uniform [that had] a superabundance of yellow lace" and rallied his force, who, even though outnumbered four to one, managed to push the retreating Federal troopers back toward Winchester. The Yankee force halted further up the pike, and Gilmor concluded his chase, fearing that the stealthy Northerners might have prepared an ambuscade.[21]

Gilmor placed two men along the turnpike and with the other handful cautiously galloped down the road. The daring Marylander ordered his group to halt, he being quite certain that there was a trap awaiting them down the pike, especially after he observed the Yankee force at the other end "pretending" to flee. Gilmor's small force then wheeled and headed back in the direction of Middletown, where they soon observed a cloud of dust moving along the road that bisected the turnpike at Middletown. Gilmor's men believed that this cloud of dust signified that a Union cavalry force was about to move into their rear, thus trapping them between two larger cavalry forces. The small group hurried toward the junction of the road and turnpike and managed to arrive before the approaching cavalry, led by Captain William Raisin with a force of seventy men from both the First Maryland and Jenkins' cavalry. Gilmor felt relieved to note that the approaching cavalry was friend instead of foe. Major Gilmor approached Captain Raisin and warned him about the situation in front of his companies. Both agreed that Gilmor, with his small eight man party, would skirmish in front of Raisin's advancing companies, the latter of which would proceed at a very cautious pace. The whole group immediately moved off and about ten miles from Winchester, near Newtown, the Union force stopped in front of them. They drew their sabers and yelled, daring the cautious Confederates to charge. Gilmor, who was still convinced that there was an ambush awaiting them a little down the pike, held up his pistol, hoping to warn Captain Raisin of the impending danger. Raisin misunderstood, thinking that the Marylander was giving the signal to charge. Gilmor heard Raisin bark "Gallop - march

- charge,!" just as he saw out of the corner of his eye a blue uniform concealed in the tall grass that blanketed the left of the road.[22]

The Marylanders were all screaming and yelling the famous "Rebel Yells" as they charged into the awaiting ambush, thereby drowning out Gilmor's pleas to "Halt! Halt! you will all be butchered! You are running into an ambuscade!" Seeing his pleas having no effect and familiar with Yankee traps, he joined his fellow Marylanders and soon made his way to the front of the column. Suddenly, a pack of Federal infantrymen stood up from their grassy place of concealment and emptied their guns into the left flank of the Maryland column, while at the same time a small body of Union troopers fired upon the Confederate left and right. To add to their predicament, two howitzers spilled their contents unsympathetically into the Southern ranks. Captain Raisin took a shot in the back of the head, and his horse, which was also wounded, fell upon him. As the Marylanders attempted to reorganize themselves and gain control of their horses, blue-coated Federals, some of whom already had unloaded their weapons into the mass of Southerners, were standing along a fence situated to the left of the road stabbing at the Confederates and their horses with drawn, blood covered bayonets. Gilmor, in the midst of the melee, ordered a charge, to which only two troopers obeyed, one being killed instantly. What was left of the cavalry force managed to wheel and quickly flee southward, along their highway of hell, all the while being hotly followed by the Union troopers. A little distance outside of Middletown a counter-charge prevented the Federals from further advance. All told, the Marylanders lost nearly half their force on that bloody day of combat; they tallied "four of their comrades killed and about thirty wounded or prisoners in the hands of the enemy." On the blood covered and strewn road after the battle, lay Captain Raisin, who "was most inhumanely beaten by the wretches into whose hands he had fallen."[23]

One day after the action outside of Newtown, Gilmor moved to the vicinity of Winchester, where it was hoped that a combined Confederate assault on the garrison there could lead to its complete capture. With his own battalion not yet organized, Gilmor was without a command and thus decided to join Major William W. Goldsborough's force, which acted as skirmishers for the assault on Winchester. Southern forces worked during June 13 and 14, 1863, slowly pushing in Union General Robert Milroy's pickets and beginning the encirclement of the besieged Federal force. During the night of the fourteenth, Gilmor made a wager with Major Goldsborough to the effect that he would be the first Confederate to enter Winchester, providing of course he was not killed. During the bright, clear morning of June 15, Major Gilmor made his way along the Millwood Road and Swartz's Mill, where he came upon "dead bodies, knapsacks, blankets, and guns strewn" about the ground. He also made his way into an abandoned Northern camp, where he observed neatly piled knapsacks, packed full of invaluable contents, while he read the letters that lay unmolested around the Union campsite. Gilmor grasped a "hundred gum-cloths" and carried his new found belongings to a woman's house near by, who he ordered to hold them until he returned. The wandering, curious Marylander made his way up to a crest which overlooked the desolate, former Union camp and set his eyes upon the black, burned body of a Union soldier, whose clothes were burnt away by an explosion. He then made his way around Winchester, arriving on the east side of town where he met General Ewell, who ordered him to scout in the vicinity of the Berryville Road.[24]

After taking note of the Union forces there, the major headed back toward Ewell's headquarters in order to report his findings. Gilmor sensed that he might come across a "Jessie Scout." The "Jessie Scouts" were a group of Federal spies and rangers established by General Fremont designed to root out Confederate guerrillas. Fremont named his tenacious scouts after his wife, Jessie Benton Fremont. A "Jessie Scout" would sometimes wear a white handkerchief around his neck, "leaving a long end hanging down over [his] shoulder." This was the sign by which other "Jessie Scouts" identified one another.[25]

On this occasion Gilmor was clad in Confederate gray, and he was certain to have properly adjusted his white handkerchief. Interestingly enough, the wily Gilmor would sometimes disguise himself in Union blue when the situation demanded. Gilmor's suspicion proved correct, and, while resting upon his horse, he was approached by a "Jessie Scout" who wielded a drawn pistol. The Northerner queried, "Where are you going?" Gilmor nonchalantly replied, "Going into town." The distrust between the two was mutual, as tension began to fill the air. The Yankee put forth another curt question, asking the stealthy Rebel whose command he belonged to. Gilmor responded in a manner that was designed to relax his antagonist while at the same time affording him an opportunity to strike as soon as the "Jessie Scout" dropped his guard. "To the same crowd you do - to Captain Purdy's scouts," was Gilmor's calm reply. The Yankee, observing the characteristics of Gilmor's physical constitution, his handsome mustache, and stocky build, plainly exclaimed, "Why, I don't remember seeing you," while admitting that he was a newcomer himself. Gilmor said "This is just my case." After a period of question and answer, the Yankee was satisfied that Gilmor was one of their own and "put up his pistol." Gilmor then rode closer to the now apathetic "Jessie Scout" and requested that he be granted an opportunity to look at the Federal's ruffles (handcuffs). The Union man obliged, and, as he stooped to remove them from his horse, the Marylander struck him with his sabre, piercing the Northerner's body near the heart. The latter, shocked, dazed and in severe pain, fell from his "noble dapple gray." Gilmor dismounted and attempted to revive him with his water and whiskey, but to no avail. Prior to the Yankee's death, he looked at Gilmor and concluded, "You sold me pretty well, but I don't blame you." Gilmor took the dead man's "magnificent gray," along with his very good saddle, which "suited [him] better than [his] own," as well as the ruffles.[26] On this occasion, Gilmor was able to outfox his Union adversary; Gilmor's war, that of a partisan fighter, involved just as much wit as it did brawn and fortune.

After his close call, Gilmor arrived at Ewell's headquarters during the late afternoon hours of June 15. From there, Gilmor and the Confederate command witnessed General Jubal Early's force seize the heights that approached the southwest sector of Winchester. Ewell, with a wooden leg as a result of a severe wound he received at Second Bull Run, was highly excited as he observed the action. He jerked about on his crutches, barely keeping erect. Then, through his field glasses he stated that he thought he saw Early leading his Louisiana infantry up one of the crests; with tears in his eyes he exclaimed "Hurrah for the Louisiana boys! There's Early; I hope the old fellow won't be hurt." As soon as he let out these cheers, a spent ball came whizzing through the air, smacking Ewell in the chest, leaving an ugly bruise. His physician, extremely startled, took the General's crutches, but even that did not prevent "Old Baldy" from cheering Early's Louisiana men.[27]

The Battle of Winchester became a Federal rout. After the guns fell silent, the Union could count "ninety-five killed, 348 injured and over four thousand missing or captured," or in other words almost half the number General Milroy boasted in his Winchester garrison. The Confederate count was a little under 270 casualties, which were easily offset by their capture of "twenty-three guns, 200,000 rounds of rifle ammunition, three hundred wagons and an equal number of horses," plus a large supply of food to boot. After the battle, Ewell ordered Gilmor to muster as many cavalry as he could find and attempt to seize General Milroy himself, who collected what was left of his force and retreated toward Harper's Ferry. Gilmor came up empty handed, as did several other parties that were sent out by various Confederate generals for the same purpose.[28]

With the Union forces cleared from their front, Ewell's cavalry crossed the Potomac River, and on the day after the action at Winchester, General Lee moved his Army of Northern Virginia across the same river. Panic soon struck western Maryland and southern Pennsylvania, as the Confederate legions appeared unchecked by the Yankee defenses. After moving across the Potomac, Ewell ordered Gilmor to take command of his fellow Marylanders in the First Maryland Cavalry Battalion, due to a severe leg injury to their regular commander, Major Ridgely Brown. Major Gilmor was then instructed to take this outfit twenty-five miles to Frederick, Maryland, and destroy the nearby Monocacy Bridge. The major marched off with his command, numbering approximately two hundred men, and encamped in the vicinity of Boonesboro, a little over fifteen miles from their destination. Gilmor sent Captain Thomas Sturgis Davis, also a resident of Towson, to Frederick on a scouting-raiding mission, where he managed to capture some Federal prisoners, before being forced to retreat by a small force of Federal cavalry. Major Gilmor, coming to Davis's assistance, managed to push the Union force out of Frederick. The Yankees ran off in full flight to Harper's Ferry. The people of Frederick gave their fellow Marylanders a kind and delightful welcome "and manifested unmistakably their sympathy [for] the South." However, much to the First Maryland's disappointment, the Monocacy Bridge was too heavily defended; thus, Gilmor and his command made their way toward Hagerstown, to receive further orders.[29]

Before his arrival at Hagerstown, Gilmor received word

that he was ordered to attach his First Maryland to General George H. Steuart's Brigade, which was already composed of the "Second Maryland Infantry [First Maryland Infantry Battalion], three Virginia Regiments, two North Carolina Regiments, and one artillery battery."[30] General Steuart's brigade was detached from the main army in order to make a twenty-five-mile detour to McConnellsburg, approximately eighty miles southwest of Harrisburg. Steuart was in the vicinity of Mercersburg when he sent a scout back to Hagerstown in order to discover the location of Gilmor's command. The First Maryland just arrived at Hagerstown when the courier issued Steuart's instructions to Gilmor, who quickly took the advance of the brigade, in order to aid the latter "in feeling its way" through the rough, hilly terrain. While moving toward McConnellsburg, Major Gilmor came upon a Pennsylvania farmer, who allowed the Marylander to refresh his horse on his farm. Gilmor proceeded to tell the Pennsylvanian that he was certain that the Confederate Army would be successful during their offensive, because the entire army, "from General Lee down, was wholly composed of Christian men - his own conversation being punctuated meanwhile with many an oath." Gilmor also told the farmer that he could overlook his cursing; after all, Gilmor admitted that "he was the rare exception" to those saints that composed Lee's Army.[31] A little after sunset on June 24, Gilmor was able to capture McConnellsburg for General Steuart, who was bringing up the rear.[32]

General Steuart's brigade remained in the vicinity of McConnellsburg for the next two days, during which Gilmor took the First Maryland throughout the southern Pennsylvania farmland for the purpose of requisitioning horses, cattle, and other articles of military necessity. Gilmor was ordered "to leave a pair of plow horses and milk cows on each farm, and to respect all other property."[33] This order was indicative of the Confederate effort to both attain supplies from the

Pennsylvania inhabitants while at the same time preserving their own honor in the eyes of the North and the rest of the world. A Southern Army that appeared civil and well behaved could also do much to strengthen the "peace party" in the North, thereby aiding the Southern Cause. Thus, Lee encouraged his men to show restraint and not to "take vengeance for the wrongs our people have suffered" and further suggested that wrongs committed against Northern people would serve as a great offense "against Him to whom vengeance belongeth."[34] The image of a Southern Christian Army was of course extremely idyllic; however, for those who formulated strategy within the Confederate government, it was nonetheless a realistic strategic measure.

After their two-day stay in McConnellsburg, the Confederate brigade headed twenty miles to the east, in the vicinity of Chambersburg, Gilmor capturing "sixty head of cattle, forty horses, some mules, and a few militia."[35] Sometime on June 26 Gilmor was detached from Steuart's brigade and took the First Maryland on a wide westward circuit, moving as far as Roxbury before rejoining his fellow Marylander's command at Shippensburg the following day. Steuart's brigade on June 28 continued on its trek toward Carlisle, as the hot summer sun beat down upon the Southern invaders, sapping the energy out of both man and beast. After a few days, Gilmor was ordered to scout in the vicinity of Cashtown, about ten miles northwest of Gettysburg, after which he eventually ended up reporting to General Ewell, who was already engaging the Union enemy. Ewell then commanded the major to take his force and support his extreme left, "where a pretty artillery fight" was already in session.[36]

Gilmor and his friend and fellow officer, Warner Welch, now a captain in Company D of the First Maryland, were able to observe the Confederate left push the Federal forces into the small, southern Pennsylvania village of Gettysburg.

They were both afforded the opportunity to observe "Old Jube" race into Gettysburg along the Harrisburg Road, preceded by "numbers of small squads of blue-coats who were straggling out of the woods and heading toward Gettysburg." As the Union retreat became general, Gilmor observed that "[soon] the face of the earth seemed covered with blue-coats." The situation along the Confederate front and right were equally devastating to the host army, as Union forces retreated into the village out of the west and north, along the Chambersburg Road and Carlisle Road, respectively. All through the day the Union soldiers retreated before their antagonists and finally ended up on the hill tops south of the village, where they began to rally and build defensive positions.[37]

Major Gilmor led his fellow Marylanders of the First Maryland Cavalry onto the Gettysburg battlefield. It was "the first official Maryland Confederate unit" to arrive on the scene.[38] Also, according to his own accounts, Gilmor claimed that he and Captain Welch were the first two Southerners to enter the Northern village. Once in Gettysburg, the duo slowly made their way through the city on horseback, observing the town's streets littered with dead bodies and Union weapons. Suddenly, a dismounted Union trooper took aim at the major, his ball missing Gilmor's head by an inch. The Marylander hurriedly picked up a loaded musket on the village street and fired at the Federal man. The Yankee fell, as Gilmor's ball found its mark. Gilmor made his way back to headquarters, where he overheard the Confederate high command discuss their tactics. Gilmor overheard Early tell Ewell that he could drive the enemy from the hills south of Gettysburg that evening, warning that, if not done immediately, by morning the Federals would be heavily fortified. As history shows, on that evening the high command did not give their consent to the cursing, tobacco-chewing Early; Major Gilmor claims that, had Early's advise been heeded, the Army of Northern

Virginia, "flushed with victory, [could] have laid Philadelphia and New York in ashes, or conquered a peace."[39]

Another Marylander, Captain Frank Bond of Company A, First Maryland Cavalry, was appointed Acting Provost Marshal of the vanquished Pennsylvania village. As a provost marshal, Captain Bond would use his command to inventory supplies and register prisoners that fell into Southern hands. He was also charged the task of seeing that proper care was taken when dealing with the wounded, both men in blue and gray. Finally, Company A would act as a police force behind the Rebel lines, discouraging looting in Gettysburg.[40] In the meantime, Gilmor, who was relinquished of his command of the First Maryland after Major Brown recovered from his wounds, "amused himself by riding from point to point to watch the fighting" at Gettysburg. On the evening of the following day the Maryland cavalier took part in his last assault on the Union strongholds.[41]

On July 4 a rain shower pelted Gettysburg, as if nature was symbolically attempting to wash away the blood spilled from the festering wounds of a bleeding nation. That evening General Robert E. Lee, who took full responsibility for the debacle at Gettysburg, ordered his army to retreat. His losses could be tallied at around twenty two thousand, whereas General George Meade, who before the battle replaced the disgruntled Hooker, could add one thousand more than Lee to his own casualty list. Of all those who fought in the Battle of Gettysburg, "one in four" were casualties.[42] As reports of the defeat at Gettysburg arrived in Richmond, sad news also flooded the capital from the west, where Vicksburg finally capitulated to Union forces. In Washington, the news of the dual victories helped to highlight Independence Day celebrations; however, throughout the South church bells rang, women cried, and men and political leaders mourned the devastating setbacks, as their own independence slowly slipped through their grasp.

However, whereas Lee's army was defeated at Gettysburg, it was still fully intact and threatened to slip back onto friendly Southern soil as it had successfully retreated after Antietam less than a year earlier. In the middle of July, Gilmor rejoined the Army of Northern Virginia as it was preparing to cross the Potomac River at Williamsport, less than ten miles southwest of Hagerstown. He placed his own command, being only one company, under the command of Major Ridgely Brown, while, with General John Imboden's consent, he began to organize about 180 sick and wounded men into a fighting force. Gilmor's "cripples," along with the Sixty-Second Virginia, worked together to disrupt a planned Federal assault on the Southern supply train. On the night of July 13, Lee's embattled army slipped across the Potomac. President Lincoln, who felt that General Meade could have made a greater effort to prohibit the Confederate retreat, stated, "We had them within our grasp...we had only to stretch forth our hands and they were ours."[43]

Gilmor then attempted to rally his "convalescent soldiers" for another attack, this time on a Union artillery battery. Gilmor, charging on foot, got within approximately one hundred yards of the Union artillery when he suddenly lost consciousness. He felt that "an affection of the heart," coupled with exhaustion from all the "exertion on foot," caused an "attack of vertigo." At any rate, he awoke to find himself again a Yankee prisoner under a large white oak tree. A major instructed two men to keep an eye on their prisoner, while he sent for "the sergeant of the guard." In the meantime Gilmor lay very still while he heard in close distance a Federal cavalry charge upon the Confederate's supply train. Gilmor asked his guard for a blanket, which caused the Yankee to have a violent temper tantrum, as he unpleasantly explained to Harry that his fellow Southerners removed the shoes from their prisoners captured at Gettysburg. Gilmor awoke the next morning drenched and cold due to an all night rain shower;

however, his lackadaisical guards were not overly concerned with either the weather or their charge, for they were on both sides of the Marylander, fast asleep and snoring in a crescendo. The sly Gilmor managed to sneak out "like a slithering snake" from between his two guards, who lay on both ends of a blanket that they covered Gilmor with during the night. Major Gilmor soon discovered where his weapons were placed, jumped upon one of the guard's horses, and led the other one back to camp near Williamsport.[44]

For the rest of July, 1863, Gilmor performed scouting duty for General Jeb Stuart in the lower Shenandoah, between Harper's Ferry and the Opequon. After Stuart moved his cavalry beyond the scenic Blue Ridge Mountains into the eastern portion of the state, Gilmor remained in the Shenandoah, organizing his battalion, which after its conception in May, still only had "one company of mounted men."[45]

Meredith Gilmor, Harry's brother, saw his luck run out shortly after the Southern debacle at Gettysburg. On July 22, the eighteen-year-old Meredith was captured by the Fifty-fourth Pennsylvania Cavalry near Johnstown, Virginia. He was sent to Camp Chase, Ohio, for confinement. Eventually, Meredith would be "transferred to Johnson's Island near Sandusky, Ohio."[46] He would remain in the Union stockade until 1865.[47]

In addition to military affairs, Gilmor also paid close attention to female friends, both within the Valley and throughout the South. It appears that the handsome cavalier was the topic of many conversations among the Southern belles, especially as news of his exploits filtered throughout the land. In one letter, a woman admirer by the name of Ella requested that the major forward an additional enclosed letter to a friend, suggesting that "by doing so he [Gilmor] will be obliging a *pure Rebel* and South Carolina secessionist-at-heart." She further queried:

> Why do you not make haste and drive the Yankees out - we are all dying to see you again when we speak of you (which is Frequently) we always say *bless his heart* - why doesn't he make haste and drive these vandals out and come to our *secesh* [sic].

She also asked Gilmor if he had heard any good news that could be forwarded to her. Ella concluded the letter by stressing the fact that "all the girls are well just crazy all of us to see the Rebels again so do make haste and come [sic]."[48]

Early October found Gilmor with his growing battalion scouting in the lower Shenandoah. The area his command covered stretched from Winchester to Martinsburg, then southeast to Charles Town. In effect, Major Gilmor's territory formed a triangle in the lower Valley. The Marylander decided to pitch camp on William Washington's place but not before ordering scouts to keep a close watch for any Federal movements on the roads near Charles Town. Two hours later, Gilmor's scouts hurried back to camp, informing him that a group of twenty to twenty five cavalrymen were spotted on their way to Smithfield; this group had been sent out earlier by Colonel Benjamin Simpson, of the Ninth (Federal) Maryland, to scout in the vicinity of the Berryville Road. Gilmor's men quickly mounted and got behind the small Federal cavalry force near Smithfield. However, the adversaries beat Gilmor to Smithfield and Summit Point and were well on their way back to Charles Town. Gilmor decided to lead his men through the autumn Shenandoah countryside in order to stop the force before it reached Charles Town. Three of his horsemen did indeed catch the group and gave battle to the Federal troop about a half mile outside of town but failed to stop them.[49]

Gilmor placed twelve men to cover his rear as the rest of his force moved west toward Summit Point. One mile from

Summit Point, at the residence of Joseph Morrow, known to locals as the "White House," Gilmor allowed his men to dismount and drink from a large spring almost fifty yards off the road. Gilmor, setting aside his thirst for the moment, rode up to the Morrow's yard in order to converse with some belles who made their welcomed appearance. Suddenly, a loud voice was heard in the near distance, "Here they are, boys; by God, we've got them now!" Before Gilmor could react, a bullet buzzed through a lilac bush in the yard, chasing off the excited women. Gilmor looked up from where the voice came and observed the front of a Union cavalry column. He noticed a force of forty-three cavalrymen, under the command of "Captain George D. Summers, of Company F, Second Maryland Regiment, Potomac Home Brigade," who was sent out earlier to aid the twenty man force that was falsely reported to have been "cut off by the enemy."[50]

Thus, Summers's force was located between Gilmor and Summit Point. Major Gilmor ordered ten of his men to conceal themselves behind a stone stable and fire at the approaching Federal horsemen with their carbines. However, the troopers refused to charge, thinking that Gilmor's unmounted horses along the road side meant that an ambuscade was prepared and waiting. Summers lost his temper with his incorrigible troopers, and perhaps at the same time lost his state of mind. He charged Gilmor, firing his pistol wildly. Gilmor remained calm and steady, and, holding his horse still with one hand, took careful aim at the excited Summers, firing and striking the captain's head. Summers fell from his horse, killed by Gilmor's fire.[51]

The Confederate force rallied and pushed the Union men through Summit Point, where Gilmor afterwards took his prisoners off by a private route to somewhere in the upper Valley. A Union report later commented upon the loss of Captain Summers, who was described as "a brave, daring soldier, a perfect officer, and thorough gentleman."

Meanwhile, Gilmor was criticized by the Northern press, which claimed that he "murdered" the Union officer. Gilmor concluded that, if he had indeed murdered the captain, then "not a few were murdered on both sides."[52]

After the incident at Summit Point, Gilmor had his command furnished with additional weapons. While at Edinburg, Virginia, two boxes of muskets, one-hundred sabres, and one-hundred belts were sent to Gilmor's "Band." On October 15, Gilmor moved a small group of troopers northward about sixty miles for a raiding mission. The objective was to destroy "the Baltimore and Ohio railroad bridge across Back Creek, which peacefully meanders in a narrow valley west of the North Mountain range."[53]

Gilmor took with him two officers, his adjutant Herman F. Keidel and Captain Eugene Diggs of Company B. The raiding party would number only forty men. At approximately two o'clock in the afternoon, the Rebels left their temporary headquarters, which was conveniently located near a distillery outside of Strasburg and traveled toward their destination. Along the way, Gilmor made the mistake of visiting a few lady friends at "Carter Hall." Gilmor, "a thorough lady's man," was persuaded by a "rebel maiden" of the residence to "linger behind in her delightful society."[54] Gilmor decided to place John C. Blackford, a private in Company A, in charge of the expedition. Blackford was not without experience, for he was "a former cavalry partisan commander whose company had disbanded."[55]

Blackford was quick to blunder, ordering the party to encamp in a narrow ravine nestled within the North Mountain. The partisans were situated in territory close to the mountains of western Virginia, where strong Union sentiment was the rule rather than the exception. A citizen scout came across the Southerners, who were awaiting the cover of darkness in order to complete their mission, and reported his findings to Union headquarters. The Twelfth Pennsylvania and the First

New York Regiment promptly sent out "two small detachments of cavalry and a small party of infantry," preceded by the citizen scout, who successfully led them to the Confederate encampment. There the Union troopers surprised Gilmor's unsuspecting men, who clumsily jumped upon their horses or decided to "take to their heels, and ran in a style exceedingly creditable to chivalrous pedestrianism;" on that evening the principle order among Gilmor's horsemen was "right-smart-git." Blackford and Diggs, as well as Adjutant Keidel, fell into Union hands, not to mention "twenty five men, thirty horses, sabers, and other weapons of offensive war 'too numerous to mention.'" Gilmor, who set out to rejoin Blackford's party after his visit to the Carter Hall, finally came to the correct assumption that his party was captured after his search came up empty. After his worst fears were confirmed, he sadly admitted that "they were the best men and horses of the command."[56]

Captain Diggs would eventually see the insides of three different Union stockades. After a stay at Point Lookout, Diggs was transferred to Fort Delaware on June 23, 1864. Finally, with a group of fellow officers, he was forwarded to Hilton Head, South Carolina, on August 20, 1864. As for John C. Blackford, after his capture he was sent to Fort McHenry on October 17, 1863. Three days later, between nine and eleven o'clock in the evening, the wily former partisan clandestinely escaped into the dark, nighttime Maryland countryside.[57]

Two days after the fiasco at North Mountain, Gilmor collected his wits and put together a sixty man force in order to determine the possibility of nabbing the Federal garrison located at Charles Town, which consisted of Colonel Benjamin Simpson's Ninth (Federal) Maryland Infantry Regiment along with a squadron of cavalry. Having sufficiently scouted the area, Gilmor determined a plan of action that he presented to General Imboden, who was at Berryville, fifteen miles southwest of Charles Town. By evening Imboden's staff agreed upon Gilmor's plan.[58]

At two o'clock on Sunday morning (October 18) Imboden's command left Berryville. Three miles outside of Charles Town, Gilmor was ordered to take his command, which by now counted some "sixty-five mounted men and thirty dismounted," and place themselves northeast of Charles Town, in order to cut off a possible Union retreat along the Harper's Ferry Turnpike. The Eighteenth Virginia Cavalry would be placed in support of Gilmor's battalion. The Federals, who were totally unaware of the stealthy Confederate forces moving about, remained within "the court-house, jail, and some other buildings," located in the center of town. Imboden asked Simpson to lay down his arms, and, after an hour of deliberation with his staff, he defiantly replied "take us if you can." A small volley of shells forced the Yankees out of their hideouts, and they formed and retreated toward Harper's Ferry.[59]

A half hour after sunset, a group of fifty Federal cavalry troopers, like rabbits surrounded by ferocious hounds, charged "in columns of fours" out of Charles Town. Gilmor's cavalrymen charged their flanks and managed to drive the majority of the escaping troopers into an open field, while capturing twenty others. After this skirmish, the Eighteenth Virginia with Gilmor's dismounted men, who were under the command of Captain Nicholas Burke (Company A), came up to lend closer support to Gilmor's cavalry. Just then a larger Yankee force came charging out of town, only to meet the same fate as the earlier group; this time thirty to forty more were bagged.[60]

Gilmor then observed Simpson's Ninth (Federal) Maryland, already formed, attempt to make its way toward Harper's Ferry, along with their supply wagons. The major's mounted force was located to the right of the Eighteenth Virginia, and his dismounted men, under Captain Burke, fired upon Simpson's infantry from the opposite side. As the Union infantrymen moved in front of the Rebel forces, Major Gilmor galloped up to the commanding officer and asked him if he was going to charge. The colonel turned to Gilmor and replied in confusion that "[his] men have never charged infantry, and I do not know what to do." Gilmor convinced the hesitant colonel to order his men to charge on foot. Gilmor hurried back to his own men and charged the enemy with their pistols drawn, which broke the infantry regiment's ranks, resulting in the surrender of most of the Union men. Many of the Federal Marylanders wished to surrender to old acquaintances who now donned Confederate gray. One Union soldier said to an old friend, "Here, Billy, I surrender to you." Truly, such incidents epitomized the War of the Rebellion as a battle of "brother against brother." Meanwhile, Gilmor saw that Colonel Simpson was able to sneak through the Southern trap, but he was unable to catch the scampering Federal before the Yankee met up with the Union force that was arriving from Harper's Ferry to assist his battered command.[61]

Two hours after the fighting at Charles Town commenced, the Union force out of Harper's Ferry, under the command of General Jeremiah Sullivan, began to enter the town, forcing Imboden's command, with its captured prisoners and booty, to retreat back to Berryville. One of Gilmor's companies, together with McNeil's Rangers, under the command of Captain John H. McNeil, protected the rear of the retreating Confederate force. With a Yankee force in hot pursuit, Gilmor was able to slip away with a squadron of men and force himself into the rear of the pursuing enemy. His charge took the Union men by surprise as he darted at the Federal guns. The Union major in charge attempted to draw his revolver when a tall, red haired man from Gilmor's outfit swung his saber at the major, who just managed to miss being decapitated by ducking under the muzzle of a gun. Then, in the distance, he heard "Fours, left wheel," and before he "could draw [his] breath" a "handsome, dark-mustached youngster, boy in looks," came charging at him with his silver saber, which "appeared as long as a fence rail" to the besieged major, who again escaped by "dropping flat under the guns axle." Concerning Gilmor's charge, the Union major concluded "that dash of Gilmor's was one of the handsomest [sic] things of the kind that occurred during the war."[62]

General Imboden reported after the action that he managed to capture "the Ninth [Federal] Maryland Regiment, and three companies of cavalry, [estimated at] between four to five hundred men and officers." In addition, the Confederates grabbed a considerable number of "wagons, horses, mules, arms, ammunition, medicines, and clothing." His estimate of the number of Union soldiers that fell into Southern hands was slightly overestimated, the actual number being 360. Still, Imboden's Charles Town operation was a splendid success. General Robert E. Lee, satisfied with the results of the operation, commented that "by a well-concerted plan" Imboden was able to surround Charles Town and "capture nearly the whole force stationed there, with all their stores and transportation."[63] As with "Stonewall's" Shenandoah Campaign of 1862, Gilmor's role in the affair at Charles Town during that autumn of 1863 was as invaluable as it was unacknowledged.

By the end of 1863, it was apparent that the Confederacy, though far from completely beaten, was now irrefutably losing their war for independence. On the battlemap, they were turned back at Gettysburg, depriving General Lee of a possible victory on Northern soil and significantly reducing Davis's already dwindling chance of gaining diplomatic recognition from Britain and France. Also, by late October, the Union was threatening to break through the Confederacy's western defenses and cut across the Deep South.

As 1864 approached, Gilmor's role in the War Between the States became much more pronounced. The partisan ranger's activities would have a greater consequence on events during this year of the war than in any of the previous three. By this time, the gap between the North and South's industrial capacity and manpower was widening even more, slowly wearing the Confederacy down. Furthermore, with the North's occupation of large, crucial regions of the South and its growing penchant to take the conflict into the heart of Dixie, the rebellious Confederacy began to increasingly rely upon irregulars such as Gilmor. Indeed, the use of irregulars against invading Yankees only encouraged the North's willingness to punish local Southern populations who abetted guerrilla efforts.[64]

This is not to imply that Confederate partisan rangers or independent irregulars had no role in the conflict prior to 1863 and 1864. Irregular fighting in Missouri during the early summer months of the war was a continuation of the violent clashes in the region in the turbulent 1850s. Western Virginia, although favoring the North, still witnessed the growth of many "Secessionist" irregular bands. Eastern Tennessee, an area loyal to the North, actually saw the use of partisan units by Federal authorities to destroy Rebel war materiel. As early as "September 1862 six regiments, nine battalions and several companies of partisan rangers had been organized in eight [Confederate] states."[65] These outfits, officially organized under the auspices of Confederate legislation, in no way lessened the debate in the Southern military and government circles concerning the utility and ethical question of implementing partisan forces in a conflict firmly embedded within gentlemanly Victorian virtues.[66]

However, the method of warfare changed in 1863 to 1864. The war evolved from a "gentlemen's war" to a far more destructive "total war." Commensurate with this change was the gradual stripping away of those Victorian values that soldiers, civilians, and government officials took with them into the war. The Union Army sanctioned the destruction of civilian property and, even though the Confederate Congress prohibited the formation of any further partisan forces in 1864, important irregular units such as Mosby's continued to operate.[67] With a change to the "total war" Major Gilmor would see his role in the fight for Southern independence greatly enhanced.

1. Robert Gilmor. Robert Gilmor, Harry's father, sparkled brightly in Baltimore's social and business limelight. (Courtesy of the Craig Horn Collection)

2. Harry Gilmor as a member of the Baltimore County Horse Guard. Gilmor was a corporal in the Horse Guard. (Courtesy of the Barry Pipino Collection)

3. Thomas Benton Gatch. Gatch was elected a sergeant in the Baltimore County Horse Guard. Gilmor and Gatch would remain close friends throughout the opening salvoes of the war. (Courtesy of the Barry Pipino Collection)

4. An unidentified member of the Baltimore County Horse Guard. (Courtesy of the Barry Pipino Collection)

[No. 33.]

REQUISITION for Forage for ~~144~~ 65 Private Horses in the service of Capt Gilmor Ashby Cavalry ~~United~~ Confederate States Army at Camp in Valley of Virginia for ninety one days, commencing the 1st of April, 1862, and ending the 30th of June, 1862

Date.	Number of horses.	Daily Allowance for Each. Corn. Pounds.	Oats. Pounds.	Hay. Pounds.	Fodder. Pounds.	Total Allowance. Corn. Pounds.	Oats. Pounds.	Hay. Pounds.	Fodder. Pounds.	Remarks.
1862										
April	65	12	"	14	"	23400	"	27300		
May	64	12	"	14	"	23808		27776		
June	65	12	"	14	"	23400		27300		
Total,						70608		72376		

I CERTIFY, on honor, that the above Requisition is correct and just, and that I have not drawn forage for any part of the time above charged.

Approved
Turner Ashby
pr [illegible]

H W Gilmor
Comdg Compy

RECEIVED at Camp in Valley of Virginia the 1st of April May & June 1862 of Capt William Miller A. Quartermaster ~~United~~ Confederate States Army, Seventy three, six hund & eight pounds of corn, pounds of oats, Seventy [illegible] pounds of hay, pounds of fodder, in full of the above Requisition.

[SIGNED IN DUPLICATE.]

H W Gilmor
Comdg Compy

5. A requisition order signed by Captain Harry Gilmor. At this time, Gilmor's company was a member of Ashby's Cavalry. (Courtesy of the Barry Pipino Collection)

6. General Thomas "Stonewall" Jackson. Gilmor served as a scout for Jackson during the famous Valley Campaign of 1862. (Courtesy of the Library of Congress)

7. Captain Gilmor of the Twelfth Virginia Cavalry. Note the large frame, strong features, and stern countenance; by this time in the conflict, Gilmor was demonstrating his ability as a company commander. He would soon ask for a larger command. (Courtesy of the Barry Pipino Collection)

8. General Fitzhugh Lee. In an official report, Lee commended Gilmor for his "marked bravery and cool courage" during the Battle of Kelly's Ford, March 17, 1863. (Courtesy of the Library of Congress)

9. James E. Taylor's sketch of Gilmor dropping Captain George D. Summers, Company F, Second Maryland Regiment, Potomac Home Brigade. This action took place near Summit Point in October 1863. (Courtesy of the Western Reserve Historical Society, Cleveland, Ohio)

10. General John D. Imboden. Gilmor played an instrumental role in helping Imboden bag the Union garrison at Charles Town on October 18, 1863. (Courtesy of the Library of Congress)

11. James E. Taylor's sketch of Gilmor in the saddle. Gilmor appears every inch to be a proud Confederate cavalier. (Courtesy of the Western Reserve Historical Society, Cleveland, Ohio)

5

"If Spades are Trumps"

Autumn slowly gave way to the bitter days of winter in the Shenandoah Valley, while, north of the Mason-Dixon line, news of the Federal debacle at Charles Town found its way into Northern newspapers. The *Philadelphia Inquirer* stated that the incident "[was] but a part of the disgraceful list of surprises so common to this region," concluding that "a little vigilance and skill exercised by our outpost commanders would render these raids very dangerous experiments for the Rebels." In the meantime, Gilmor and his command headed back up the Valley in search of forage. For his own efforts in protecting General Imboden's retreat to Berryville after surprising the Federal garrison at Charles Town, Gilmor discovered buckshot in his leg and counted three horses wounded, one falling as he attempted to recapture Joseph Stansbury of Company A. However, a slight leg wound was not about to hinder the partisan activities of Harry Gilmor. Undaunted, he approached 1864 with an even stronger determination to fight for the Southern Cause.[1]

After Charles Town, Colonel William H. Boyd, First New York Cavalry, provided Gilmor with a new challenge in the Valley. On the early dawn hours of Sunday, November 15, Boyd, placed in charge of detachments representing seven different commands, moved out of Charles Town for a raid up the snow covered Shenandoah. Gilmor noticed Boyd's force as soon as it slithered its way out of Charles Town and quickly reported the activity to his superiors. He also informed them of the important fact that the Federal raiding party contained infantry and artillery, in addition to cavalry. The Marylander rounded up fifty men from his command and traveled into "Fort Valley" (or "Powell's Fort"). Fort Valley, located just north of the Massanutton Mountain, is a small valley surrounded on four sides by mountains, thereby providing occupants with natural fortifications. Within the valley proper, Major Gilmor decided to make Burner's Springs, normally a resort spot for the residents of the quaint little valley, his base of operations.[2]

Only one day after taking up headquarters Gilmor mustered thirty of his best men, including his cousin, William, of Company C, for a scouting mission in the vicinity of Millwood, where Boyd's cavalry was shadowing his left flank as he made his way up the Shenandoah. While Gilmor's force clandestinely approached Millwood, he and William Doran, also of Company C, slipped unnoticed into the Shenandoah town. There, the stealthy Rebel duo were informed by a friend that a large Federal cavalry force, consisting of both the First New York and Major Henry Cole's Potomac Home Brigade of Maryland Cavalry, had already entered the town and were stationed in and around the church. Gilmor left Millwood, formed his men who were encamped outside of town, and briskly galloped southward toward Front Royal, warning the citizens in the locale of the impending Yankee movement before making their way back to the "fort."[3]

For both the men in Boyd's command as well as Gilmor's rangers, the harsh winter weather was equally unsympathetic. Severe, frigid high winds beat down upon all who dared to brave the cold. Most troopers had to walk along their mounts in order to avoid freezing in the chilly environment. Also, heavy sleet and rain storms left "every bush, tree, and blade of grass glittering and loaded down with ice;" the scenic beauty of such a phenomenon belied the hazard that it posed to the rangers, for every time a scout took a step the crunching sound beneath his feet foiled any attempt for surprise. To compound their difficulties, swollen streams had to be crossed, more often than not leaving Gilmor's rangers covered with ice cold water that froze instantly when it touched their clothing. The cold notwithstanding, Gilmor decided to leave the friendly but cold confines of Burner's Springs and travel west twelve miles, where he observed Boyd's main force moving "up the [Shenandoah] Valley Turnpike," the vanguard of the Yankee column already in New Market.[4]

While the Federal column moved up the Valley, Major Gilmor decided to slip to the rear and destroy the bridge over the North Branch of the Shenandoah River, thereby cutting off the Yankee retreat route. The bridge was protected by a squadron of Union men who were sheltered in "cedar boughs and fodder." On their way to the bridge they were tempted to visit the 2,400 acre Mount Airy estate owned by Dr. Andrew Russell Meem. "'Mount Airy' [was] a 'home away from home' for many Southern soldiers," most of whom had their wounds of war treated by the women of the estate.[5] However, perhaps calling into memory the disastrous October expedition to the Baltimore and Ohio Railroad, when Gilmor decided to visit the ladies at "Carter Hall," this time he displayed self-restraint and passed by the inviting estate. Due to the valiant resistance of the Union squadron on guard at the bridge, Gilmor's attack was repulsed, leaving William Gilmor with a wound to the right arm as a result of hot Federal fire. Gilmor's effort was not in vain, for the rangers managed to come away with "about fifteen prisoners and twenty-six horses."[6]

Gilmor's men finally made their way over hazardous roads to Luray, where they found Confederate cavalry general, Thomas Rosser. The tried and weary rangers thought that they would be afforded some rest after the day's contest at the bridge and their tiring journey to Luray. However, they were denied when Rosser ordered them to discover Boyd's exact disposition, which was estimated to be in the vicinity of New Market. Major Gilmor's command soon discovered that Boyd had already begun his retreat down the Valley and had just passed through New Market. Gilmor was again ordered to seize the bridge and harass Boyd's rear. Much to his chagrin, Gilmor found that the flooring of the bridge was removed by Boyd in order to cover his retreat; not to be denied, Gilmor's command did manage to continue to aggravate Boyd's rear all the way to Woodstock. Four of Gilmor's more indefatigable troops followed Boyd more than thirty additional miles down the Valley to Winchester, where they plugged at Yankees "from a house, wounding one of the First New York Cavalry very seriously." When an angry vengeance party of Union men searched the dwelling, they found Gilmor's men attempting to conceal themselves in some fashion "beneath the floor." As punishment, the four partisans were forced to march back to the Union camp barefooted, which doubtless caused as much humiliation as it did physical suffering. During his raid up the Valley, Boyd managed to capture "twenty seven prisoners...about ninety fat cattle, fifty tents, three four-horse teams and a quantity of tobacco and salt."[7]

By late December and early January of 1864, the Confederate Army of Northern Virginia was lacking some of the vital necessities of warfare, most important of which was food. As a result General Lee ordered General Jubal Early to make a cavalry raid into Hardy and Hampshire Counties, both of which were located in western Virginia, in order to gather cattle and meat for his hungry legions. At the forefront of the expedition was Lee's nephew, Major- General Fitzhugh Lee, whose force was to be augmented by one of John Hanson McNeill's partisan ranger companies as well as Gilmor's battalion, both of whom would aid Lee in scouting and raiding. Early's order to Lee was as blunt as it was demanding, especially in light of the weather and mountainous terrain. Lee was instructed to leave the Shenandoah Valley by crossing the Great North Mountain into Hardy County, then do no less than "dislodge an infantry force at Petersburg, cut the Baltimore and Ohio Railroad at the mouth of the South Branch of the Potomac and Patterson's Creek," and all the while collect as much of the area's beef cattle that could be had. The artillery battery that was to support Lee's efforts had to be sent back due to the inability of his command to transport them down the ice covered mountains.[8]

After Gilmor received word that he was going to play a role in the foraging expedition into western Virginia, the partisan mustered a force of seventy-five effective men, under the command of Captain David M. Ross, Company C. Gilmor's men were still haggard as a result of their recent activities against Boyd. Nevertheless, Gilmor ordered Ross to take the command and move to Moorefield, Hardy County, and wait for him there. In the meantime, Gilmor and some fellow officers from Fitzhugh Lee's staff decided to seek shelter and wait out a terrible snow storm that was breaking through the valleys of western Virginia. After celebrating the bringing in of the New Year of 1864 "in regular old Virginia style" at a pro-Rebel household during the night, the small group of officers again set out after breakfast. Gilmor and his comrades soon came upon a distillery owned by John Basore, which was nestled within "a gap in the Cove Mountain." The owner was previously ordered to sell none of their "spirits" to any Rebel soldier on the expedition. Deciding to try their luck, Gilmor and the officers entered Basore's dwelling only to find a curious woman present, her husband being away at the mill. One of the party proceeded to introduce Gilmor, who was decked out in a "new uniform as well as a wide-brimmed slouched hat that sported a long plume and gold band with crossed sabers on front," as none other than General Robert E. Lee. "Lee" informed the hostess that he "was almost perished with cold and would kindly desire something to drink, provided it was good." She did more than just answer the "General's" request. The kind hostess treated the stealthy officers to a bottle of peach brandy that her mother gave to her when she married John Basore thirty three years earlier. After their coup at the Basore's residence the officers set off again. A short time later, the "high humor and capers" of Gilmor's group finally caught up with the Marylander as he attempted to race some friends to a house where dinner was about to be served. Gilmor's horse was just about to leap a fence when it slipped and fell broadside, knocking the wind out of its dazed rider, who was left in much pain and was barely able to catch his breath during a sleepless night after the accident. Perhaps Gilmor's fall was a result of childlike carelessness, or, on the other hand, it may have been a supernatural hoax played by Mrs. Basore's departed mother, who did not take kindly to the trick played by the Marylander and his allies at the expense of her naive, but well-intentioned, daughter.[9]

Gilmor awoke in much pain the next day and "had to be lifted upon his horse," but he managed to rejoin his command and was also placed in charge of Captain McNeill's company of rangers. With these two commands, Lee ordered him "to hold the gap on the Moorefield and Petersburg Road, and also protect [his] flank and rear." Gilmor, however, was able to accomplish much more. He moved his command into northern Hampshire County, where he came across the eight hundred man Union garrison located at Springfield. After the major made a faint to the garrison's rear, the Union force panicked and evacuated the city during the night without offering a struggle, allowing Gilmor's command to enter unmolested and remove "about three thousand pounds of bacon, some hard bread, horseshoes, nails, &c., and destroyed by fire the forage and other stores in addition to the troops' winter quarters." Overall, Lee's raid was successful, for he managed to take "forty Union wagons, 110 prisoners with their arms, &c., and 460 head of cattle;" unfortunately for his uncle's hungry soldiers, almost half of the cattle were lost moving eastward over the precarious mountain conditions at night. He also managed to destroy the Baltimore and Ohio railroad bridge over Patterson's Creek and also damaged the one over the South Branch. Lee's command had marched 555 miles "in weather of uncommon severity," and as a result he commended his men "for the endurance displayed and hardships undergone."[10]

Robert E. Lee appreciated the effort put forth by his troopers in western Virginia, but also informed Early that according to his sources there existed in Hardy and Hampshire Counties additional cattle that were not requisitioned during the recent expedition. Lee thus ordered Early to organize another raiding expedition, suggesting that "care should be taken to select men well acquainted with [the region], and who know where the cattle were to be found." Lee named three men, who, "by their energy, intelligence, and knowledge of the resources of the country were qualified to aid the expedition," one of whom was Captain Ross of Gilmor's Band. On January 28, 1864, Early set off on another raiding expedition, this time "with Rosser's brigade, two units of mounted scouts, a brigade of infantry, and a battery of four guns." Meanwhile, a cold Union private in Company A, The Ringgold Cavalry Company 22nd Pennsylvania Cavalry, who was previously scouting and picketing in the rugged terrain, wrote to his beloved Esther. Aungier Dobbs mentioned that "a big scare" occurred in his near vicinity, however, "it [the scare] is subsiding."[11] The "big scare" was undoubtedly the first Rebel raid, and little did the Monongahela Valley native realize it, but another Rebel expedition was well in the works.

Gilmor's battalion, together with McNeill and Elijah V. White's respective commands, served as cavalry support for Rosser's efforts in the western Virginia raid. Soon, most of Gilmor's battalion and McNeill's entire command were ordered to move back to the Allegheny Mountains with the objective of rounding up cattle. Rosser's order sending McNeill back on a cattle expedition did nothing to enhance the already strained relationship between the two, a feud that would reverberate into the highest pinnacles of the Confederate government a few weeks after the expedition. Gilmor, with only his "most reliable scouts" plus White's men, remained the vanguard of the Rebel column. After capturing a Union wagon train numbering some ninety wagons, Rosser marched on Petersburg, only to find that the Union garrison stationed there had already fled without taking their valuable "stores, forage, and ammunition." Rosser completed the remaining "part of his mission, destroying the Baltimore and Ohio railroad bridges and rounding up some eight hundred head of cattle."[12]

During an assault on one of the bridges, Gilmor had another very close call. A Union man was able to get a clear shot at the Marylander from within close range, but, after the Federal's bullet passed through Gilmor's two bulky overcoats and pack of playing cards in "his left side pocket," it stopped. Only one card remained untouched by the ball's potentially deadly path, "the ace of spades!" Gilmor would be constantly reminded of his "lady luck" by General Rosser, who whenever he saw the fortunate Marylander would inquire jokingly "if spades are trumps."[13]

Gilmor's activities during Boyd's raid up the Valley, as well as his role in Early's raids into western Virginia, epitomized his growing importance as a partisan fighter. During Colonel Boyd's raid Gilmor kept a constant vigilance upon the Yankee force, attempted to destroy bridges in his path of retreat, and harassed the Yankee's rear. Also, his attack on the Union garrison at Springfield and rounding up of cattle during Early's food expeditions further personified the role he played as an irregular. Regardless of the hostile attitude directed toward guerrilla units on the part of many prominent Confederate generals and political figures, they still found many such units of great utility in abetting their war efforts; it would be a bitter-sweet marriage that would last the duration of the conflict.

Around the ninth of February, General Jeb Stuart ordered Gilmor to cut the Baltimore and Ohio Railroad with the objective of preventing additional Union forces from traveling eastward and bolstering the ranks of the Army of the Potomac. Realizing that such a strike depended more upon surprise than numbers, Gilmor selected only twenty-eight men for the operation. His small force moved northward into the lower Valley, which was a proverbial "hornet's nest" of Union commands and strong picket guards. Gilmor fully appreciated the huge Union cavalry force situated at Charles Town, which, if alerted to his activities, could easily cut his retreat route back up the Valley. Furthermore, he had to deal with the Union line of pickets that extended from the Shenandoah River westward to the North Mountain. However, to Gilmor an order was an order, and so he meandered his way through the picket force and decided to assault the Baltimore and Ohio at a spot halfway between Duffield's Depot and Kearneysville. The two locations were approximately four to five miles apart, and both harbored numerous picket guards. The stretch of railroad that connected these two places bisected thick, dense patches of woods, which would serve to enhance surprise and allow a quick get away.[14]

Upon reaching their destination, the Rebel party was unable to remove the securely fastened rails. This being the case, Gilmor ordered his men to place several large logs upon the track, and, in order to lessen the impact of the train smashing into the log barrier and possibly causing undue injury, Gilmor had two men move two hundred yards up the track from which direction the train would arrive and place fence rails across the track. Gilmor's men then took up their position in the thick woods along the track, but not before he warned them "not to molest citizens or ladies" during the train assault. As the early evening advanced, an express passenger train appeared, having left Camden Depot, Baltimore, for Wheeling the day before.[15]

The engineer, upon observing the fence rails, was able to slow the train to such an extent that when it struck the log barrier it easily rumbled off its track, not even awaking many of the sleeping passengers. After seeing that the engineer was uninjured, Gilmor looked for the mail car in search of an "iron safe that he was informed contained a large amount of public money." Instead he entered the smoking car which contained a large number of armed cavalrymen. Gilmor ordered the startled Northerners to surrender their weapons and vacate the car. No sooner had the Marylander barked these instructions when a large Irishman attempted to strike Gilmor with his saber. Fortunately for the partisan, the saber first struck the low ceiling of the car, grazing Harry slightly in the arm, leaving only a bruise. Gilmor struck the disgruntled Union man on the head with the barrel of his rifle, and, grabbing the Federal by the collar of his shirt, pushed him out the front door. The Yankee trooper was by now of course extremely angry, and, after throwing two of Gilmor's comrades from atop the train platform, he in turn was hurled down to the ground by Gilmor. Unfortunately for the Federal trooper, his head struck a rock, the impact of "which stilled his breath forever."[16] After this incident, Gilmor attempted to break into the iron safe which occupied his attention since running the train off track. However, his efforts came to naught, for the express messenger had the key and had escaped earlier, and, to add to his distress, he and some of his command could not break the Herring Patent lock. Gilmor, after rounding up the passengers, ordered the train destroyed, save for the sleeping car, which would be used to house the lady passengers. It was during this time that the major was informed that some of his men, against his express orders, had robbed several of the passengers. This infuriated the

Marylander, who "threatened to shoot any one caught in the act of robbery." At any rate, Gilmor had no time to discipline his men, for he was also warned that the Wheeling train, with more Union troops aboard, was in close proximity. His men fled toward Smithfield, about eight to ten miles to the southwest.[17]

The news of the train robbery made its way into the *New York Times* only three days after it occurred. The New York press labeled Gilmor's group "a guerrilla band" and "raiders," which did nothing to brighten their reputation among Confederate officials. Furthermore, the *Times* reported that one of the eyewitnesses suggested that "the aggregate amount of money taken from the passengers was not less than thirty thousand dollars." In addition to this testimony, other passengers reported that valuables, such as "watches, diamonds, rings, and breastpins" were seized by the "raiders." Even though the press admitted that details were lacking in order to make a positive identification of who was in charge of the raid, or, who the horsemen actually were, they did however mention that one of the riders stated that "Major Harry Gilmer [sic], of the Confederate Cavalry, was in command of the expedition, [and] that he knew and conversed with him." The *Times* also wrote that some of the passengers concluded that the raid "was done by a local predatory band organized for the purpose of plundering at every opportunity." In addition to the *Time's* report, the *Baltimore American* did nothing to help the waning reputation of their native son, stating that the robbery was undertaken "with all the grace and sang froid of experienced highwaymen." Also, the paper said that the robbers "thrust the muzzles [of their guns] under the noses of their victims whilst they were being plundered," even carrying off "pocket knives and toothpicks," among much more valuable booty.[18]

To make matters worse, a few days after the Baltimore and Ohio train robbery, seven Confederate cavalrymen, all of whom were members of Gilmor's "Band," managed to rob a two wagon Jewish caravan near Woodstock, in the Shenandoah Valley. Gilmor's men stole "six thousand in gold, two wrist watches, a great coat, fur collar, Hebrew prayer book, in addition to a number of silver coins and medals." In the days following the robbery, Confederate authorities sent two detectives into the area in order to investigate the incident. However, according to a letter written from a Southern major in Harrisonburg to the provost-marshal in Richmond, Gilmor, drunk at the time, confessed to bribing the detectives not to turn the guilty parties over to authorities. Also, it was alleged that the intoxicated partisan boasted that he "could manage the whole detective force of the government." In March General Imboden was ordered to investigate this so-called "Hyman Robbery." His inquiry uncovered substantial testimonial evidence from men of Gilmor's battalion that incriminated the partisan in the affair. For example, one of Gilmor's men claimed that the Marylander "acknowledged ...that he had arranged the affair of robbing the Jew, had put the men concerned all right, and had stood off and seen the thing well done." In another invidious bit of testimony, Gilmor's quartermaster, a Captain Owings, claimed that "Gilmor gave him $160 in gold to buy a horse with, and told him that most of it was taken from a Jew, and that he had arranged the affair."[19] While Imboden's investigation proceeded, Gilmor remained in prison, for after the Baltimore and Ohio affair attracted such negative attention from the Northern press, Confederate officials had no choice but to arrest the Marylander. Indeed, "for a time Gilmor's future in the Confederate army was uncertain."[20]

General Lee, who was the consummate "gentlemen's general," was disgusted by the Baltimore and Ohio train robbery outside of Duffield's Depot. Such thievery was too readily comparable to the distasteful exploits of some of the lawless guerrilla bands that preyed upon helpless citizens;

only in this case the incident occurred right under the watchful eyes of the Northern press. Lee, in a message to Secretary of War Seddon, stated his disgruntlement and concern over the implications of the matter.

> As far as I know no military object was accomplished after gaining possession of the cars, and the act appears to have been one of plunder. Such conduct is unauthorized and discreditable. Should any of that battalion be captured the enemy might claim to treat them as highway robbers. What would be our course? I have ordered an investigation of the matter and hope the report may be untrue.[21]

Incidents such as the train robbery became increasingly common among many guerrilla bands operating in the northern Shenandoah Valley and western Virginia.[22] Such affairs, like scouting missions and raiding enemy encampments, also began to personify partisan activities in a negative sense. This led many within the Confederate military and governmental circles to question if all partisan units, with the exception of Mosby's, were not more of a liability than a military asset to the Southern "Cause."

The behavior of Gilmor's men in both the incident on the Baltimore and Ohio as well as the "Hyman Affair" could not have come at a worse time. By February and March 1864, the reputation of partisan commands was at an all time nadir, and Confederate authorities were moving steadily toward a consensus that something had to be done in order to check the misbehavior and other negative aspects of irregular units. A key event that served to spur the passage of legislation concerning partisan rangers was Colonel Rosser's letter to General Lee, in which he expressed his unfavorable opinion in regards to the general military utility of irregular units. Reminiscing about his recent disagreements with Captain

McNeill during Early's second food raid into western Virginia, Rosser made sweeping statements referring to "all irregulars" as nothing more than a "nuisance and an evil to the service."[23] General Jeb Stuart concurred with Rosser's assessment, citing Mosby's Rangers as the only exception to the rule. Soon General Lee "recommended that the law authorizing the Partisan corps be abolished."[24] On February 17, 1864, legislation was passed which prohibited the legal military organization of irregular units and further "directed that all partisan commands organized under the April 1862 law [Gilmor's being one of them] were to be united with other organizations into battalions or regiments."[25] However, "the legislature granted [Secretary of War] Seddon the authority to permit certain units to operate within Federal lines."[26] Thus, Gilmor's military career, which had just taken a horrific down swing, now became entangled in the Confederate debate over the usefulness of partisan forces.

While the troubled partisan remained under arrest at Staunton, Gilmor maintained a lively correspondence with friends and well-wishers. One comrade from Mount Airy, who was downcast, wrote to the imprisoned Gilmor, "I am so unwell this morning that I must beg of you to send me a bottle of brandy." In another letter, George Treaver, a good friend of the Marylander, writes that he is in need of a good horse. Treaver admits that it has been difficult to purchase one, requiring "bushel basketsfull [sic]" of inflated Confederate currency to purchase "a few pounds of horseflesh." Attempting to humor the major, Treaver states that "if [he] had the recuperative energy of many of the *Band*, not omitting its gallant and *strategic* chief, [he] might scale this little difficulty." Treaver, fully aware of what the newspapers were saying about the imprisoned Gilmor, as well as his waning reputation with Southern authorities, suggested that his chances are good that the major would lend him a horse. After all, continuing in the same jocular tone, you are presumably "just rioting with greenbacks, with all your pockets full, notwithstanding the many holes which *Apple Jack* and *lovely women* keep tearing in them, and [also you are] just rollicking on good horses." Treaver agreed to pay Gilmor for the horse as soon as possible, but if it is stolen, he assured his potential creditor that he would give him "one horse worth about eight hundred dollars," a gold watch, "one pair of very high legged boots, [and] a lock of hair." Encouraging Gilmor to accept the deal, while simultaneously teasing his friend, Treaver makes reference to the train robbery:

> Now Harry here is a first rate speculation - a d-mned sight better than throwing railroad cars off the track and *not getting into the safe*, and I shall be surprised at your want of common sense, if you don't bite like a trout.[27]

Undoubtedly, as Gilmor read Treaver's letter, a warm smile and an occasional boisterous laugh served as a welcome reprieve from what would have been a typical mundane day in his Staunton confines.

On March 21, 1864, General John D. Imboden released Gilmor from arrest, thereby allowing the major to "resume his sword." The order must have been a temporary one, for in late April, as a result of the train robbery, Gilmor was tried by court-martial in Staunton. Colonel Richard Dulany, of the Seventh Virginia Cavalry, presided over the proceedings. Just prior to the hearings, George Treaver penned another letter to his embattled friend, encouraging Gilmor to "...take it for granted that you will come off with flying colors. You have my sympathy and I shall stand up for you through thick and thin." He also advised Gilmor to use Major General Fitzhugh Lee's recently published report concerning the Battle of Kelly's Ford, in which the Marylander is spoken of proudly, in his defense. Treaver then informed Gilmor that "these *matters all* have weight in military trials."[28]

While the evidence was being collected for the upcoming trial, General Lee informed Richmond of his conviction that Gilmor's battalion should be disbanded, stating that "experience has convinced me that it is almost impossible, under the best officers even, to have discipline in these bands of partisan rangers." Lee also suggested that irregular commands encourage "desertion and marauders, and commit depredations on friend and foe alike." However, Samuel W. Melton, Major and Assistant Adjutant-General in the Confederate capital, had other plans for the Marylander. Melton stated that Gilmor's battalion consists of Virginians and Marylanders and Gilmor himself "is represented to be a good officer and his men willing to come into general service." Melton requested that his command be mustered into the Maryland Line. In addition to Melton's recommendations, in late April Gilmor was acquitted and released from arrest by General John C. Breckinridge. Interestingly, Breckinridge decided to release Gilmor without first gaining General Lee's approval of the court-martial verdict. Then, the former Vice-President of the United States issued Special Orders Number One, restoring Gilmor's command.[29]

To further add to Gilmor's delight, he was given back his old command, only with a new name. Secretary Seddon approved Melton's suggestion, and on May 5 Gilmor's "Band" was officially "mustered into service as cavalry" and ordered to report to General Arnold Elzey, who was attempting to organize the Maryland Line. The Maryland Line was a plan by which Marylanders within the Confederate ranks would constitute an exclusive Maryland military organization. "Gilmor's Battalion" officially became entitled the Second Maryland Cavalry Battalion, and "citizens of other states who were enlisted in his [command]" were granted the opportunity to transfer out on their own recognizance.[30]

After his release from arrest at Staunton, Gilmor was ordered to travel northward, collect the men of his battalion, and perform his military role as a de facto irregular. Even though he was nominally mustered into service under a regular command, the major would continue his partisan activities, as was the case with not a few partisan commands that came under the February legislation. General Elzey was hard pressed in his efforts to organize the Maryland Line, and found groups of Gilmor's new battalion located at different places in the Shenandoah Valley. Fifty dismounted men belonging to Gilmor's command were located at Staunton, and an additional thirty men, who were in jail in Charleston, reported to General Elzey's headquarters at Camp Maryland. Elzey, who apparently had some of these men provided with horses, sent the two groups of Gilmor's partisans to Imboden's command, requesting that he "retain the mounted men in the lower Valley, on such duty as [he] may direct." It was during this time that the lower Shenandoah was bustling with activity as a result of the recent Union movement up the lush springtime Valley. Gilmor would reunite with his battalion, which, after being sent to Imboden's command, was serving as "pickets between Mount Jackson and Edinburg." The Marylander quickly organized his small force, preparing them "for the work we had to do."[31]

Gilmor's waning reputation as a result of the February train robbery in no way discouraged Marylanders from joining his command. On May 10, 1864, General Elzey ordered two privates that were "transferred from the Twelfth Virginia Cavalry to the Maryland Line" to report to Gilmor for temporary assignment. In the spring of that year, Company F of the Twelfth Virginia, Gilmor's former company, would be restored to his command. In 1863 this company had been temporarily assigned to Gilmor's command while he was recruiting his force, only to be returned to Colonel Arthur Harman's Twelfth Virginia later that summer. Indeed, as late as September 1864 eleven Marylanders who were former members of a South Carolina Regiment and were "old soldiers [who] have been in the service since March 1861," petitioned Gilmor for an opportunity to join his battalion.[32]

The negative attention Gilmor received from Confederate authorities also did not lessen his standing in the eyes of the Southern belles. In a letter from one of his many female admirers, a mysterious Eve tells the cavalier that "it may surprise you when I tell you I have long loved you with the utmost fondness." Four days later she again wrote to her knight, once again refusing to disclose her full identity. She wrote teasingly, "You say you are puzzled to know who this fair correspondent of yours really is, true you would not recognize her did you see her, yet she has often stood near you, and listened to your manly voice." Eve described herself as "rather tall, graceful in [her] movements, dark eyes and hair, fair complexion, and somewhere between eighteen and nineteen years of age."[33]

Back in the Shenandoah Valley during the Spring of 1864, Major Gilmor and the Confederacy confronted another Federal invasion. This time nine thousand Union soldiers under the command of Major General Franz Sigel invaded the Southern bread basket. A native German, Sigel appeared every inch an officer that embodied that European region's esteemed military tradition. However, his appearance concealed a general who would prove himself indecisive, and history would judge the German as a "walking military disaster, who bawled out orders in German when rattled." Sigel would demonstrate greater utility to the North through his rallying of German-born citizens to the Union's efforts.[34] By the middle of May, Sigel's column lethargically made its way up the Valley, all the while being constantly menaced by irregulars. While near Strasburg, Sigel decided to divide his command, sending out two cavalry detachments, both of which numbered approximately one thousand troopers, toward the Luray Valley and west of the Massanutton Mountain, respectively. These cavalry forces shadowing Sigel's flanks would serve to protect his main column against the guerrillas, particularly against Mosby's men, who were a threat from the east.[35]

Gilmor left headquarters at Staunton and traveled the short distance to the vicinity of his battalion. Along the way, he was startled by firing and the sight of retreating Southern pickets. The pickets were being forced in by Union cavalry under the command of Major Charles Otis, of the Twenty First New York. Otis's large force managed to push aside Imboden's pickets as well as Gilmor's men, who managed to retreat beyond Mount Jackson, just before Otis decided to call off his hounds. Gilmor, as usual, was in the thick of the action. His last fight had been with Colonel Rosser in western Virginia back in January, and his thirst for adventure had to again be quenched. Determined to remain behind and "plug away" at the Yankees as they pursued his retreating men, after awhile, he decided that it would be wise to rejoin the rest of his command. When he turned to gallop away, he received a ball from a carbine in his lower right back. Almost immediately, he felt a paralysis in his lower back, and right hip and leg. However, fortunately for the Marylander, the bullet "first struck the top of his [horse's] crupper" (that portion of the harness that is tied to the saddle and around the tail of the horse, preventing the saddle from moving toward the horse's neck). Had it not, the projectile would have passed straight through Gilmor's body, more likely than not killing him. After the action, the wounded Gilmor collected his men and traveled to Mount Airy, where he was kindly cared for by the hospitable host, Mrs. Meem, whom he described "[as] the sweetest and kindest woman in the world." Gilmor was among several wounded during the Federal assault, which also claimed the lives of many horses.[36]

After a short retreat into New Market, Imboden

orchestrated a masterful counter strike. The Confederate general, supplemented with John Hanson McNeill's men, managed to rout one of Sigel's Union cavalry wings in the vicinity of Wardensville. At the same time Gilmor's command was sent into the Luray Valley, in order to harass the other cavalry detachment under Colonel William Boyd's command.[37] While on his way to Luray, Gilmor, still in pain due to his wound, passed through "Fort Valley," where he encountered a small Union picket guard who was present in and around a barn. The major did not wish to attack the party for fear of arousing the larger Union force known to be in close proximity, and besides, a local citizen piloted Gilmor's command to a location where they could observe the entire small force in the morning. Much to Gilmor's chagrin, the small Union party escaped right out from under his nose, making their way intact to Milford during the early morning hours. To compound his frustration, during the morning a battered Union straggler told Gilmor that the small party at the barn was composed of Union men all right, but their effectiveness was significantly reduced by drunkenness, as the Union men threw caution to the wind and engaged in a drunken brawl that evening. The blue-coated soldier himself bore many bruises on his face, which testified to the veracity of his statement. Gilmor shook his head and "cursed his timidity" for not assaulting the barn that night. He then decided to pursue the careless Northern troopers by crossing over the Massanutton Mountain. After reaching the summit, he and five of his troopers took the vanguard of the march, and by the time they were at the base they became separated from the main column by over two miles. The half dozen Confederates then spotted the dismounted Yankees next to the Shenandoah River. With his main force still over two miles away, Gilmor, "losing his senses," charged the Union camp, with his "equally crazy" comrade, William Kemp, leading the way. Nevertheless, several of the more pathetic, "hung-over" Yankees put up their hands to surrender, while another fled toward the river bank. However, a Union sergeant soon jumped upon his horse and rallied the men, informing them that they only had five or six men. Kemp drew his pistol and plugged the sergeant, just as he came within a saber's length of his major. Gilmor and his followers came to their senses and retreated hastily toward the base of the mountain, followed closely by twenty-five Federal troopers. They were saved by the main force that was just making its way to the base of the Massanutton, and together they pushed the Yankees into the Shenandoah River, its waters claiming nine of the Federal men. Because of his timidity and later carelessness Gilmor contended that "this was the worst managed affair I ever undertook." The Marylander counted three wounded after the day's fiasco came to a welcome conclusion.[38]

During a terrific rainstorm, Gilmor's battalion forded the overflowing and hazardous Shenandoah, and after making its way to the eastern shore, decided to await Colonel Boyd's arrival. Gilmor soon discovered from "fleeing citizens from Rappahannock County" the troop numbers contained within Boyd's command. He also learned that they had been moving along lethargically east of the Massanutton Mountain. In addition, Gilmor came to the realization that Boyd had moved southward beyond Luray, much farther up the Page Valley than expected, and, according to the citizens, he told them that he wished to join Sigel at New Market in a couple of days.[39] After sending this vital information off to Imboden, Gilmor prepared his men for battle. The Marylander surmised that, if Boyd's force was beaten by Imboden in the southern portion of the Page Valley, the Union colonel would have to retreat northward down the valley where Gilmor's troopers would be ready and waiting. Gilmor's plan was well thought out. However, due in large part to the intelligence Gilmor had obtained, Imboden was able to prepare an ambuscade for

Boyd's force well south of where Gilmor's men were waiting; "on his way from the Luray Valley to New Market" Boyd unwittingly entered the awaiting Southern ambush.[40] He was completely defeated by Imboden, who reported that he managed to "cut him [Boyd] off from the roads, and drove him into the Massanutton Mountain. Numbers [of men were] captured, together with about half their horses," and Boyd was counted among the Federal wounded during the affray.[41]

After his defeat of Boyd, Imboden traveled back to New Market. Meanwhile, the unfortunate Sigel, who observed a double dose of misfortune befall his two cavalry detachments at Wardensville and east of the Massanutton Mountain, marched with his main command of approximately 6,500 men upon General Imboden's cavalry located at New Market. Imboden managed to delay Sigel's advance until General Breckinridge arrived with a three thousand man force, including some two hundred cadets from the Virginia Military Institute in Lexington. After a hole in the Confederate line developed, Breckinridge ordered that the young cadets be thrown into the fight in order to mend the opening. The cadets turned the tide of battle in favor of the South. During the mid-afternoon hours of May 15, 1864, Sigel ordered a retreat. After the Battle of New Market, Breckinridge rode over to a group of weary Virginia cadets who were resting after the action which claimed "one fourth of their numbers as casualties" and said "well done, Virginians, well done, men."[42]

Sigel's debacle had an influence upon future military operations in the Valley and can be interpreted a number of ways. First, his decision to send two cavalry forces to shadow his flanks as he moved up the Valley was due in large part to his difficulties with the partisan units located there. This decision significantly weakened his main force, thereby setting the stage for his crushing defeat at New Market. Thus, it can be concluded that irregulars were directly influencing Union decisions and fortunes in the Shenandoah. Also, the charge of the young cadets at New Market, as well as the overall Southern will to continue their struggle against ever increasing odds, demonstrated that even though the infrastructure of the Confederacy was disintegrating, the flame of independence and patriotism still burned within its spirit and soul. Also, Sigel's defeat represented the last Union attempt to conquer the Shenandoah Valley and defeat its army through traditional methods of warfare. On the heels of the New Market blow, a new Union general, with a new style of warfare, would be sent into the Valley to attempt to succeed where Sigel had failed; General David Hunter's new method of warfare carried the war's ugly destructive powers directly to the Shenandoah's populace to a much greater degree than ever before witnessed in the Valley. In the Shenandoah Valley during the summer of 1864 the final chapter of the "gentlemen's war" came to a conclusion, turning to a tragic new one entitled "total war."

Almost sixty two years of age, David Hunter, a "stern looking" virulent abolitionist, was given a fifteen thousand man command and ordered to move his force into the Valley and "destroy its railroads, cross the Blue Ridge to smash the Confederate supply depot at Lynchburg, and continue east toward Richmond" as one part of General Ulysses S. Grant's plan to "cut Lee's supply lines and flank him out of his trenches" in eastern Virginia.[43] Hunter faced a Confederate Army of only 8,500 men in the Valley, now under the command of General William E. "Grumble" Jones, which paled in comparison to the Federal's force. Nevertheless, even before he started up the Valley on May 26, he was already being harassed by guerrilla forces in the lower Shenandoah region.[44]

Meanwhile Gilmor made his way behind Hunter's column and operated in the area between Middletown and Martinsburg, a stretch of land along the Valley Turnpike that ran from south to north a length of forty-five miles. He soon received word from his scouts that a wagon train consisting of "eighty-three men and sixteen wagons" was at Winchester, just five miles north of Gilmor's force, which was concealed in a thick wooded area near Bartonsville. Gilmor, who had been keeping a close eye upon the supply train since it left Martinsburg, decided to allow "[it] to pass by and enter Newtown, where [he] would charge them in the rear." Gilmor's force moved along parallel to the train, and, when he saw the rear guard enter the quaint Shenandoah village, his fifty-three man force struck. The attack was a success. Gilmor managed to capture the wagon train, killing one Federal officer and wounding nine more. Gilmor burned twelve of the sixteen wagons, leaving only "a small part of the medical stores, forage, and one wagon" behind to be reclaimed by the disgruntled Federal commander of the train, who returned a short time later with a large number of infantry. The mortally wounded Federal officer was a Captain Brett, of the First New York Veteran Cavalry, who, according to his superior officer, "although having no command he took his place in the ranks and fought like a hero."[45] Gilmor's Second Maryland, like hornets awakened from a nest, began to sting Hunter's army as it moved up the Valley.

After his successful raid upon the small Union supply wagon train, Gilmor and his men rode back into Newtown, only to find the villagers very concerned over the fate of their dwellings. Hunter earlier "had issued a circular to the citizens, telling them that if any more trains were attacked or pickets captured," he would burn every house in the vicinity of the depredation. Seeing the grave concern on the villagers' expressions, Gilmor could bear no more, and he penned out a message to General Hunter, warning the Northerner that if he carried out his threat to torch the town he would execute "thirty-five [Union] men and six officers" that he held as prisoners. The following day a force of three hundred blue coat cavalry troopers rode into town and their officers announced to the hapless citizens the fate that was about to befall their barns and dwellings. Then an unidentified person handed Gilmor's note to the officers, who were at least emotionally relieved, for now they had an excuse not to burn the village.[46] Newtown was saved due to Gilmor's efforts and to a lesser extent to a handful of caring Union officers, who still were endeared to the mores of the "gentlemen's war" and humanity. As time went on, their example would prove an exception to the rule.

Despite Gilmor's assault upon one segment of Hunter's medical supply train, and many other raids that followed the major's example, the indefatigable Federal general continued to push resolutely up the Valley. On June 5, Hunter pitched into Brigadier General William "Grumble" Jones's forces at Piedmont, located ten to fifteen miles north of Staunton. Hunter, with the numerically superior force, defeated the Confederates, capturing nearly a thousand gray coats and killing or wounding five hundred more. Among the dead Union and Southern bodies that littered the field of battle after the fight was none other than the Confederate commander, "Grumble" Jones. Only one day after Piedmont, Hunter, flushed with triumph, marched unmolested into Staunton, where "Black David" continued his path of destruction, burning "a large amount of public stores, consisting of shoes, saddles, harness, and clothing," in addition to the "extensive establishments for the manufacture of army clothing and equipments" which were torched.[47]

Two days after entering Staunton, Hunter's command was augmented "by the [arrival of] forces under Generals [George] Crook and [William] Averell," and on June 10 renewed his march toward Lexington. With his enlarged force of eighteen thousand men, Hunter was readily able to force General John McCausland's two thousand mounted men aside. McCausland retreated into Lexington, where, according to Hunter's reports, his Confederate adversary concealed sharpshooters in the Virginia Military Institute Buildings and placed artillery behind buildings. Hunter described McCausland's desire to fight within the town as "an unsoldierly [sic] and inhuman attempt...to defend an indefensible position...by screening himself behind the private dwellings of women and children." On June 12 Hunter avenged Sigel's debacle at New Market by torching "the Virginia Military Institute and all the buildings connected with it." During that same day, Hunter put to the torch Governor John Letcher's residence, who by proclamation attempted "to incite the population of the country to rise and wage a guerrilla warfare" upon the invading blue legions. Hunter's troops, who went hungry during the march up the Valley as a result of guerrillas cutting off supply trains, released days of pent-up anger upon the town of Lexington, which resulted in the torching of her prized historical institution as well as the wholesale looting and terrorizing of her populace.[48]

General Hunter then marched off toward Lynchburg, hoping to seize its rail center and carry out the remaining objectives in Grant's overall scheme. By this time, "[Confederate] General [John C.] Breckinridge had moved from Rock-fish Gap to Lynchburg by a forced march, as soon as Hunter's movements towards [sic] that [city] were discovered."[49] Breckinridge, the victor at New Market a little over a month earlier, was in bed with a leg injury that he received at Cold Harbor. However, the former Vice-President of the United States quickly made contact with Gilmor, ordering him to attain information concerning the strength and disposition of Hunter's forces and also carry out operations along his column. A short time earlier, Gilmor had observed the results of "Black David's" wrath on the beloved Mount Airy estate. The Meem's acreage was littered with dead "hogs, sheep, and poultry," all of which were shot by the General's men. Doubtless, the seed of hatred was budding in Gilmor's heart for this Yankee General, whose extent of destruction in the Valley had no equal up to that time. With a new horse that he purchased for four hundred greenbacks ($3,500 Confederate currency), Gilmor was ordered "to go through Hunter's line and make a circuit of his rear."[50]

In the meantime Hunter, from his headquarters outside of Lynchburg, listened with great anxiety to the sound of trains entering and leaving the Lynchburg rail center "without intermission." To add to his concern during that humid summer night of June 17 was the "repeated cheers and the beating of drums, [which] indicated the arrival of large bodies of troops." However, during nightfall not one telegraph entered Hunter's headquarters suggesting that "General Lee had detached any considerable force for the relief of Lynchburg."[51] Even though Hunter did not realize it at the time, he was falling victim to an old ruse; the Lynchburg garrison "ran an empty train up and down the tracks" all night long, while band music played and cheers were shouted welcoming the phantom soldiers into town.[52]

However, around the mid-afternoon hours of June 18 General Jubal Early, who had by now arrived at Lynchburg, struck with a vengeance; he no longer needed the mirage of phantom soldiers. Hunter believed that his command was depleted of adequate ammunition, and, furthermore, with the addition of the veterans of "Old Jubal's" Second Corps to the Lynchburg garrison, the Federal officer concluded that he was outnumbered. As darkness fell upon western Virginia that night, General Hunter began to withdraw his entire force, leaving only "a line of pickets close to the enemy, with orders to remain until midnight, and then follow the main body." Gilmor, who was still on the prowl around Hunter's forces, correctly interpreted Hunter's train movements as a sign of a general retreat out of the Lynchburg area.[53]

The middle of June was intensely hot, and the roads upon which Hunter used as his path of retreat were covered with dust several inches thick. The inclement weather notwithstanding, Early ordered Gilmor to take his force, now numbering only about forty effective men, and strike at Hunter, stressing that "hundreds" of the blue-coats could fall into the hands of the Marylander's troopers. Gilmor thought to himself that such orders were "all very well to talk about." He realized that Hunter's "rear guard was large and well handled," and he further appreciated that his own force was already "overworked, and could not hold out for long." Early would hear none of it, and, according to Gilmor, "like all infantry officers, he thought cavalry ought to know no flagging."[54]

The rear of Hunter's force was overtaken at Liberty, about twenty five miles from where he started his retreat. Here, Gilmor with 250 Virginia men coupled with his own command attacked a rail barricade that was located on a hill crest that served to protect Hunter's rear guard. While Gilmor assaulted from the left, General Stephen Dodson Ramseur's sharpshooters plugged away at the Union men from the right, eventually charging their "house-burning enemy." The weight of the attack was too much, and the rear guard was forced away from their protective barricade.[55]

During Hunter's retreat toward the Kanawha Valley Gilmor continued to serve as Early's scout and also harassed Hunter's retreating legion. In an attack upon the rear of the Yankee column near Salem, Gilmor was able to "assist in command of a dismounted battalion" that Imboden ordered forward. Once Hunter managed to retreat into the rugged terrain of western Virginia around June 21, Early called off the pursuit. The next day he rested his force, "which had marched sixty miles, during the three days' pursuit, over very rough roads."[56]

Hunter's decision to retreat into western Virginia rather than retrace his steps back down the Valley was due to his fear of the irregulars lurking in the Shenandoah; Hunter feared retreating "with Early in his rear and guerrillas on his flanks."[57] Thus history repeated itself in the Valley during that humid spring and summer of 1864. General Franz Sigel, when studying the horrific results of the guerrilla units upon his rear and flanks, decided to divide his force just north of the Massanutton Mountain, in order to protect his column against these pesky irregulars. Both generals' decisions had two underlying characteristics: both were determined in light of partisan activities, and both ended in disaster. Sigel's division of his forces to protect his flank contributed greatly to the New Market debacle. However, Hunter's decision to leave the Valley and move westward opened the way for "Old Jube" to move his men northward and take the war directly to the Northern capital.

As demonstrated by the first two months of summer in the Shenandoah Valley during the war's fourth year, the conflict had changed. The conflagration was no longer that "gentlemen's war" where handsome men in Union blue marched off from Boston and New York and Philadelphia to the gay cheers of crowds to "whip Johnny Reb in six weeks." The war in 1864 was no longer a war that could be observed from picnic blankets upon a distant hill as was done at Bull Run. By the middle of 1864, the South's back was to the wall, and irregular fighters were used to offset the roaring, irresistible Union tide. Meanwhile disgruntled Northern soldiers and officers took revenge upon the Southern Shenandoah countryside and villagers that housed such guerrillas; "Black David" Hunter's path bore testimony to the changing face of the war. Gilmor was a major participant in the new "total war" and his activities personified an irregular fighter. The partisan ranger claimed that "Hunter's gang left in their track more suffering women and children than did all their predecessors in Virginia." He further claimed that "such lawless atrocity caused our authorities, when we afterward invaded Pennsylvania, to pursue a course so different from that adopted by us on former invasions."[58] By the middle of 1864 the gutted barns and burned remains of houses as well as the vacated farms littered with dead animals brought the reality of a "total war" to the people of the Shenandoah. As Gerald Linderman notes in his classic *Embattled Courage*, even though "the broadened belligerence was not terror by twentieth-century standards - its focus was the destruction of property rather than people," it nevertheless contradicted popular expectation of warfare; the new mode of battle "was indeed a warfare of frightfulness."[59]

When the Johnny Rebs of the Valley marched off to battle in 1864 they perhaps had in the back of their minds that the Cause for which they fought was slipping through their grasp. More personally, they all had to wonder if they indeed would have homes or farms to march back to after that fight was over.

6

"Brave Hearts That You Can Depend Upon"

By early summer of 1864, the Confederacy reeled under the pressure from two large Federal advances into its territory. As Union General William Tecumseh Sherman dueled with Confederate General Joseph E. Johnston in Georgia, Generals Grant and Lee stood at a deadlock before the gates of Petersburg.[1] The South needed to follow-up their triumph over General David Hunter at Lynchburg with another victory. After "Black David" retreated from the Shenandoah, the Southerners were granted a golden opportunity to again invade the North via the Valley and score a win on enemy soil. By 1864, with their armies either depleted or on the defensive, such a Southern invasion force would invariably require the support of the much maligned irregulars. Major Gilmor, who had previously aided in the defeat of two Federal commanders in the Valley, would now be permitted to take the fight to the Yankees in his native state of Maryland.

As General Jubal Early was poised to give battle to Hunter's forces at Lynchburg, General Lee granted "Old Jube" permission to take the war to Northern soil and menace the Federal capital. Such an assault could serve to either draw Federal attention and resources from their efforts before Petersburg and Richmond or, conversely, cause Grant to launch an attack of attrition upon Lee's Army of Northern Virginia. This could leave the Union general vulnerable to counterattack. Early's raid could also glean supplies from the abundantly rich Northern lands and thereby alleviate the shortages in the Confederacy's depleted armies. Lastly, a Confederate occupation of Washington, or even a strong Southern drive toward the capital, could prove damaging to Lincoln's hope for re-election in November. Already prevalent within the North was a growing war-weariness and sad defeatism due in large part to Grant's appalling losses in northern Virginia as well as the North's failure to finally crush the rebellion. Many were calling for Lincoln's ousting in November, and a Democratic President could cut the South loose from the Union.[2]

While at Staunton, Early reorganized his army and reshuffled his command in order "to promote efficiency in battle and on the march."[3] Early had an infantry force that numbered approximately ten thousand men, and even this tiny command's effectiveness was considerably reduced by hunger and many disgruntled soldiers who demanded shoes for their blistered and blood stained feet. The remaining elements of his army, numbering around four thousand, were composed of both artillery and cavalry. After taking care of his regular units, Early told Major Gilmor of his role in the invasion north of the Potomac. On June 28, 1864, Early's new streamlined army, now renamed the Army of the Valley, pulled out of Staunton and moved deliberately down the Shenandoah; he was, for the most part, unopposed.[4]

After Early told Gilmor of his role in the invasion, the six-foot tall Marylander leaped upon his horse and galloped down the Valley to Winchester, days ahead of Early's main army. There he prepared his Second Maryland Cavalry for the movement across the Potomac and their subsequent role in Early's invasion. Gilmor had about one hundred men who were armed with only sabers and pistols. In the meantime, with sunburnt complexions and faded butternut uniforms, Early's army came marching down the Valley. They were preceded by General John C. Breckinridge's infantry corps.

Gilmor insured that no information made its way to the Yankee lines concerning the Southern advance, and, as a result, on July 2, Early's army, undetected, pulled into Winchester.[5]

At Winchester, Early ordered General John "Tiger John" McCausland to take his command west over the North Mountain and destroy the bridge on the mouth of the Back Creek. Such demolition would prohibit a Federal force from rapidly moving upon Early's left or rear as he progressed eastward across Maryland. In addition, "Old Jube" commanded Breckinridge to march down the Valley and strike Union General Franz Sigel's force at Martinsburg, while Early's other infantry corps moved to assault the Federal garrison at Harper's Ferry. Gilmor's Second Maryland was placed at the vanguard of Breckinridge's infantrymen. When Gilmor's cavalry came within five miles of Martinsburg, it was attacked by a numerically superior Union cavalry force, which caused Gilmor to order a retreat south of Bunker Hill. When the retreating Marylanders made their way one mile south of Bunker Hill, Gilmor, fearful that the Union force would plunge into Breckinridge's advancing infantry, requested one hundred sharpshooters. Breckinridge agreed, and, with the sharpshooters, as well as additional Rebel soldiers, Gilmor managed to push the Federal troopers back toward Martinsburg.[6]

A half mile outside of Martinsburg, Gilmor warned Breckinridge that Sigel's men were taking up positions on the outskirts of town. Also, Gilmor informed the former vice-president of the United States that he was able to observe burning stores within the town proper. Obviously, Sigel was preparing to evacuate the town, and during the night he slipped out of Martinsburg, moving his garrison southeastward to Harper's Ferry. Just as Breckinridge was about to enter Martinsburg, General Early told the victorious Kentuckian "to secure for the use of the entire army such public stores as may have been left by the enemy." Early, cognizant of the lack of shoes among his tiny infantry command, specifically mentioned the acquisition of shoes from the vacated Federal stores that were not already destroyed by fire.[7]

After destroying major railroads in the vicinity of Martinsburg, on July 5 Breckinridge, along with Gilmor's partisans, moved across the Potomac near Shepherdstown. By the next day, Early's entire force was on the north shore of the Potomac. Meanwhile, Sigel's command, as well as the original force stationed at Harper's Ferry, retreated eastward to Maryland Heights, a strong defensive position with several heavy guns that "blocked the Confederates' most direct route to Washington."[8] Early studied the possibility of an assault upon the Heights, and, while he contemplated the question, he sent "Tiger John" McCausland to Hagerstown in order to place a $200,000 levy upon the Maryland town. While on the march, McCausland dropped a zero on his ransom tribute, and the Hagerstown people were able to save their city from the torch by paying the twenty thousand dollar fee.[9] While McCausland was exacting payment at Hagerstown, a courier carrying a message from General Lee informed Early of a plan to release Southern prisoners from the Federal prison located at Point Lookout. Lee directed Early "to take steps to unite them with [his] command, if the attempt was successful."[10] From the time "Marse Robert" asked President Davis to consider this operation in late June to the actual delivery of Lee's message to Early on July 6, particulars of the plan remained extremely nebulous. Worse yet, even Early was not aware of the plan until well into his campaign in Maryland. However, "he had to be vigilant and mobile in the event he learned that his cavalry could assist the released prisoners."[11] In addition to audaciously moving into Northern soil with the intent of threatening the Federal capital with an already small force, Early would now have to coordinate his efforts with the "prison breakout" at Point Lookout, situated some eighty miles south of Baltimore on the extreme "southern tip of St. Mary's County, Maryland."[12]

However, information concerning the Point Lookout plan did break the deadlock in Early's mind concerning a possible frontal assault on Maryland Heights. Instead, he decided to march through important passes in both the South and Catoctan Mountains north of the Heights and then proceed to Frederick, Maryland. From this vantage point, Early could aid in the Point Lookout operation while at the same time marching toward his operation's main objective - menacing the Yankee capital.[13]

Sometime on July 7, Gilmor, who had just been given command of the First Maryland Cavalry, reported to Early at his headquarters near Sharpsburg. The general ordered the partisan ranger to serve as the vanguard of his army as it maneuvered its way through the Maryland mountains to Frederick. On July 8, as Early continued to move forward, McCausland dashed off from his right flank and demolished telegraph and railroad lines between Maryland Heights (in Early's rear and on his right flank) and Washington and Baltimore.[14] As Early's main army approached Frederick, Gilmor skirmished with small Union detachments that attempted to hinder the Confederate advance. In one such encounter with some Yankee troopers along the base of the Catoctan Mountains, Gilmor's brother, Richard (First Lieutenant, Company C, Second Maryland), was wounded by a piece of shell that exploded over his head, leaving "an ugly gash in the calf of his leg."[15] Also, in a fight to "clean out" a portion of the Eighth Illinois Cavalry that managed to slip into the Confederate's rear, Captain James L. Clark (Captain, Company F), received a bullet that "struck his jacket button and made it concave, but inflicted no injury." Clark, Gilmor admiringly claimed, "behaved nobly, and after that incident was a perfect tiger for a fight."[16] By nightfall on July 8, the Southerners, foot-worn and exhausted, retired for the evening outside of Frederick.

News accounts of Early's incursion into Maryland were filled with wild rumors and gross exaggerations concerning both the activities and strength of the Confederate raiding party. In addition, the Southern placement of levies upon Hagerstown and later Frederick only exacerbated the panic-laden reports, which were based more upon exaggeration by agitated citizens and reporters rather than objective reporting. Based upon observations he made of the Confederate occupation of Hagerstown, a startled Marylander concluded that the Southern invaders "seem to have adopted a different course from the one they pursued last summer," for this time they "make no distinction between rebel sympathizers and Unionists" when plundering property. Another report stated that about four hundred Southern marauders were "scouring the country north of the river, stealing horses [and] robbing stores, ... but showing no disposition for fight." Finally, the *New York Times* printed a statement provided by a person who suggested that "it is believed that the rebel force is not far short of thirty thousand." When all told, Early was lucky to muster half that number, and even less when excluding those ineffective for combat purposes.[17]

In the early morning hours of July 9, General Early prepared to engage Union General Lew Wallace's force at Monocacy Junction. Wallace's command was all that stood between Early's raiding party and a capital that boasted strong, but poorly manned, fortifications.[18] Meanwhile, after seeing that Early's left flank was secure, General Bradley Johnson's brigade, along with Gilmor's command, was ordered to strike eastward across the lush Maryland countryside. In just four days, Johnson, also a Marylander, was ordered to:

> cut the railroads and telegraphs north of Baltimore, sweep rapidly around the city, cut the Baltimore and Ohio Railroad [sic] between Washington and Baltimore, and push on rapidly so as to strike Point

> Lookout on the night of the twelfth. [He] was to take command of the prisoners there, some ten or twelve thousand, and march them up through lower Maryland to Washington, where General Early [would be waiting].[19]

The Marylander told his commanding officer that "the march laid out for him was utterly impossible for man or horse to accomplish." In just four days, both man and beast in Johnson's brigade were ordered to cover almost three hundred miles, destroy telegraph and railroads along the way, and partake in the land and sea operation to release their fellow Southerners from Point Lookout on July 12. Whatever the odds, Johnson resigned that "he would do what was possible for men to do."[20]

Thus, Johnson and Gilmor were detached from Early's main army and galloped eastward toward Westminster, Reisterstown, and Cockeysville, the latter being situated on the Northern Central Railroad. Westminster was almost twenty five miles from their point of origination, and Cockeysville was located no more than fifteen miles north of Baltimore. While Johnson's brigade halted for a rest at New Windsor, a short distance southwest of Westminster, Major Gilmor, allotted only twenty freshly mounted troopers, was ordered to move ahead and enter the Maryland village. There this tiny force managed to drive out a much larger Union command, seize the telegraph, cut the wires, and picket the town, while the blue coats scampered off toward Baltimore.[21]

Major Gilmor, with his exhausted troopers, made William F. Given's residence his temporary headquarters. Then, a little before dawn on Sunday, July 10, he received orders from Johnson, commanding the partisan to take his force and gain "possession of the railroad [North Central] and village of Cockeysville." Johnson, with his brigade, was to follow a short distance behind his fellow Marylander. Gilmor, as ordered, was able to seize Cockeysville, "burn the first bridge over the Gunpowder River [bridge over which the North Central Road crossed], and set pickets in the direction of Baltimore." Around nine o'clock that morning, Johnson's brigade arrived and demolished the rest of the bridges located in the vicinity of Cockeysville.[22] Through his quick assaults and destruction of railroad and telegraph lines, the cavalier from Maryland was performing to a maximum his role as a partisan ranger in Jubal Early's raid on Washington.

As Gilmor and Johnson were destroying bridges and telegraph wires, forty miles to the west, Early defeated General Wallace's force at Monocacy Junction and received a payment totaling $200,000 from the people of Frederick under threat of putting their town to the torch.[23] Early's victory over Wallace achieved the dual purpose of reopening the Confederate route to Washington and, judging by both the resistance and uniforms of some of the Federal soldiers along the Monocacy, it became apparent to Early that elements of the Sixth Corps were being sent from Grant's army to the capital's defense. Thus, Early achieved one of his main objectives of the campaign - divert attention from the Petersburg and Richmond siege. On the other hand, the fight delayed "Old Jube's" march and thereby allowed time for more Union soldiers to fill the empty rifle pits, parapets, and trenches of the capital's defenses. After Early's victory against Wallace his men marched twenty miles to Rockville, where they rested for the night. During those early afternoon hours of July 10, Lincoln telegraphed to Grant his dissatisfaction and pessimism concerning the Union forces located in and around Washington. The president concluded that troops due in from Pennsylvania and New York "will scarcely be worth counting." Earlier, Lincoln was even more pessimistic, stating "let us be vigilant but keep cool. I hope neither Baltimore or [sic] Washington will be sacked."[24] It was indeed a paradox, for, while his own armies were bleeding the Confederacy on two fronts, Lincoln could only "hope" that the numerically and qualitatively weak Federal forces in and around his capital could stave off a small Confederate raiding party numbering less than ten thousand effective men. While the Union president was expressing his concern, wildly exaggerated reports concerning the strength of Confederate forces in eastern Maryland flooded into Federal circles. Soon Union authorities ordered the "streets of Baltimore to be barricaded."[25]

Meanwhile, in the eastern half of Maryland, at Cockeysville, Johnson detached Gilmor, who took with him all men "with serviceable horse" that he could muster from the Second Maryland plus "fifty of the First Maryland under [the] command of Lieutenant William H. Dorsey (Company D)." The major also transferred some of his horsemen to Johnson's brigade to serve as scouts. All told, Gilmor had no more than 135 men in his command.[26] Gilmor's small force belied both the nature and importance of his orders, for he was "to strike the railroad at [the] Gunpowder river, on the Philadelphia, Wilmington and Baltimore railroad, and [in addition], destroy communication between Baltimore and the North" by cutting telegraph wires in the area.[27] Furthermore, Gilmor's activities around Baltimore would serve to shroud Johnson's movements farther south. After detaching Gilmor from his brigade, Johnson was to move southward from Cockeysville, cut the Washington Railroad at Beltsville, and then race to Point Lookout, located some eighty, arduous miles from Baltimore. Gilmor and Johnson were, according to plan, to rejoin Early in the vicinity of Washington on July 14.[28] It was hoped that Johnson's ranks would be augmented by the released Confederates from Point Lookout, whose pent-up anger and frustration would be unleashed upon the defenders of Washington.

After his detachment from Johnson's brigade, Gilmor gave the impression that he was moving toward Baltimore, and then dashed off in the direction of Towsontown. Near Meredith Bridge, Gilmor quickly assigned the bulk of his command to Captain James P. Bayly, while still other troopers of his small force searched the countryside near the Old York Road for horses and feed. Leaving his command during a most precarious time, Gilmor and a few friends and officers made their way to Glen Ellen, his father's estate. At this sentimental locale he spent "a few hours" visiting relatives and dear friends, perhaps reminiscing about the past and discussing Early's present operation. As he was about to leave his father's aristocratic estate, he told a close relative of the nature of his objectives around Baltimore. The neighbor replied in a rather pessimistic fashion that Gilmor "would never return alive." In an operation that was already logistically "impossible" due to the amount of land to be traversed as well as the time allotted, Gilmor and Johnson both wasted valuable time by visits to friends and relatives. Undoubtedly such escapades held sentimental value to these renowned Marylanders. However, these visits were equally detrimental to the overall success of their operations. Furthermore, by leaving his command at such an important time, Gilmor was placing his troopers in extreme jeopardy - his action was clumsy and unnecessarily reckless.[29]

In the late evening hours, Gilmor and his comrades who ventured off to Glen Ellen rejoined the troopers that the major put under Captain Bayly's charge at Meredith Bridge. Several miles from Cockeysville, the July night, with its sultry summer air drenched with humidity, struck oppressively down upon Gilmor and his gray clad horsemen as they continued on their mission. Gilmor slowly gave way to sleep when the sudden barking of dogs awoke him. As he turned to study the rest of his column, the major observed that some of his men who surrendered to sleep while in the saddle had unwittingly allowed their mounts to wonder off the road and into the woods. Other Southerners who gave way to exhaustion fell from their horses onto the dusty roads. Gilmor thus decided to allow his men to rest at a nearby farm owned by Joshua C. Price.[30]

On the morning of July 11, Gilmor and his men continued their destruction of telegraph wires around Baltimore. While his column was approximately twenty-five miles northeast of the city, there was a welcome lull in the action. Suddenly, a single shot was heard in the distance, and, a short time later, a lone Confederate came galloping back to the column informing a startled Gilmor that his ordnance sergeant, Eugene W. Fields, had been killed. The duo had previously been sent out to serve as Gilmor's advance. The remainder of Gilmor's column came upon the mortally wounded Fields, who was lying prostate in front of Ishmael Day's property. Fields's pale "face and chest were filled with buckshot," each entry into the sergeant's flesh marked by a sickly, dark bluish-purple spot. It was alleged that Day was proudly flying a United States flag from his house when Fields challenged the Union man to remove that "damned old rag." Day refused. Fields dismounted in order to rip down the Yankee flag himself, only to be greeted by Day with a load of buckshot, which dropped the trooper. Gilmor and a few men stared at Fields's dying body, while several walked about cursing; others watched their commander give a drink of water to the wounded man. Gilmor then observed flames leap from the Day residence, and, before he could turn, reddish-orange flames leaped from the barn and some of the out-buildings, as gray clad troopers ran about the property. The vengeance minded Rebels also managed to steal some cash and silver from the Day property. Gilmor had his wounded sergeant placed in a carriage and hurried off to Wright's Hotel. Mrs. Day, hardly a supporter of Gilmor and his Cause, suggested that "had [Gilmor's] father taught him the art of handling the plough, perhaps he would not have become a highway robber."[31]

The Confederate cavalrymen pushed southeastward

toward the small post office town of Magnolia, which is situated in the southwest corner of Harford County, and is only fifteen miles from Baltimore. "Within a mile and a half from where the Philadelphia, Wilmington, and Baltimore Railroad crosses the Gunpowder [River]," the early morning train from Baltimore came churning up the track and arrived at Magnolia Station. Gilmor ordered twenty men to capture the train, which was accomplished after they "fired a volley into it."[32] Gilmor, not wishing by any means to repeat the February incident on the Baltimore and Ohio Railroad, warned his men not to plunder. The engineer managed to escape the partisan's grasp, or else Gilmor claimed that he would have ridden the train all the way to Havre de Grace, all the while destroying bridges along the way. Such an activity would have laid waste to some seventeen miles of track in northeastern Maryland.[33]

According to one account printed in the *Baltimore Sun*, some of Gilmor's men resorted to a type of exchange thievery. Even though the passengers "were treated very well," some of Gilmor's men forced the civilians to trade personal items for those belonging to the horsemen. For example, a doctor was ordered to barter his boots "for a pair of dusty cowhide riding boots, or rather leggins, as they were minus the soles." The eyewitness also stated that one of the cavalrymen approached him, and removing "his tobacco stained and rusty-looking felt [hat]," said to the nervous train passenger, "Here, I want that hat." The rebel next requisitioned his haversack and blanket, "and soon, I, together with the majority of the prisoners, had no article of value left." The irregulars also showed clear signs of chivalry, for not only were "the lady prisoners remarkably well treated," but the Rebels also returned photographs and other items to the passengers that were perceived as unimportant.[34] Many of Gilmor's troopers were clothed in uniforms that were dusty, pungent, and hole ridden, and as such they naturally coveted the fine articles possessed by the passengers. However, implicit in the above eyewitness account is a group of rugged partisans who were remarkably well-behaved. Whereas Gilmor maintained loose discipline over a command that included men of questionable military value and ethics, his Second Maryland is in no way comparable to Quantrill's raiders. Irregulars such as William Quantrill, "Bloody Bill" Anderson, and Champ Ferguson represented a class of guerrillas who actively pursued murder and destruction for sadistic thrill.

As his men rounded-up the passangers, Gilmor, to his chagrin, discovered that the alert engineer disabled the train's engine before fleeing the scene. So, the Rebels were forced to torch the train where it rested, while simultaneously putting to flame the freight house located at the station. The major also was able to capture Major-General William B. Franklin and a handful of other Union officers. After this unexpected but delightful episode, Gilmor called to the Union infantry force which was guarding the drawbridge over the Gunpowder to capitulate. The guerrilla also demanded the surrender of the *Juniata*, a Union gunboat situated to protect the bridge and its Federal garrison. After sending some sharpshooters forward in order to edge the Yankees into accepting surrender, the ten o'clock train from Baltimore arrived and was also quickly captured by Gilmor's awaiting troopers. Gilmor kept the engine of the locomotive running while his men unloaded the passengers' belongings. He also ordered his sharpshooters to force the Union infantry force located near the Gunpowder River onto the bridge proper. Like herding cattle, the sharpshooters began to plug away at the startled Yankees, forcing them to retreat onto the narrow bridge and toward the *Juniata*. Before most of the scampering blue coats could make it one-fourth of the way across the bridge, the Marylander lit the train afire and slowly reversed the flaming mass onto the bridge. The Union men who were fleeing for safety toward the *Juniata* were forced to leap into the river below before being burned and crushed to death by the ominous, flaming train, which stopped in the middle of the bridge before burning it through and falling into the awaiting waters, teaming with panicked Federal soldiers. Gilmor could only speculate as to the number of Yankees who drowned in the waters below but concluded that "as the life boats from the Gun Boat were some time getting there I have no doubt half of them went to the bottom. Hope so at least."[35]

"Gilmor allowed the gunboat to take the passengers across the river and paroled most of the soldiers [officers] except for General Franklin and four others."[36] Gilmor's operations on the Philadelphia, Wilmington, and Baltimore Road at Magnolia on July 11 disrupted train service on that stretch of track for almost two weeks. As with Early's raid in general, Gilmor's activities on the Gunpowder River and the destruction of railroads and telegraph lines around Baltimore created panic among the people of the countryside, some of whom made their way to Washington and Baltimore. On July 12, one day after the Gunpowder Bridge affair, the *New York Times* reported that "fears are entertained that a number of mills, factories and foundaries [sic] around the city will be destroyed." The *Times* also printed, in typical numerical exaggeration, that "as far as known, the whole cavalry force in Baltimore County, which has done this mischief, does not exceed eight hundred, under the command of the notorious Harry Gilmore [sic]." One report in the *Baltimore Sun* listed Gilmor's force at between one thousand and 1500 men.[37] Furthermore, Bradley Johnson's torching of Maryland Governor Augustus Bradford's residence in retaliation for Hunter's firing of Governor Letcher's dwelling in Virginia only served to heighten fears and tension.[38] Most of these reports and the lion's share of the gossip concerning Early's raid on Washington, along with the Johnson-Gilmor raids, were nothing more than gross hyperbole. However, the fear of the populace, whose homes dotted the rural countryside, was very real. Such terror was symbolic of the new war that dawned in 1864, one that no longer could be viewed from a picnic lunch upon some lush grass covered hill. Moreover, it was a conflict that refused to respect the sanctity of personal property, as the "gentlemen's war" had done earlier.

On July 11, Early moved his main army from Rockville toward Washington, hoping to arrive there before large numbers of Union men were able to pour into the capital's defensive works. "While marching, the men were enveloped in a suffocating cloud of dust, and many of them fell by the way from exhaustion."[39] Earlier that same day, elements from General McCausland's cavalry actually defiantly galloped onto District of Columbia soil; the last time a hostile party entered the District of Columbia was the British Army during the War of 1812, and on that occasion the red coats set fire to the White House. However, the gray coats in 1864 were out of luck, for the "feebly manned" Washington defenses at midday on July 11 became "lined with troops" by the early dawn hours of July 12. When Early learned that "two corps had arrived from Grant's army and that his whole army was probably in motion," he decided to "reluctantly give up all hopes of capturing Washington."[40] In addition, Early had to be concerned with the presence of General David Hunter, who, as reported by a Northern paper, was crossing the Baltimore and Ohio Railroad, and would thus be ominously close to "Old Jube's" rear. However, the audacious Confederate general decided to remain in front of Washington on July 12 and send skirmishers against Fort Stevens. During the fighting, a tall, slender man dressed in black made his appearance at the fort and stood over the parapets in order to observe the action. On that day, President Lincoln was granted the opportunity to observe those haggard forces that placed such a scare into the hearts of his fellow Washingtonians.[41]

With his forces unable to seize the capital, Early recalled Johnson's Brigade, which, after cutting the Washington

Railroad at Beltsville, began to move southward in order to carry out the second phase of his operation, the liberation of the prisoners at Point Lookout. If Johnson would have successfully made the trek "over eighty miles in only seventeen hours," he would have found no sea support. He later learned that "on the night of July 10 the *Tallahassee*," the steamship ordered to take part in the prison break-out, had "received orders to abandon the expedition" after word of the operation found its way into the enemy camp. Johnson returned in time to protect Early's rear from Rockville to Poolesville and covered his retreat across the Potomac at Leesburg on July 14. Early, reminiscing about his retreat across the Potomac seventeen years after his indefatigable forces marched upon the Federal capital, claimed that "if the Federal commanders in Washington and General Hunter had been possessed of the requisite enterprise and daring" they could have captured his entire force. Instead, "Old Jube" was allowed to escape and would continue to serve as a menace to the Union efforts for many more months.[42]

Gilmor, still operating in eastern Maryland, had not learned of Johnson's recall. After destroying two trains, one freight house, the bridge over the Gunpowder River, and the capture of General Franklin, Gilmor moved his command in the direction of Baltimore. In the vicinity of Towsontown he was warned by Southern sympathizers that Union forces were expecting him in Baltimore and that an additional Federal cavalry force, composed of "emergency volunteers" as well as veteran cavalry, was prowling the countryside in search of his small command. Gilmor determined to give battle to these mounted Yankees who were outside of Baltimore, their numerically superior force being situated between Towsontown and Baltimore. The Marylander recalled that his men were tired and nervous. However, one ardent Southerner, who had unquestionable faith in his commanding officer, stated with conviction: "No fear; he'll take us through all right; only stay by him, and there's no danger."[43]

Gilmor ordered William Kemp (Second Lieutenant, Company C) to take fifteen men and assault the enemy's advance guard and drive it back along the York Road toward Baltimore. Then, Kemp's small force was to rapidly retreat, hotly pursued by the entire Yankee cavalry force. At the last minute, Kemp's command was to dodge off to the sides of the road, allowing Gilmor's command to charge the unsuspecting Federals. Kemp dashed at the Yankee advance guard with an intimidating "Rebel yell," which was echoed by Gilmor's cavalry force waiting in reserve. Gilmor recalled, when he heard the brave howling of his men, with their drawn sabers, "what joy it affords to command men like these - brave hearts that you can depend upon under all circumstance!" Gilmor's horsemen, yelling and screaming in a monstrous crescendo, convinced the Yankees that an entire regiment was coming down the road in front of them. The blue-coats quickly retreated into Baltimore, completely fooled. Neither the Confederates nor the Federals suffered a casualty in the affair.[44]

However, as a soldier's fortune in war can change as easily as the shifting wind, so Gilmor, blessed with an easy triumph over a larger Union cavalry force, now became struck with ill fortune. Before operating against the Federal cavalry force near Baltimore, he placed his five Union prisoners, including General Franklin, in the charge of Nicholas Owings, his quartermaster, along with twelve other reliable men. A few hours after driving the Union force to Baltimore, Gilmor's command came upon Owings and the dozen men who were supposed to be guarding the prisoners. Gilmor and Captain James Clark (Company F) were in the advance, and they rode up to Owings and his crew, all of which were laying on the road sound asleep. The major turned to Clark and sternly stated "I'll bet Franklin is gone." Gilmor dismounted and woke up his sleeping guards by asking where Franklin and his comrades were located. One trooper told his commanding officer that they were in the fence corner, and, when Gilmor turned his eyes to view his five captives, they were gone - off into the dark wooded countryside. Gilmor became irate and "swore with unusual energy." He would later recall that he "was right glad that my pious friends were not there to hear me when I found that Franklin had indeed escaped; I fear they would have considered me somewhat ruffled." After sending out search parties for the escaped officers, Gilmor gave up the pursuit and led his exhausted column toward Rockville, where he was to rejoin Early's army. However, he found that Early's forces had already retreated to Poolesville. Gilmor's men rode all night to Poolesville, where Gilmor rejoined Johnson.[45]

Gilmor counted only six men captured and one man killed (Sergeant Fields) during the operation, and both Generals Early and Breckinridge complimented Gilmor on the success of his operations around Baltimore. The Marylander and his relatively small band of partisans were able at one point to prohibit communication between the Federal capital and the North due to their destruction of telegraph lines. Early regretted that he could have spared no more troopers to give the major after Gilmor told of his drive near Baltimore. "Old Jubilee" also responded that Gilmor deserved a promotion. Gilmor would later contend "that [he] preferred [his] battalion to any regiment in the army; it was the right kind of stuff." Gilmor was however "entitled to a lieutenant colonel's commission," for his Second Maryland contained six companies. All the Marylander had to do was apply for it, but, according to Gilmor, "it was not worth the trouble." This attitude which soothed the import and pomp of military status is confirmed by Major Henry Kyd Douglas, a noted Gilmor contemporary, who claimed that the ardent Marylander "was just as likely to use [a commission] to light a pipe as to have preserved it or taken any care of it."[46]

As he was preparing to cross the Potomac into Virginia,

General Early turned to Major Douglas and said, "in his falsetto drawl, 'Major, we haven't taken Washington, but we've scared Abe Lincoln like hell!'"[47] "Old Jube's" jocular comment held undeniable veracity. Not only had his tiny army frightened "Old Abe," but it caused not a little consternation among Union military and government officials. With the sending of the Sixth Corps to Washington's defense Early achieved a major military objective, and the "large number of beef-cattle and horses" acquired from Maryland farms bore testimony to the fulfillment of another goal in his offensive.[48] Early also significantly weakened Lincoln's chance for re-election in November. However, Sherman's victory at Atlanta and Sheridan's triumph at Cedar Creek later in the year would ultimately secure Lincoln's return to the White House.

Undoubtedly, if Early's tenacious force could have entered Washington, or even have laid siege to the Union capital, the impact upon the outcome of the war would have been profound. Word of Confederate forces in Washington might have permanently lowered Northern popular morale, which was growing more impatient daily. However, to have accomplished these military tasks Early would have needed many more men, men that the South did not have. Early was unable to seize Washington for the same reason that Gilmor failed to grasp Baltimore; the smallness of their forces made their operations more conducive to diversionary activities, and it prohibited such capable, daring commanders from exploiting a military situation for larger gain. For the Confederacy in general, it meant that the self-proclaimed nation could slowly bleed to death in this new "total war" of attrition.

12. James E. Taylor's sketch of Gilmor throwing a Union man off a train platform during the infamous Baltimore and Ohio Robbery of February 1864. This train robbery was a disaster for Gilmor, causing his arrest and trial by court-martial. (Courtesy of the Western Reserve Historical Society, Cleveland, Ohio)

13. Signed Photo of Harry Gilmor. (Courtesy of the Barry Pipino Collection)

14. Colonel John Singleton Mosby. Gilmor, like all southern irregular commanders, stood in the shadow of the "Gray Ghost of the Confederacy." (Courtesy of the Library of Congress)

15. General David Hunter. "Black David" gave the Shenandoah Valley its first taste of "total war." (Courtesy of the Library of Congress)

16. General Jubal Early. During Early's famous raid on Washington, Gilmor marched his small command for operations around Baltimore. (Courtesy of the Library of Congress)

17. Patch from the Centennial Reenactment of Gilmor's Raid Around Baltimore. (Courtesy of the Barry Pipino Collection)

18. General William W. Averell (seated). On August 7, 1864, one week after the burning of Chambersburg, Pennsylvania, General Averell's command smashed the Confederate force responsible for torching the Pennsylvania village. (Courtesy of the United States Military History Institute, Carlisle Barracks, Pennsylvania)

19. Captain James Louis Clark, Company F, Second Maryland Cavalry. Clark was captured by General Averell's troopers in the Moorefield Valley on August 7, 1864. (Courtesy of the Barry Pipino Collection)

20. James E. Taylor's sketch of Gilmor fleeing through the streets of Winchester after General Phil Sheridan's force broke into the city on September 19, 1864. Gilmor, bedridden and caught by surprise, galloped through the streets without "a hat, coat or shoes, his naked feet hanging loose below the stirrups." (Courtesy of the Western Reserve Historical Society, Cleveland, Ohio)

21. Private Archie Rowand. A member of the famed "Jessie Scouts," Rowand's efforts in January and February 1865 led to Gilmor's capture. (Courtesy of the Barry Pipino Collection)

22. General Philip H. Sheridan. After Gilmor's capture in early February 1865, Sheridan warned Union authorities that Gilmor "is an energetic, shrewd, and unscrupulous scoundrel and a dangerous man. He must be closely watched or he will escape." (Courtesy of the Library of Congress)

23. Gilmor after his release from Fort Warren. Gilmor's captivity in Fort Warren from February to July 1865 was a marked antithesis to his imprisonment at Fort McHenry three years earlier, as shown by his worn appearance. (Courtesy of the Barry Pipino Collection)

7

"...Acts of Atrocious Barbarity"

General Early's failure to penetrate Washington's outer defenses during his invasion of Maryland in no way lessoned his desire to avenge General "Black David" Hunter's pyromaniacal path of destruction in the Shenandoah Valley. While Jubal Early's force was stationed at the friendly confines of Martinsburg, news of Hunter's terror in the Valley slowly found its way into "Old Jube's" headquarters. The tobacco chewing, profane Southern general concluded that "Hunter had been again indulging in his favorite mode of warfare."[1]

Indeed, while Early's soldiers were knocking at Washington's front door, Hunter was applying the torch to several private dwellings situated within the quaint Valley. Alex Boteler, a former Confederate congressman, Andrew Hunter, Virginia state senator and "Black David's" cousin, and Edmund Lee, a relation to the esteemed commander of the Southern armies, all witnessed their private dwellings fired by order of Hunter. General "Tiger John" McCausland shared Early's indignation with Hunter's abuses and took to heart the stories alleging that Hunter boasted "that he 'would humble the Virginia women before he left the state.'" Many people in the Valley suggested that Hunter felt that the Virginia women were "worse traitors than their husbands."[2] Major Gilmor, whose partisan career afforded him a key role in the new "total war," concluded that he "could fill pages with the acts of atrocious barbarity against the unprotected women of that valley."[3] The tempestuous accounts of Hunter's excesses bore testimony to the "total war" of 1864. Early's order to put the torch to Chambersburg opened a new chapter in this modern war - Southern retribution for Hunter's sins in the Valley.

In addition to retaliating for "Black David's" campaign of fire in the Valley, Early decided to place a levy on the Pennsylvania village, like he did at Hagerstown and Frederick earlier that summer. This time the collected monies would be sent directly to those Southerners whose houses were put to the torch by Hunter, instead of being sent to the Treasury.[4] Also, "Old Jube" realized that another raid on Northern soil could serve as the *coup de grace* for Lincoln's chance at re-election in November, for more than a few Northerners were calling for his ousting and an end to hostilities.

Early's selection of Chambersburg to bear the brunt of Confederate vengeance grew more out of practicality than due to any personal animosity he had with its citizens. Early surmised that Chambersburg, with its relatively large population base of approximately seven thousand people, could provide a nice sum of greenbacks if he levied the town. Furthermore, Chambersburg, located in Franklin County, was geopolitically only fifteen miles north of the Maryland-Pennsylvania border. It was surmised that a small Rebel force could move quickly into the Cumberland Valley, levy, and if need be, fire the town, and then scamper back to safety in Virginia. As one Southern soldier admitted, "it so happened that it [Chambersburg] was the nearest and most accessible place of importance for us to get to. It was the unfortunate victim of circumstance."[5]

The waning days of July found David Hunter's army sprawled along the northern shore of the Potomac from Hancock, Maryland, southeast to Harper's Ferry, where the bulk of his force was stationed. Early's army, with McCausland's cavalry brigade along his left flank, was disposed directly in front of Hunter's blue-coats along the southern shore of the river. On Friday, July 29, at Hammond's Hill, western Virginia, the two cavalry brigades that were to make the raid into southern Pennsylvania were hastily organized. McCausland's brigade was composed of 1300 men, including cavalrymen from three Virginia cavalry battalions. The other cavalry brigade assigned to the mission was under the command of Brigadier General Bradley T. Johnson. Johnson's brigade numbered a little more than McCausland's, and together they would attempt to turn Hunter's right near Hancock. McCausland's and Johnson's brigades were to be bolstered by two batteries of artillery, Braxton's battery and the Baltimore Light Artillery, respectively. After turning Hunter's right, the Southern brigades were to proceed rapidly to Chambersburg. There McCausland was to "demand of the municipal authorities the sum of $100,000 in gold or $500,000 in U.S. currency, as compensation" for Hunter's recent destruction in the Valley. Early further ordered McCausland to "lay the town in ashes in default of payment."[6] Gilmor, with both the First and Second Maryland Cavalry Battalions, was ordered to move to the vicinity of McCoy's Ford and scout the remaining local fords along the Potomac, in order to find a safe crossing. The Maryland partisan ranger was also charged the task of serving as the vanguard of the Confederate invasion force, which numbered a modest 2,600 men.[7]

At one o'clock on the humid, muggy night of July 28, Gilmor's command set out to seize a foothold along the Maryland side of the Potomac a short distance north of Williamsport. Such an operation was a necessity if McCausland's larger force was to enter Maryland soil. It was early dawn when Gilmor's battalions reached the river and he soon observed that the northern shore was only lightly guarded by pickets. The major ordered two squadrons of sharpshooters to keep the Yankee scouts busy while he and

Second Lieutenant William Kemp (Company C, Second Maryland) took the lion's share of the battalions safely across the river. A short time after seizing the crossing, "Tiger John" McCausland ordered Gilmor to push northward and place two picket forces to the west and east along the National Turnpike.[8]

With their passageway into Maryland thus clear, McCausland's command began to cross the Potomac on the morning of July 29 and was completely on Maryland soil by noon. The Potomac at this point was quite wide and deep, and "it was a novel sight to see [the] men scattered over the river with a firm grip on their horses' tails, slowly toiling to a small island" situated at midstream.[9] McCausland's plan, after forming his command on the National Pike, was to march to Clear Spring and then turn off the Pike and move his troopers to Mercersburg, Pennsylvania, located some thirteen arduous miles northwest. Gilmor was ordered to force the Yankee cavalry from Clear Spring and drive them eastward to the Conococheague Creek. There, he was to engage the enemy until both McCausland and Johnson's brigades were safely through the small Clear Spring village. Afterward he was to guard McCausland's rear as his column made its way toward Mercersburg.[10]

As the Southern invaders were slipping across the Potomac, Union Major General Darius Couch, commander of the Department of the Susquehanna, could count only "one hundred and thirty five [men] under his command."[11] In addition to Lieutenant McLean's small command located near the Potomac, Couch could tally a company of Independent Philadelphia Scouts, who stood guard in the vicinity of Emmitsburg. With him at his headquarters in Chambersburg, Couch had only the Patapsco Guards, Independent Company of Maryland Volunteer Infantry, which numbered sixty men, along with a piece of field artillery, Battery A, First New York Light Artillery. The lack of soldiers along Pennsylvania's southern border was due in large part to Early's Washington

Raid. Couch watched helplessly as Pennsylvanians from his department were sent to stifle Early's raid on the Federal capital. Moreover, a short time prior to McCausland's move across the Potomac, Couch sent General William W. Averell, whose command was situated at Hagerstown (Maryland), two companies of mounted, "one hundred days' men." On the very next day, some "six companies of one hundred days' infantry" that were to be sent to Chambersburg were rerouted to Hagerstown.[12] Thus, with a little over one hundred men, Couch was expected to prevent a totally unexpected invasion; the stage was set for disaster.

Meanwhile, fifteen miles south of Couch's headquarters, Gilmor's battalions, coupled with additional Southern soldiers that General Johnson sent to aid his fellow Marylander, were able to readily push the Yankee forces through Clear Spring. It again appeared as if Gilmor's luck was as strong as his will, and in this operation he was apparently continuing his uninterrupted success. However, as easily as the shifting wind, the soldier's fortune in war often changes. With his force numerically weakened after Johnson's men left to rejoin their command, Gilmor could count only two hundred lightly armed troopers, but they nonetheless kept pressure on the reeling Yankees. Gilmor, however, had as yet to force the Federal force across the Conococheague, and furthermore he did not know if all of McCausland's command was safely through Clear Spring. The Marylander decided to assault the Yankees once more, which would give the impression that he was attempting to clear the way for McCausland's men to march upon Hagerstown, located eight miles to the east. This time Gilmor's command galloped directly into a Federal ambush. The concealed Northerners punished Gilmor's command, claiming seventeen killed or wounded Confederates. Among the dead was a young Baltimorean, Adolph Warfield (Company F, Second Maryland), whom Gilmor described as brave.[13]

Just before nightfall on July 29 McCausland's exhausted troopers arrived at Mercersburg after forcing McLean's smaller party through the Pennsylvania town. McLean did manage to reorganize his command, and he promptly placed a picket force at Bridgeport, while the remnant of his beleaguered force fell back to Saint Thomas. In the meantime McCausland's Confederates halted in order to refresh both man and beast and allow the stragglers a chance to rejoin the main army. Some incorrigible Southerners took the opportunity to loot Mercersburg's shops and threaten her townspeople. Gilmor's battered command managed to make its way to McCausland's camp around ten o'clock that evening, and he no sooner arrived when McCausland ordered the march renewed. "Tiger John" told Gilmor that he wanted to be in Chambersburg by sunrise and he additionally wished to have his two battalions guard his rear. Just before daylight, after a grueling all night march in which McLean's force was driven back on Chambersburg, McCausland again sent for the major. Gilmor, who had not laid down for sleep in over two days, approached McCausland, who was allowing his command a respite to feed their horses in an open oat-field. McCausland told Gilmor to join Major James W. Sweeney's Thirty-sixth Virginia Cavalry Battalion for an assault on the town at daybreak. Sweeney's dismounted command would serve as the vanguard of the thrust into Chambersburg.[14]

Well within view to the east lay the quaint village of Chambersburg, whose small shops and handsome private dwellings bore stark contrast to the gutted dwellings left behind by Hunter's flames in the Shenandoah. On this day the Pennsylvania village, relatively unmolested by Southern hands during the Gettysburg Campaign of 1863, would fall prey to the deadly "total war" of 1864.[15]

As ordered, Major Sweeney's Thirty-sixth Virginia Cavalry Battalion and Gilmor's horsemen entered Chambersburg approximately six o'clock in the morning on

July 30. The Marylander then ordered his men to block escape routes out of the Pennsylvania village. While inside the city limits, Gilmor approached a few Pennsylvania women, "who exercised their tongues upon [him] rather freely," to which he reciprocated in a most provocative manner, returning oath for nasty oath. After he and General McCausland ate breakfast at a Chambersburg hotel, the latter ordered Major Gilmor to arrest some fifty of Chambersburg's more affluent citizens. Gilmor's men seized the wealthy Pennsylvania gentlemen, explaining to each "that by order of General Early $100,000 in gold or $500,000 in currency was required to ransom the town;" the failure to pay would result in the town's firing in retaliation for Hunter's destruction in the Valley. Most told the trooper that there was probably no more than fifty thousand greenbacks at hand.[16] Gilmor was about to seize another man, when one of McCausland's aides arrived at Gilmor's side and ordered the major to report to "Tiger John" immediately. McCausland, perhaps fearful that Averell's force was in close proximity, told Gilmor that they were out of time, the town must be put to the torch, and that he would be the one in charge of firing the town.[17]

Even before Gilmor had a chance to organize his men and send them to the various blocks of the town to perform their upsetting deeds, long pillars of smoke could be viewed in the near distance rising toward the heavens.[18] These fires were ignited by undisciplined Southern troops, who were motivated more by terror and plunder than sheer retaliation for Hunter's incendiarism in the Shenandoah. In one instance a group of soldiers broke into a drug store and stole its supply of turpentine. The men then proceeded to place the sticky, highly combustible liquid on cotton balls, which they "lighted and threw into shops and houses" as they galloped by.[19] Some of the more incorrigible Rebels searched for a prize of even greater value than either jewelry or greenbacks - liquor. After relieving a Mr. John Treher of "two hundred dollars in gold and silver, and [an additional] one hundred dollars in currency, they also stole all his liquors." "Spirits" only served to exacerbate an already chaotic situation.[20]

Scenes of plundering and drunken disorderliness were observed objectively with terror and justifiable horror by Chambersburg's people. However, the systematic destruction of the town was also viewed with equal disgust. As one observer reported:

> No time was given to remove women or children, or sick, or even the dead. No notice of the kind was communicated to any one [sic]; but like infuriated fiends from hell itself the work of destruction was commenced. They [Rebels] did not have anything to learn in their horrid trade - they proved themselves experts in their calling. They divided into squads, and fired every other house, and often every house, if they presented any prospect of plunder. They would beat in the door with iron bars or heavy plank, smash up any furniture with an axe, throw fluid or oil upon it, and ply the match.[21]

Such livid scenes were made even more indelible by the many women who pleaded with the Confederate soldiers not to burn their dwellings.[22]

The plundering and horrific exploits of many Southern troops are confirmed by General Bradley Johnson. According to Johnson, both before and after the town was ordered put to the torch "drunken soldiers paraded the streets in every possible disguise and paraphernalia, pillaging and plundering and drunk." Also, some Confederates "exacted ransom of individuals for their houses, holding the torch in terror over the house until it was paid." Some Pennsylvanians paid upwards of two hundred dollars to save their dwelling from a terrible end. Johnson disgustingly concluded that "the grand spectacle of a national retaliation was reduced to a miserable huckstering for greenbacks." Johnson tersely stated that it was "impossible to preserve the discipline of this brigade."[23]

Amid the scenes of terror and anguish some miniscule traces of humanity and mercy were observed. In one instance, a group of Confederate soldiers approached a city block that had thus far been unmolested by flame. The entourage approached the first block on the street and informed the owner that his dwelling must be put to the torch. However, the gentleman's wife hurried to the door and "placed one hand upon a curious Rebel officer while she used the other to point to the shrieking women and children scampering by their dwelling." Then, she proceeded to ask the Southerner if his need for vengeance was satisfied. The stoic woman told the officer that her husband could purchase another dwelling, but requested that he spare some of the dwellings for those homeless, frantic people on the streets. The lady, Mrs. M'Lellan, concluded her plea by asking the Confederate, "when you and I and all of us shall meet before the Great Judge, can you justify this act?" M'Lellan's selfless courage was awarded, for the officer turned to his men and waved them away; the entire portion of the town was saved.[24]

In another instance, Gilmor and two of his men approached a large dwelling situated on a hill northwest of the burning town. The Marylander and his comrades marched to the front door and told a woman who responded to the knocks "that [he] was there to perform the extremely unpleasant duty of burning her house." The woman began to shed tears but did not request that her house be spared. However, she did ask for time in order to remove valuable articles. Gilmor, in the meantime, spotted a hardy breakfast sitting upon the dining room table. Unbelievably, the woman unselfishly asked her unwelcome guest to help himself to the luscious fare. Major Gilmor, always willing to be in the company of an amicable female hostess, welcomed her hospitality and accepted the offer. Gilmor finished the meal and moved his large, stocky frame from the table; he perhaps felt inwardly confused, maybe even slightly ill. How could he torch a person's dwelling who displayed kindness in the face of hostility? "[He] had half a mind to disobey orders in regard to this house." The glossy-eyed woman re-entered her dining room, and Gilmor nonchalantly asked the name of her husband. She responded, "Colonel Boyd, of the Union Army." The Marylander excitedly stated, "What! Colonel Boyd, of the First New York Cavalry?" Gilmor then happily told the woman that her husband's dwelling would be spared. He explained that her husband "had gained a high reputation for kindness and gentlemanly conduct among the people of the Shenandoah Valley." Thus, Gilmor was reciprocating kindness for kindness; on this day Boyd's dwelling would not have to suffer for Hunter's sins.[25]

A short time after midday the Southerners fled Chambersburg, leaving behind mass hysteria, sorrow, and a town whose burning houses sent pillars of black smoke into the July, summertime sky. Several miles outside of the blackened city Gilmor turned around to study the destruction that he and his fellow Confederates brought to Chambersburg. Turning his attention from the red and orange flames, he noticed multicolored specks that dotted the lush green countryside that surrounds the town. A closer observation revealed that these were people, now homeless, who had but memories of a once happier life.[26]

Irrefutably, many of the tempestuous Northern accounts of Southern behavior are immersed in sensationalism and subjectiveness. However, equally undeniable is the fact that, when the colorful adjectives and aggrieved sentiment of the reports are removed, at the core exists the story of a community that experienced a heart wrenching terror at the hands of the enemy. For, after the last butternut-faded uniform was out of sight, the people of Chambersburg could only view with grave sadness and harsh bitterness the ruins of their community. "Damage to the town itself amounted to four hundred buildings burned, 274 of them homes, at an estimated value of about $1.5 million."[27] All told, eleven square blocks were engulfed by the flames, and, ironically, only one civilian perished in the day's affair.[28]

News of the burning of Chambersburg sent tremors that rocked both borders of the Commonwealth. As the Southern force was making its way southward, the *Post-Pittsburgh* reported that "it [was] believed that the invasion is of a character too gigantic to be regarded as a mere raid." Furthermore, the paper stated that General Couch had arrived in the city and would be consulting with Pittsburgh's government and military officials in order to make preparations in case the "gigantic" 2,600 man invading force "should turn its course towards the Monongahela valley." The newspaper was concerned that Pittsburgh, which produced over one thousand cannon, "about ten percent of the projectiles bought by the government," as well as a host of other war related goods, would serve as a viable objective.[29]

Meanwhile, on the opposite side of the state, Philadelphians hustled to newspaper offices in order to attain reports of the invasion.[30] The *Philadelphia Inquirer* reported that "the Rebels committed all kinds of depredations, robbed the citizens, and hardly gave them time to leave their houses" before torching them. The *Inquirer* also incorrectly printed that Gilmor was killed by some townspeople for plundering their ravaged city.[31] To the north, the *New York Times* was drawing analogies between southern Pennsylvania and the western frontier of Colonial America.

> One would almost imagine himself once again among the savages on the frontier during the early days of

> our country, when he reads of the brutality and utter disregard of all merciful feelings, so glaringly displayed in yesterday's proceedings [burning of Chambersburg]. It is to be hoped that a final and bloody reckoning will be dealt out to the reckless and abandoned invaders, who, disclaiming the practice of their boasted precepts of 'chivalry,' so brutally apply the torch, and render homeless three thousand helpless citizens.[32]

The reporter was actually comparing early America's frontier to the new total war. For in his mind, Indian attacks along the frontier were both impersonal and aimed at civilian centers; furthermore, such assaults by the "wild savages" placed fear into the hearts of the early settlers. The new total war was equally as impersonal; the enemy no longer cared to respect the sanctity of civilian property, and this new war, not unlike Indian attacks along the frontier, spread terror throughout the countryside. The *Times'* reporter, however, missed the mark by contending that the South was "disclaiming the practice of chivalry." Chivalry was dead. Its decomposing corpse could be seen in the burned out private dwellings that dotted the Shenandoah Valley and in what was the quaint village of Chambersburg.

Not the least to comment upon the torching of Chambersburg was Pennsylvania Governor Andrew Curtin. In an address before a special session of the General Assembly, Curtin listed Pennsylvania's contribution, both military and pecuniary, to the Union's war effort. He further stated that Pennsylvania had not drained the Union army in the field by calling upon its men "to save her cities from being devastated by small bands or ruffians composed of their own inhabitants." Curtin next turned his attention to those men who ridiculed or hindered Pennsylvania's efforts to defend her southern border from attack. "These men," the Governor added, "are themselves morally responsible for the calamity over which they now chuckle and rub their hands." Curtin was undoubtedly referring to those military and political authorities who ordered large numbers of Pennsylvania men to be sent off to defend Washington, leaving his own state with only a scant defense. Pennsylvania, selflessly giving so much of its manpower and wealth to the cause of liberty, had a right to expect assistance from her sister states and the Union government, he asserted.[33] Therefore, the torching of Chambersburg not only had repercussions across the state, but it also unleashed pent-up frustration and divisiveness within the Union ranks.

After traveling west to McConnellsburg, Pennsylvania, the Confederate brigades moved southward toward Hancock, Maryland, arriving there on the afternoon of July 31. Here, General McCausland ordered a levy of $30,000 placed upon the Maryland town, adding that the village would share the same fate as Chambersburg if the money would not be had. General Johnson and his fellow Marylanders raised serious objections and refused to carry out the order, contending that Maryland shed blood loyally for the Cause and her villages do not deserve to come under the torch. Johnson ordered Gilmor to place two men at each Hancock dwelling for protection. For an instant, it appeared that a standoff was about to ensue between McCausland's and Johnson's respective brigades, when, suddenly, a shell exploded outside of town. General Averell's force had arrived. The two brigades would have to settle their differences at another time or else face being butchered by the vengeful minded Yankee troopers.[34]

The Confederate brigades managed to leave Hancock just before Averell's unit could inflict heavy damage. Gilmor's battalions protected the brigades' rear as the column made its way along the National Road toward Cumberland, Maryland. However, blocking the Confederate movement was Union

General Benjamin Kelley's command, which was situated in a strong position two miles outside of Cumberland. McCausland told Gilmor to take his command and attempt to find an alternative route to the Potomac River. The Southern raiding party was in dire straits; General Kelley was in front blocking their retreat route in that direction and General Averell's force was still hot on their trail to the north. Unless they could slip out of this deadly vice, McCausland told Gilmor, "I fear it will be too late to save our guns and wagons," not to mention "a good many men."[35]

Gilmor made his way approximately a half mile before he discovered a suitable place for crossing into Virginia. After seizing a Union man to serve as a guide and also sending the important information back to McCausland, Gilmor and his men made their way to the point over which the brigades hoped to cross. Their guide, with a revolver always to his head, led them to Oldtown, Maryland. Oldtown was situated not only near a fordable place on the Potomac, but it was also located along the path of the Baltimore and Ohio Railroad and in close proximity to the Chesapeake and Ohio Canal. Thus, Major Gilmor realized that a significant Union force would be stationed there. He decided to rest his command in the wooded area and await the arrival of McCausland's embattled brigades.[36]

On the morning of August 2, Gilmor and a few others reconnoitered along the bank of the Potomac. The Marylander and his comrades saw that Colonel Stough's command, the 153rd Ohio National Guards, were ordered to disrupt the Southern attempt to cross into Virginia. Also, Gilmor's couriers reported that an iron-clad battery, placed on the railroad on the Virginia side of the river, served as another major obstacle near the ford. Furthermore, the Northern force had already destroyed a small bridge which crossed the canal above Oldtown. However, they did leave another one intact near the ford. Soon Johnson's brigade arrived on the scene, followed shortly thereafter by McCausland's. The Southerners would have to penetrate through the strong Yankee positions if they were to make it to the safe haven of Virginia.[37]

The Southerners hastily prepared a new bridge over the canal which enabled McCausland to move his troopers into a better angle by which to assault Stough. McCausland's men, once on the other side of the canal, dismounted and forced Stough's men to the opposite side of the river. Many of the blue-coats retreated without further fight, leaving the Ohio colonel with "only five officers and seventy-seven enlisted men," some of whom either raced to the iron-clad train cars for safety or scampered to a large blockhouse with their commander. The iron-clad train was moved closer to the ford, where it could bring deadly fire upon the Confederates who dared to cross the Potomac.[38]

Gilmor's Second Maryland Battalion was able to make its way across the river but were pinned to the opposite bank. Gilmor, seeing his force paralyzed due to the hot fire from the Federal train, went back across the river to speak with Johnson, who was in consultation with McCausland. The Marylander told his two commanding officers that artillery had to be brought upon the iron-clad train if the brigades were to be crossed. They agreed but told the major that the artillerymen would be killed due to the hot fire from the train before they would even be able to position their weapons. The resolute Gilmor would not hear of pessimism, and he galloped off to find Lieutenant John McNulty, of the Baltimore Light Artillery. Gilmor, with men from his command and McNulty's, took two pieces of artillery hurriedly across the bridge that the Union forces left intact. Making it safely across, artilleryman George McElwee, carefully took aim, despite fierce fire from the Union guns. His first shot destroyed the boiler of the train, which caused a deafening explosion. The well-aimed shell had its effect, for the Northern soldiers in the train went scampering to safety, deserting their comrades in the iron-clad portion of the Union bastion. McElwee, with confidence significantly bolstered, struck the pivot-gun of the iron-clad by the third shot. The Yankees thus retreated out of the train and scampered into the surrounding wooded countryside. Seeing the mighty iron-clad demolished by shelling, the Union troops along the river bank joined their comrades in flight.[39]

By this time, the bulk of the two brigades were able to make their way to the Virginia shore, but still they had to cling precariously to the dirt and sand of the Potomac beach. Hindering their advance was the block-house, which Gilmor and his men were unable to see from the Maryland shore. Johnson ordered a charge from the beach against the block-house, only to suffer heavy losses. Another assault was in the planning, when somebody suggested that Johnson simply ask the block-house to surrender. After all, even though the Southerners were pinned to the beach, they could still give their even more immobile enemy the impression of superior numbers. Thus, the Confederate officers sent two of Gilmor's men, a Sergeant T. Kidd (Company F, Second Maryland) and another man with a terse message penned by Johnson: "You will surrender the block-house and your force at once. If you do not you will not receive any terms."[40] Stough conceded but "only if his men would be immediately paroled," their personal belongings remain intact, and "a hand-car [be provided] with which [he could] transport his wounded men to Cumberland."[41]

After destroying the block-house, lighting the armored train ablaze, and demolishing important track around Oldtown, the Southern men galloped to Springfield, West Virginia, where they rested for two days. After resting both man and beast, General McCausland decided to attempt to disrupt the Baltimore and Ohio Railroad by assaulting the important railhead situated at New Creek. The attack failed due to strong Union fortifications. Then, the Confederates, dressed in their butternut, rag-tag uniforms that reeked of smoke, headed in the direction of Moorefield, West Virginia.[42] Arriving within Moorefield Valley on August 6, McCausland and Johnson decided to afford their men rest within this beautiful Valley that had thus far escaped the destruction of the Civil War. "Johnson's brigade, with the guns, bivouacked on the west bank of the South Branch; McCausland's Virginians crossed the river and settled down on the east bank." According to General Johnson, "McCausland directed no scouts along my front and I sent none out, he being my commanding officer."[43] The indefatigable, vengeful-minded Union men under General Averell's command were drawing near, while in the meantime Johnson's men were just retiring to sleep.

As dawn blessed the early morning hours of August 7 Averell's force slammed into Johnson's sleeping brigade, where Gilmor's two Maryland battalions were situated. Alerted to the Federal presence in his camp, Gilmor made his way to alert the First Maryland, which was stationed a short distance away. It was too late. Yankee horsemen, with long, blood-stained silver sabers, were relentlessly hacking away at the dazed Southerners. Some within the First Maryland offered encouragement to one another by crying "Stand firm, men; stand firm." As the Yankees were slashing their surprised foe, some yelled "Surrender, you house-burning scoundrels!" while others screamed with equal conviction, "Kill every damned one of them." Retribution was the order of the day as far as Averell's troopers were concerned.[44]

After Johnson's brigade was taken by surprise and roughly handled, Averell punished McCausland's men in similar fashion. The Federal rout of McCausland's command could have been even more complete. However, due to Averell's worn down horses, he called off pursuit of the battered enemy. By the time McCausland and Johnson reorganized their command at Mount Jackson, Early's main camp, they could tally their losses. Between their two commands they counted "the loss of some four hundred horses, all four guns, and 420 men captured, as well as 150 killed, wounded, and missing."[45] The casualties to Gilmor's command were equally devastating. From his Second Maryland, Gilmor counted "forty-five men and six officers lost." Among the officers were two captains, Henry D. Brewer (Company E) and James L. Clark (Company F), both of whom were captured.[46]

Indeed, the list of men who were either captured or killed by the Yankee forces were closely associated with Gilmor. Private William Gilmor of Company C, Harry's cousin, was captured and sent to Camp Chase, Ohio, for confinement. He would eventually find himself in the Federal stockade at Point Lookout. Arthur Gilmor, Harry's brother, was also captured. Like William, Arthur was sent to Camp Chase and later transferred to Point Lookout. On March 26, 1865, he would die on the ship *City of Albany*. Finally, Gilmor's companion, Second Lieutenant William Kemp of Company C, was killed in the action in the Moorefield Valley. Gilmor also noticed that the First Maryland suffered even heavier losses.[47] Even General Early had to admit that his setback at Moorefield "had a very damaging effect upon [his] cavalry for the rest of the campaign."[48]

Early's raid into southern Pennsylvania and the torching of Chambersburg perhaps displayed to General Ulysses Grant the vitality of "Old Jube's" army. Early appeared almost at will to be able to move his force northward into Pennsylvania and Maryland and thereby pose a threat to the Federal capital. Thus, "Grant could no longer contemplate bringing the Sixth and Nineteenth Corps back to him at Petersburg."[49] Furthermore, when word of the firing of Chambersburg reached the White House, Lincoln became irate. Already suffering politically due to the length of the war and Early's recent Washington raid, "Old Abe" told Union Army officials that if these raids were not terminated President-elect McClellan would be waiting to take over the reigns of government come next March.[50]

More importantly, the Chambersburg incident represented "total war" by Early upon the people of that village. The act itself was not only to serve as retribution for General Hunter's excesses in the Shenandoah Valley earlier but also to prevent future Union tactics in the South's breadbasket. For the Southern men who fought against Hunter in the Valley that summer, "Black David" started the new "total war" of fire; they were simply retaliating by scorching Chambersburg. However, perhaps beyond the frame of reference of most of the hardy men who served in Early's army during that humid summer was the fact that, if the South could not win the "gentlemen's war" from 1861 to 1863, they could never hope to become a victor in the new "total war" of 1864.

Even though the South could never become a victor in the total war with the Union, not a few Northerners were seriously asking if they could ever defeat the Confederacy, total war notwithstanding. Indeed, Early's raid on Washington demonstrated that, as long as the South held the Shenandoah, they would always have a sharp sword pointed directly at the heart of the Union. Thus far, Northerners watched the ignominious defeat of two generals in the Valley during the summer months of 1864: Franz Sigel and David Hunter. Sigel's debacle bore testimony to the strength of the partisan rangers in the Valley, and Hunter's defeat epitomized a lack of enthusiasm coupled with gross negligence. Another crushing Union defeat in the Valley followed by an Early raid could spark complete defeatism in the North, especially when Northerners' emotions were at an all time nadir. Many were already asking how long it would take "another Sigel or Hunter" to place another embarrassing stamp of defeat upon the dignity of the Federal Army.

As sections of Chambersburg still smoldered, Grant ordered General Philip H. Sheridan to replace Hunter and rid the Valley of the audacious Early. Inconspicuous in appearance due to a short, stout frame, Sheridan nevertheless had a special charisma and magnetism with the men of his command. As one Union trooper stated, "he was the only commander I ever met whose personal appearance in the field was an immediate and positive stimulus to battle."[51] Furthermore, Grant and Sheridan were both united in the conviction of bringing total war to the Valley to a degree not yet realized. Sheridan, given a 37,000 man force, was charged with the task of destroying both Early and the lush valley that served as his army's source of sustenance and base of operations.[52]

On August 10, 1864, Sheridan marched his Army of the Shenandoah southward, up the battle-weary Valley. General Early retreated before his advance, finally halting at Fisher's Hill, three miles south of Strasburg. Early's small force, numbering to the tune of thirteen thousand effectives, was stretched thin along the width of the Valley. "Old Jube's" left flank shouldered the North Mountain and his right touched the Massanutten Mountain. Major Gilmor, after the debacle at Moorefield Valley, took what was left of his two battered Maryland Cavalry Battalions and reported to Early at Fisher's Hill. The irascible Confederate general ordered the Marylanders to scout his front. In the meantime, Sheridan, who had just formed his command along Cedar Creek, decided to retreat. The exposure of his flanks coupled with partisan ranger John Singleton Mosby's assault on his wagon train at Berryville convinced Sheridan that his position was too hazardous.[53]

On the very next day, August 17, Early learned of Sheridan's retreat to the north and ordered a quick pursuit. Between Kernstown and Winchester, the advancing Southerners came upon Sheridan's cavalry and a body of infantry. The Union infantry force was deployed on Bower's Hill, and, to their left, Sheridan's cavalry took up their position. Only a mile to their rear was Winchester. As dusk fell upon the Valley, the Confederates, in a three-prong assault, charged the Federal lines. General Gabriel Wharton formed the left wing, and, together with General Stephen Dodson Ramseur's force in the center, operated against the Federal infantry. On the Southern right flank, General John B. Gordon attacked Sheridan's cavalry. The Rebels struck with determination, and the Union line soon began to show signs of cracking, when disaster beset the Confederate forces. In the heat of battle, Gordon's left bludgeoned directly into Ramseur's right in a corn field. Under the darkened sky in a shadowy corn field, the Southerners began to unload into the eerie, dark figures that lurked about, failing to realize that they were comrades instead of foes.[54]

Ramseur noted the terrible situation and sent Gilmor, who had volunteered earlier to serve on his staff, into the fracas in order to organize the lines. The Marylander, assisted by Major Holmes Conrad, managed to restore order and prevent disaster. Afterwards, according to Gilmor, he unwittingly wandered upon a line of twenty-five Yankee infantrymen, who were lying along a stone fence that concealed them from their enemies. Gilmor, realizing that an attempt at a sudden departure would probably startle the unsuspecting Yankees and lead to his capture, or worse, slowly approached the prone blue-coats from the rear. Once within their lines, he confidently yelled, "Boys, don't fire! Don't fire! They'll surrender," to imaginary Confederates hiding in the surrounding woods. The Yankees glanced at each other with disappointed expressions, but to a man each raised his hands and abandoned his weapon, and Gilmor "marched his captives back to the skirmish line."[55]

Next, Gilmor discovered a small force of approximately sixty Union troopers of the First New Jersey Cavalry moving along the Millwood Turnpike. He rode back to the skirmish line in order to report his findings but was informed that no Confederates could be spared to capture the Yankee force.

Not to be denied, Gilmor, again taking Conrad, moved off to capture the blue-coat cavalry force. Conrad, future Assistant Attorney General under President Grover Cleveland's Administration, galloped onto a wooded hill overlooking the Turnpike and the troopers below. Meanwhile, Gilmor daringly approached the Yankee column. Once the Marylander was poised in front of the commanding officer, he stated that the Federals were surrounded and, that if they refused to surrender, his (imaginary) "men" concealed behind that wooden stone fence on the hill would unload on the Yankee horsemen. The Union commanding officer refused to surrender, defiantly telling Gilmor that he wished to parley. Gilmor sternly replied by repeating his threat that his "men" would empty every New Jersey saddle. Then, a voice was heard within the troopers' ranks; a lone horseman exclaimed that, to fight it out was useless, they were completely surrounded and would be "easy pickings" for the Southern men. The lieutenant turned around to hear the protest and, turning back to the Maryland officer, accepted Gilmor's terms. He ordered the Yankee horsemen to dismount and lay down their arms, while Conrad searched for a few Southern skirmishers to take the Union horsemen into captivity. In a morose mood, the Yankees were led into captivity, never realizing that they were captured by only two men.[56]

On the next day, Early's army occupied Winchester, as Sheridan's force formed a new line of defense in the lower Valley. "Little Phil's" line stretched from north to south from Charles Town to Berryville, respectively. While moving northward, down the Valley, Sheridan's men managed to torch important wheat and hay supplies that dotted the Southern breadbasket. In the meantime, while the two armies jostled for position like two knights in a medieval tournament, the horses captured from the New Jersey command along the Turnpike were sent to Gilmor's dismounted men at Newtown. Gilmor's cavalry battalions, still feeling the effects of Averell's raid on August 7, were replenished by the addition of these new mounts, thereby allowing his dismounted men to take to the field of battle. Gilmor's command, numbering approximately 175 men, was attached to General Lunsford Lomax's brigade, serving as his advance guard.[57]

On August 21, 1864, Early, instead of moving his command north of the Potomac River and thereby allowing Sheridan to move into his rear, assaulted the Federal positions at Charles Town and Berryville. Gilmor took part in some of the inconclusive fighting and skirmishes around Charles Town over the next three days and was also given temporary command of the Nineteenth and Twentieth Virginia Regiments of Colonel William L. Jackson's brigade. Further, he performed "scouting duties for General Lomax in the direction of Martinsburg and Shepherdstown."[58]

Four days after his attack on the twenty-first, Early moved his infantry and artillery northward towards Shepherdstown, in order to faint a raid into Maryland. While the infantry and artillery was making its way toward Shepherdstown, General Fitzhugh Lee, with Gilmor in front scouting for the enemy, was to make its way for Williamsport. Gilmor was charged the task of not only gleaning the enemy's disposition, but if possible also crossing the Potomac River and occupying Williamsport before Lee's men arrived. In order to screen the movement toward the Potomac, Major General Joseph Kershaw's infantry and "Tiger John" McCausland's horsemen pounded away at Sheridan's lines.[59]

Early engaged Federal forces along the way and managed to clear an invasion route into Maryland. However, it would be too risky to proceed into enemy territory with such a large Federal force to his right which could easily move into his rear. He decided to return to his original line situated at Bunker Hill, as Sheridan moved to his former position. Thus, after nearly three weeks of sparring, Early and Sheridan's positions were almost the same as they were in early August. "Little

Phil," showing no more audacity or creativity than Hunter, led Early to appraise his new nemesis in negative tones. To Early, Sheridan appeared little more than just another incompetent Yankee general sent into the Valley. With this mind set, Early began to display even more risk with his small army, sending various commands out on numerous excursions and wearing his men down with brutal marches and counter marches. Even his army in the vicinity of Bunker Hill was precariously scattered and vulnerable. Such recklessness led Henry Kyd Douglas, a member of Early's staff, to reflect that he "never could understand why Sheridan permitted Early to play this reckless game under his nose." He further suggests that Sheridan, contrary to the reputation he later gained, was "both timid and lacking enterprise," during this period.[60] However, even though Early was showing boldness and adventure, Sheridan was biding his time, building his forces, and planning the destruction of "Old Jube" and his Valley. Sheridan was the savior that the North wanted, and the demon that the people of the Shenandoah would come to dread.

A short time after partaking in Early's faint to the north, General Lomax ordered Gilmor to take his two cavalry battalions and assist Colonel William Jackson's brigade, whose pickets were being driven in by "two hundred Union cavalrymen" south of Leetown. Lomax's scouts were correct in reporting that approximately two hundred Union horsemen were harassing Jackson's pickets daily; however, on this day, instead of a force of only two hundred, all of Sheridan's cavalry was deployed in that location. Expecting to find only two hundred blue-coats south of Leetown, Gilmor's men confronted well over five times that number. In one instance, a large body of blue-coats overcame Gilmor's ranks and mixed in with them, forcing the Rebels to either fight against superior numbers or beat a hasty retreat. In the wild melee, an unidentified Southerner saved Gilmor's life twice, both times emptying the barrel of his pistol into Federal troopers just as they were about to kill the Marylander. All that could be heard were the horrid screams of men and the clash of sabers, intermingled by an occasional crack of a pistol. Gilmor's troopers managed to retreat, in a disorderly fashion, through Smithfield to relative safety. On this cool Sunday afternoon, the Northern cavalry claimed twenty-six men in Gilmor's command. Among the casualties was Harry's cousin, Hoffman (Company F), who was struck in the arm by Union fire. Also, Captain John D. Clarke of Company F was captured by Union authorities and imprisoned at Fort Delaware. Even the people of Smithfield felt the Union fury, as three houses in the little hamlet were put to the torch by the Northern troopers.[61]

As the calendar revealed the first few days of September, Gilmor's battalions were encamped between Smithfield and Bunker Hill. Here they skirmished with large bodies of Union cavalry, while supporting sharpshooters and serving as scouts in the major skirmishes along the Opequon Creek. These small battles saw both Union and Confederate forces beating each other back and forth across the Opequon, whose muddy waters witnessed the countless battles that claimed so many lives.[62]

In the early morning hours of September 3, Gilmor moved his two battalions from their new position at Stephenson's Depot and formed them in preparation for an assault upon General William Averell's division between Bunker Hill and Darkesville. Gilmor was ordered to place his cavaliers along Colonel Jackson's flanks, as "Mudwall's" dismounted troopers marched northward along the Valley Turnpike toward Averell's position. As soon as the Southerners encountered heavy resistance, Gilmor quickly moved his forces to either the Union left or right flank, as if he was about to outflank the Federal troops. This movement, combined with fierce charges by Jackson's skirmishers, was enough to intimidate the Yankee men into retreating down the Valley Pike toward

Darkesville. The technique worked well, and the Yankees were even driven beyond their reserve picket camps.[63]

However, just south of Darkesville, the irresistible gray tide came upon a low ridge, covered with barricades of fence rails, which formed a ninety degree angle with the Valley Pike. Concealed behind this improvised bastion were Yankees armed with deadly Spencer seven-shooters. According to Major Gilmor, these were "terribly effective weapons," a conviction shared by not a few of his fellow Southerners. Gilmor, noting the strength of the new Union position, requested that General Lomax send forth a new regiment, replete with long-range guns. Lomax responded by sending up the Eighteenth Virginia, of General John Imboden's brigade. Lomax ordered Gilmor to assault the barricades with the Eighteenth while he would hold the First and Second Maryland Battalions in reserve. Gilmor led the Virginians in a charge, which attracted hot fire from the concealed Union troopers. However, after observing that the Rebel ranks remained intact and moved irresistibly forward, the startled Yankees vacated their barricades, while they cheered their adversaries' courage. They jumped upon their mounts, which were hidden in a nearby wooded area, and proceeded to be chased by the indefatigable Southerners all the way through Darkesville.[64]

During the pursuit, Gilmor and the Virginians soon came upon General Averell's cavalry, which was formed in perfect order a little distance north of Darkesville. Just as Gilmor ordered the bugler to sound the recall, the Yankee general detached a regiment to cut off Gilmor's retreat southward, while at the same time pummeling the Marylander's command with artillery. Gilmor's troopers retreated back to the Union barricades south of Darkesville, were he found Lomax waiting with his two cavalry commands. Lomax ordered Gilmor to stymie Averell's advance with both the Eighteenth Virginia and the two Maryland Battalions, in order to give him adequate time to retreat to Bunker Hill. Gilmor managed to slow Averell's advance only by desperate counter-charges and "volleys from the Eighteenth Virginia's carbines."[65]

Before Gilmor's command could safely retreat to Bunker Hill, they had to cope with a large mill-dam that was situated along their escape route up the Valley Pike. The mill-dam, stretching a distance of some three hundred yards, allowed for only two avenues by which to cross its waters; one route, the Valley Pike, traversed the dam at its mid-section, while the other, a road, crossed a shallow stream below the dam. With the blue coats pushing on, Gilmor ordered the Eighteenth Virginia to cross the road below the dam and the Second Maryland to cross over the dam by way of the Valley Pike, while he, with the First Maryland, would hold off the Yankees. Averell, on the other hand, hoped that many of the Confederates would not be able to make their way across the dam before his forces arrived and thus could be forced into the dam's waters by his charging Federal troopers. After seeing the Second Maryland and Eighteenth Virginia safely over to the south side of the dam, Gilmor and the First Maryland had to cross by way of a marsh situated near the dam, for by the time they attempted to cross the Valley Turnpike the route was already covered by a Union regiment hidden in a clump of trees.[66]

Once he reached the other side, Gilmor reorganized his men, despite the incessant Union fire. He waited for a chance to charge a Federal cavalry force that dared to cross over to the south side of the dam. Before long, a regiment galloped across the dam; Gilmor patiently waited until the last Yankee was on his side, before he ordered the First and Second Maryland to charge. The Yankee lines broke, and the blue-coats retreated toward the Valley Pike. All the Union men were unable to make the crossing and were bludgeoned into the dam's deep waters by the furious Marylanders, who relentlessly charged them. After the Eighteenth Virginia was quickly recalled to its brigade, Gilmor attempted to form his fellow Marylanders behind a brick church. Then, to their disgruntlement, Southern shells began to land in their midst, killing two Marylanders and wounding five others. A courier was quickly sent to warn the artillery officer of his deadly error. Lomax actually ordered the shelling, not realizing that it was friend instead of foe that was being mangled by the artillery fire. After their friends stopped blasting them, Union shells began to find their mark within the Confederate ranks. Gilmor, seeing that his men were receiving "the very devil" from both the blue and the gray, decided to retreat to a peach orchard located some three hundred yards away. Gilmor ordered Captain Burke (Second Maryland) and Captain Gus Dorsey (First Maryland) to take the Second Maryland across the Valley Turnpike and attack any group of Yankees that were preparing to cross. Out of the corner of his eye, Gilmor then noticed a large group of Union troopers moving towards the First Maryland in the orchard.[67]

Gilmor also noticed that his Second Maryland was charging a Yankee regiment along the Valley Turn Pike. If the Federal force on the Turn Pike was to coordinate its efforts with the large body of Union cavalry already on the south side of the dam, the Second Maryland would be squeezed between them. Gilmor became frustrated. His entire Second Maryland was in dire straits. Where was Lomax's command, and why wasn't he coming to his assistance?[68] To further add to his distress, the First Maryland refused to charge. The major, raising his sword above his head, attempted to rally them, when a ball tore into his left shoulder and passed out beneath his jaw bone. The force of the bullet almost toppled the large Marylander from his horse and caused his saber to fall to the ground; noticing the approaching blue-coats, who were getting ever closer, he galloped back to the First Maryland, scolding them for their disobedience. Finally, they agreed to charge, when two men noticed the severe hole in

Gilmor's neck and his sickly, disjointed limp arm dangling by his side. One man grabbed his horse's bridle and led the wounded major to the rear. Once out of immediate danger, Lomax had Gilmor placed in an ambulance and sent out of harm's way. Before leaving, Gilmor told the Confederate general that Captain Welch (Company D, First Maryland) would be placed in temporary command of his men.[69]

On that humid day in September patience undoubtedly was beginning to wear thin among the battered men of the First Maryland. They were not only beaten back by superior Yankee weaponry and numbers but were ordered to hold the ground north of the dam while Gilmor's own Second Maryland and the Eighteenth Virginia retreated. Once on the south side of the dam, they refused to follow Gilmor's first order to charge. It is possible that one disgruntled man in the First Maryland, exhausted by the day's affair and deeply angered by his commanding officer's relentlessness, decided to take matters into his own hands by shooting his major. Gilmor could have finally pushed this man to his breaking point, a point at which he was finally willing to jettison personal loyalty and obedience for a far more tangible Cause - survival.

Gilmor's wounded body was sent at a quick pace up the Valley, to Charlottesville, where he was placed in a hospital. Here he received a letter from a James F. Cook, who wrote that he was sorry to learn about Gilmor's wound, concluding wryly that he hoped the ailing Marylander would "have a shorter stay with the Surgeons than I have had."[70] Perhaps in order to be closer to his command and local friends, Gilmor convinced his caregivers to allow him to move back down the Valley to Winchester. At Winchester, Gilmor spent a day in the York Hospital, where his wound was treated, before requesting permission to be cared for at a private residence. Soon, a letter from a "friend" by the name of Delia arrived at Gilmor's location. Delia, writing from Mount Airy estate, said that "we were indeed sorry to hear of your misfortune my kind friend." Furthermore, she wrote that they "feel that every effort will be made by the good people of this town [Winchester]...to speed your recovery." The kind Delia encouraged Gilmor to visit Mount Airy for assistance, and she also added that Hoffman, Gilmor's cousin, who was wounded about a week prior to Harry, was in their care at Mount Airy. Concerning Hoffman, Delia optimistically concluded, "we have great hopes of finding the balls and being able to extract it [sic] in a few days..."[71]

While at Winchester, General Lomax informed the ailing Marylander that he was promoted to colonel and that the First and Second Maryland Cavalry Battalions were going to be consolidated, with him at the helm. Gilmor, gratefully accepting the promotion, requested only his former command, the Second Maryland. He suggested that not a few officers in the First would have serious reservations concerning consolidation. As he predicted, many officers in the First protested and tendered their resignations. Also, further lessening the morale of the new regiment, the acting Lieutenant Colonel, Gus Dorsey, was wounded about a month later, and the ranks began to dwindle. The First Maryland would eventually be returned to its independent status due to the vehement protests of its officers.[72]

In Winchester recovering from his wounds, Gilmor still managed to receive word of Early and Sheridan's movements in the lower Valley. On September 19, "Little Phil's" force broke through the Rebel defenses on the outskirts of town and smashed into the city proper. Sheridan's drive through Winchester caught the recuperating Gilmor by surprise, for he did not even have time to completely dress before fleeing ahead of the Yankee troops. On this day the Marylander appeared as "a sorry figure," dashing through the chaotic Winchester streets without "a hat, coat or shoes, his naked feet hanging loose below the stirrups." The tall colonel's legs were far too long for the stirrups. After his narrow escape from Winchester, Gilmor traveled throughout the Valley. He made several stops at dwellings of various friends and Southern sympathizers, before arriving at the Mount Airy estate.[73]

Gilmor's condition and his sense of despair were at an all time low as the fall months slowly approached. The proud cavalier had to sometimes be assisted off his horse, and on more than one occasion he felt weak and faint in the saddle. Furthermore, the pain emanating from his shoulder was severe, and his arm had to be kept in a sling. In one instance Gilmor thought that he was finished and became somewhat fixated upon death, until a Southern woman with brandy gave him an emotional charge. During this time he wandered to and fro in the Valley, visiting headquarters, rallying men, and observing contests between Early and Sheridan. In November, Early requested that Gilmor, arm still in a sling, enter Sheridan's line and note if any of his army had been detached eastward to Grant's Army of the Potomac. Gilmor took six of his men, all of which were in the Second Maryland, on the two-day trek into Sheridan's lines. While on their way, Gilmor's clan, stealthily decked in Union blue, captured four Yankee men, who were on their way to camp in order to cast their votes for President Lincoln in their command's presidential ballot. Gilmor and his comrades captured the four Northerners, seized their tickets, and marched directly into camp and proceeded to cast their votes for "Old Abe." In one of history's ironies, Gilmor and his fellow Rebels were to vote for a man whose election sealed the Confederacy's fate. Lincoln's election was a firm mandate from the Northern people: continue the war until the rebellion was completely quelled.[74]

As the injured Gilmor made his way up and down the Valley during that fall, he made note of the torched, smoldering dwellings and the utter destitution of many who once shared a wholesome existence in the Valley. At a friend's house, Gilmor ate cakes made of chopped horse feed. There was neither meat nor flour to be had on this farmer's acreage; his flour mills were torched and his cows, horses, and hogs were gone. The Marylander's eyes witnessed only a mere microcosm of Sheridan's onslaught in the Valley, as "Little Phil's" army claimed the destruction of 1,200 barns, seven furnaces, eight saw mills, seventy-one flour mills, and the irreplaceable loss of 435,802 bushels of wheat.[75]

Gilmor's battered body and bruised spirit embodied the war-ravaged Shenandoah Valley; Harry Gilmor's wounds were caused by fighting superior numbers and weaponry, and the Valley's wounds and scars were the result of total war. The new colonel, after a furlough that was issued in November, would return to action in December of that year. However, the Shenandoah would never quite return to the way it was, as generation after generation kept alive their hatred that was sparked by Sheridan in the Valley during those last ominous months of 1864.

8

"Hush Up, or I'll Blow Your Brains Out"

In early February, 1865, a deep blanket of heavy snow buried the rolling hills and narrow valleys that constituted the rugged topography of western Virginia. A layer of ice, reflecting the sparse moonlight, added to the treacherousness of the lonely mountain roads, as free-floating, large chunks of the frigid material clogged the streams and rivers, making passage within this vicinity extremely hazardous. Nestled within this area, three or four miles south of Moorefield, was the snow covered residence of a Mr. Randolph. The innocent nature of this mountain dwelling belied the presence of Colonel Harry Gilmor, a guest of the dwelling, who was in a childlike sleep in one of the Randolph's bedrooms. Before retiring that evening he placed his pistols on a chair next to his bed; little did he know that within five miles to the north a contingent of over three hundred Yankees were hot on his trail, with the objective of terminating his military contributions to the "Southern Cause."

The capture of Gilmor brought to a culmination years of Federal efforts to deal with this elusive Southern irregular. It also marked an end to the career of one of the most feared partisan fighters of the Civil War.

Although General Philip Sheridan had been successful in driving "Ole Jube's" main force from the Shenandoah, he was still, nonetheless, plagued by the destructive activities of partisan bands. Partisan fighters such as Gilmor operated in areas inhabited by a populace overwhelmingly sympathetic to their efforts. These irregular forces depended upon "quick strike and disappear" tactics along Federal wagon trains, supply depots, encampments, communication networks, and railways. This meant that hundreds, if not thousands, of additional Union troops were forced to be deployed to protect such key military essentials, thus sacrificing their opportunity to be used in major campaigns. For instance, Sheridan stated in postwar comments that, even though he maintained a large numerical superiority over Early's army during the Shenandoah Campaign of 1864, irregular forces in his rear "compelled such heavy detachments to guard the border and his line of supplies that their actual strength was about equal."[1] Therefore, even in preparing major military campaigns, Sheridan was forced to take into account the disposition of such irregular forces.

Sheridan, who became obsessed with putting a halt to irregular activities, organized his own unit of scouts. Through espionage activities, these scouts infiltrated partisan camps and from there proceeded to glean valuable information concerning future activities as well as disposition and numerical strength of their forces.

Sergeant Joseph E. McCabe, of the Seventeenth Pennsylvania, attracted "Little Phil's" attention due to his insatiable thirst for hazardous missions, where he daringly carried dispatches through enemy lines and raided Jubal Early's embattled forces. With his tenacity proven, Sheridan charged McCabe the task of organizing this scout battalion. McCabe was named Chief of Scouts; however, the entire force of some forty-five to sixty men, all adorned in gray and each provided with two revolvers, was placed under the command of Major Harry Young, First Rhode Island Infantry. Sheridan thus sent his scouts, who would fall under the general label of "Jessie Scouts," against the Confederate partisan rangers. "He was beginning to fight fire with fire."[2]

The "Jessie Scouts" employed several techniques that aided their infiltration into Rebel camps and acquisition of information. In addition to their method of identifying each other via a white handkerchief, a "Jessie Scout" would also be certain not to forget his passes that were gleaned from captured Rebels. Finally, the "Jessie Scouts" acquired a great deal of basic knowledge concerning the Confederate Army, especially officers.[3]

To "sweeten the pot," a scout was paid an amount of money from the Secret Service Fund directly correlated to the importance of the duty performed and the information attained from the Johnny Rebs. For example, Scouts George D. Mullihan and Abe Atkins successfully delivered a message from Sheridan to General T.A. Torbert after a one hundred-mile trek through hazardous territory, where the two stealthy Yankees entered three Confederate camps and managed to enjoy breakfast with the Rebels. They completed the mission in a day, and Mullihan received one hundred dollars from the Fund for his efforts. Sheridan, with his new military organization of scouts and spies, set out to tackle Harry Gilmor.[4]

In the meantime, Gilmor, who was on furlough due to the wound he received back in September, was casually escorting two young ladies on a trip through the war-weary Southern cities of Lexington, Lynchburg, and Richmond. Afterwards, the partisan ranger reported to General Early's headquarters at Staunton a few days before the Confederacy celebrated its fourth Christmas as a self-proclaimed independent nation. Early ordered Gilmor to take his Second Maryland Cavalry Battalion to Hardy County, located in western Virginia, and also take charge of other partisan forces in the vicinity under Blake Woodson and Jesse McNeil. Then, when weather would permit, Gilmor was to use this combined force of approximately three to four hundred troops to operate against the Baltimore and Ohio Railroad located some thirty-five to forty miles north, with the objective of interrupting the passage of Union troops eastward.[5]

While on his way to the rugged terrain of western Virginia, the partisan received a letter from his sister, Ellen. She wrote, "I am most miserable about you for fear you should attempt to come home, *never never* do so." Undoubtedly, she was implying the time that her brother was captured by Union authorities when he attempted to visit friends and family members in Baltimore during the late summer of 1862. She further admonished the Marylander:

> *never take horses unless from the enemy, respect private property always,. and try to be kind and polite to every one, you will lose nothing by it. [Also], try to get with those who are honorable, principled men and who [will] not lead you astray.*

Ellen also told Harry to "stick to your command and stay in the right place..." She concluded by writing "...Be a good boy and do your duty may God bless and protect you, is the prayer of your devoted sister Ellen."[6] Ellen's letter showed keen insight, for she realized the poor reputation of partisan commands, and undoubtedly she read the news reports that labeled her brother "notorious." She further understood that many on the Union side wanted her brother captured, dead or alive. Also, she must have taken into account her brother's reckless habit of leaving his command when she warned him to remain with his men and "stay in the right place."

The weather turned intensely cold and inclement during the last week of January 1865, and the conditions of the streams, rivers, and roads west of the Shenandoah Mountains prohibited both Gilmor, and his nemesis, Sheridan, from attempting extensive strikes upon the enemy. Gilmor could not make a raid without "killing up [his horses]," and his soldier's better wisdom suggested that he "keep [his] stock in good order, and have the men well clothed in readiness for a raid," whenever the unsympathetic western Virginia weather would break.[7] Sheridan disdainfully reported in a letter that he "had scarcely ever felt such cold weather as we are having here," and he expressed concern for an expedition he sent out into the harsh winter wilderness.[8]

The winter weather was equally brutal to both the "Men in Blue" as well as the "Rebs." During this time, troops under Southern Generals Thomas Rosser and Lunsford Lomax were disbanded in the general vicinity of Hardy County and were about gathering horses, in anticipation of the spring campaigns.[9] Thus the "Jessie Scouts," provided with passes gleaned from captured Confederate prisoners and clad in Confederate gray, were presented with the fortuitous opportunity to stealthily infiltrate the ranks of Rosser and Lomax's cavalry. From there they would be able to fraternize with Gilmor's troops, with the hope of attaining the whereabouts of either his camp or even the headquarters of the partisan ranger himself. Gilmor, all too familiar with the "Jessie Scouts," was constantly on the lookout for these relentless troops.

Sheridan learned from a group of "Jessie Scouts" that Gilmor was around Harrisonburg during late January, and he quickly sent Scout Archie Rowand and another "trustworthy" agent into the frigid wilderness in order to attain the elusive Gilmor's exact location. In a little less than a week, the exhausted, snow covered Rowand and his courageous comrade returned to Sheridan's headquarters. The dauntless scouts managed to learn through their espionage activities Gilmor's place of residence, which they placed at three or four miles south of Moorefield, Hardy County, "the center of a very disloyal section of West Virginia." To add to "Little Phil's" delight, Young's scouts also gathered the numerical strength of his irregulars as well as their rendezvous point.[10]

Confident of success, Sheridan ordered Gilmor's capture, to put an end to this "link between Maryland and the Confederacy," that he represented. He mustered a force of three hundred men, armed with "sabers and pistols," and placed them under the command of Lieutenant Colonel Edward W. Whitaker of the First Connecticut Cavalry. Whitaker's entire force was composed of men from the Third Cavalry Division. This large force was to proceed fifteen miles to the rear of a small detachment of some twenty, hand-picked "Jessie Scouts" under the command of Major Young. Young's men, dressed in Confederate Gray, deceptively would inform Gilmor's troops that the large body following them was Yankee cavalry, "hot on their heels." Major Young was charged with the duty of discovering Gilmor's location and then capturing this Confederate, partisan chieftain. With Major Young's men dressed in Confederate gray, and with Whitaker's "Yankee" troopers close behind, this ingenuous plan easily deceived Gilmor's partisans, who were ordered to keep him informed as to the enemy's movements.[11]

On February fourth, at six o'clock on a very frigid morning, these two forces, working in close collaboration, left headquarters at Winchester and entered the Moorefield Pike. At Wardensville, only ten miles into Hardy County, the cold men welcomed a forty-five minute respite, where they doubtless chatted about loved ones back home, Sherman's destructive march through South Carolina, or their chances of success in their present mission, over warm cups of coffee, supplemented by rations. Then they mounted and rode the additional twenty-five arduous miles to Moorefield. A little over eighteen hours after beginning their expedition, Lieutenant Colonel Whitaker decided to halt his column four miles from Moorefield, while Young continued on into the winter hamlet. Perhaps his conservatism was well founded. During the latter part of their trip through the western Virginia mountains the mounted men gazed at a winter, night-time sky that grew increasingly ominous and threatened to dump another load of snow onto the troops and inhabitants of Hardy County. He rested both men and horses and decided to set off again at four o'clock in the morning and strike Gilmor's camp at daylight, on the following day.[12]

Meanwhile, Young and his hardy group of men were dumfounded. Neither the location of Gilmor nor his camp was to be had, at least during the first few hours of their search of Moorefield proper. Young sent back a messenger to inform Colonel Whitaker of this sorrowful news. Adding to Whitaker's distress, the snow clouds, that had been accumulating previously, now began to release their burden upon western Hardy County. Nevertheless, in the early dawn hours the indomitable Whitaker pushed on an additional four rigorous miles to the outskirts of Moorefield, arriving in a devilish snow-squall.[13]

In the meantime, Young's men continued their search of Moorefield, which was quaintly nestled a few miles east of where the South Branch of the Potomac River breaks into two smaller streams. During the early morning hours, candles began to flicker in the frosted windows of Moorefield's dwellings, where Young's scouts, like hounds in search of a rabbit, startled some of the approximate five hundred residents. The heavy snow concealed Moorefield's excellent brick sidewalks and roadways, the latter neatly "banked with small river stones;" Moorefield's streets were the best of Hardy County and could equal the streets that lined the North's most prosperous cities. Along Main Street, Young's men confronted only the dark, lonely windows of brick business buildings, which were not yet open during these early hours.[14]

Sometime during the night, several "Jessie Scouts" stumbled across one of Gilmor's guerrillas and informed him that they were Confederate pickets from the Lost River area and wished to warn Gilmor that "the Yankees were way off at Wardensville, clear 'cross county." This partisan told the scouts that Colonel Gilmor was staying at the Randolph residence, a "leetle stretch" south of Moorefield. He then ran off to tell Gilmor, who was preparing to retire to bed with his cousin, Hoffman, that the Yanks were way off "yonder, toward Wardensville." Young's men, handsomely adorned in Confederate gray and communicating with a crude "Southern drawl," easily fooled the partisan's followers.[15]

Where his will proved irresistible, Whitaker's patience wore thin, and, with no word concerning Gilmor's whereabouts, he sent word to Young to move his party southward, along the South Fork. Meanwhile, after leaving a portion of the Second Ohio Cavalry in Moorefield to continue the search for Gilmor or his men, Whitaker took the lion's share of his men a short distance to the west, crossed a stream, and veered left, down along the South Fork, preceded, along the eastern bank, by Young's twenty man entourage.[16]

As the snowstorm subsided and as light first began to bless the western Virginia countryside, out of the corner of their eyes, along the right flank of their slender column, Whitaker's troopers began to observe mounted men. Soon, many Rebel horsemen could be seen dashing southward across the fields and hills that cushioned Whitaker's right shoulder, in the hope of warning Gilmor before the Yankees made an unwelcome, surprise arrival. After ordering a messenger to report these sudden movements to Young, Whitaker pushed his men hard, in order to reach what he perceived to be Gilmor's camp before the Rebel horsemen arrived and sounded the alarm.[17]

A short distance south of Moorefield, Young's blood hounds began to bustle with activity, hastily searching each dwelling. The scouts then came upon two houses, one belonging to a man named Williams and another to Mr. Randolph. Scout Nick Carlisle, along with Rowand, who first pinpointed Gilmor's location south of Moorefield, took eight men to search the Williams's house. Major Young, with eight scouts, including George Mullihan, who first enlisted in the Union Army at the age of thirteen, went to search the Randolph residence. A large group of horses were stabled nearby, which immediately attracted their attentive eyes.[18]

Young impatiently knocked at the door, and after a brief wait a servant woman hesitantly answered the Union knocks. "What soldiers [are] in the houses?" Young queried. By the wording of the question, it appeared as if Young and his followers simply wanted a clue as to where, in the vicinity of this neighborhood, Gilmor and his troops might be located. In a very innocent manner, the woman responded, "Major Gilmor is upstairs." Young and Mullihan, startled by this succinct response, glanced at each other in disbelief - they finally found their treasure.[19]

Waving his pistol in the air, Young quietly but sternly ordered five men posted around the Randolph dwelling, while he, Mullihan, and two other anxious scouts hurriedly brushed aside the startled woman and raced upstairs, burst open the door, and entered the room where Harry and his cousin, Hoffman, were in a sound sleep. Neither the twenty scouts in the vicinity of his house nor the immediate commotion on Randolph's front porch managed to wake him from his sleep. However, when Major Young rudely shook Gilmor and then proceeded to point his cocked six-shooter directly at Gilmor's head, the Marylander suddenly awoke. With Union guns drawn upon Gilmor, a scout seized the partisan's pistols, which were placed under his uniform on a chair far out of reach. Gilmor, who vowed never to be captured alive by the Yankees, desperately analyzed his immediate predicament. With blood shot eyes, blurred vision, and the normal fatigue of a person just awakened, he weighed the possibility of escape. However, he was brought back to attention by the sensation of a cold pistol barrel pressed against his temple and the blunt inquiry, "Are you Colonel Gilmor?" The startled Gilmor honestly replied, "Yes, and who in the devil's name are you?" The question was of course hollow, for Gilmor, much familiar with the "Jessie Scouts," knew who they were. After properly identifying himself, Young ordered Gilmor and his cousin to come along, and the partisan ranger grudgingly complied.[20]

Young gave Gilmor and his cousin an opportunity to dress, but, after observing Gilmor deliberately delaying, he nervously barked "be lively!" While Gilmor and his cousin were dressing, Mullihan ran to the partisan's stable and saddled Gilmor's black mare and his cousin's horse. Not far in the distance sporadic fire was heard, as Gilmor's irregulars began to fire upon the scouts on the outskirts of town. Gilmor in a disgruntled manner moved his tall, stout frame onto his mare and at once ordered it to take off. Mullihan, suspecting that the cunning Gilmor would attempt an escape, caught his horse's bridle rein and desperately dug the heels of his boots into the snow for traction, in order to halt Gilmor's startled mare. The incorrigible Gilmor attempted a second escape and was thwarted again. This time, a panting, startled Mullihan firmly told his superior, Major Young, "Unless you exchange Gilmor's horse with one of the other men's, I will shoot it out from under him!" Young then turned to Scout Jack Reily and ordered, "You take Gilmor's horse, he'll ride yours," and turning back to Mullihan curtly asked, "Satisfied now?" Seconds later, he told Mullihan to keep an eye on Gilmor, since he was still worried about a possible escape.[21]

Even though they managed to capture Gilmor, Whitaker and Young realized that they were still within a hornet's nest of enemy activity. Gilmor's mounted men began to collect on a bluff that overlooked the small group of houses below as well as Whitaker's entire right flank, and soon the enemy began to conjugate on his right and in his rear. Some of Gilmor's more loyal troops attempted to recapture their detained leader. As soon as a handful of scouts led Gilmor and his cousin across the South Fork and placed them at the head of Whitaker's column, three Rebels dashed, "guns a'blazen," at the Yankee column from across the stream. One ball narrowly missed striking Gilmor in the face. Witnessing his men's courage and relentlessness, he began to offer encouragement, "Give them the devil, boys!" Then somebody pushed a pistol near Gilmor's head and barked, "Hush up, or I'll blow your brains out!" The threat was to no avail, for Harry continued to encourage his fellow Confederates' valiant effort to rescue him.[22]

Seeing his own position untenable, and waving the opportunity to rout Gilmor's men from their favorable positions, Whitaker decided to make a hasty retreat. To cover his rear, Whitaker called upon Lieutenant Brown, also of the First Connecticut Cavalry, with some thirty-eight Yankees, who boasted fifteen Spencer rifles among them. This force handily checked the Confederate charges upon the column's rear. As he passed through Moorefield a Yankee prisoner and witnessed the ladies running out of their houses to wish him a last farewell, Gilmor confessed, "I tried to be cheerful, but it was hard to bear."[23]

Whitaker moved his column along the South Branch to Romney; Gilmor and his cousin rode in the front, and less dangerous Southerners captured along the way were placed in the middle of the column. While resting eight miles from Romney, Gilmor's troopers made one last desperate attack, which was easily repulsed. Not wishing to stop at night with his prisoners, Whitaker pushed his men hard. The night was so frigid that both friend and foe were forced to dismount their horses and walk some of the trek. After passing through Hanging Rock Gap, around midnight on February 5, the expedition came to a well-deserved halt along the Big Capon bridge, where they remained until daylight. According to Gilmor's memoirs, three miles before reaching this point a squabble flared between Young and Whitaker, which allowed him an opportunity to escape. Young wished to take Gilmor and his comrades directly off to Winchester, without the large column. After Whitaker refused him, Young took his scouts off to Winchester, thereby abandoning the column. In one instance, Whitaker was left alone with his orderly and surgeon, with Gilmor, relatively lightly guarded, in close proximity. However, "an unaccountable fit of trembling, not from fear," seized Gilmor as he planned to lunge for Whitaker's pistol. Thus, Gilmor lost his one chance to flee. At any rate, apparently Young later had a change of heart, because he was found waiting for Whitaker's column at the Big Capon bridge, and, as a result, Gilmor's chance of escape was again significantly reduced.[24]

Interestingly, neither Sheridan nor Whitaker makes an account of Gilmor's allegations. Whitaker, in his official account of the raid and capture lists nothing but praise for Young and his scouts:

> I cannot commend too highly the zeal and hearty cooperation evinced by Major Young, commanding General Sheridan's scouts, who accompanied me. To his personal gallantry is due the successful 'bearding of the lion in his den.'[25]

At daybreak, Whitaker and his men, prisoners in hand, completed the remaining portion of their successful expedition. The colonel arrived back at Winchester just before noon on the sixth of February.[26]

After offering praise to fellow officers, Whitaker reflected on the success of the entire expedition:

> Having ridden near 140 miles in a little over forty-eight hours, over a mountainous country, across swollen streams filled with floating ice, and within the enemy's lines, the object of the expedition was fully accomplished without the loss of a man.[27]

Despite his efforts in bringing the partisan into captivity, Rowand was not decorated by Union officials. Gilmor's partisan comrades quickly avenged the capture of the Marylander. On the night of February 21-22, Jesse McNeill's irregulars raided Cumberland, Maryland, capturing "Major General George Crook and Brigadier General Benjamin F. Kelley."[28]

Upon arriving at Winchester, the captive Gilmor was separated from his cousin and other captured Confederates and given his own private hotel room, which was extremely cold and minus any furniture, save for a chair and an old bedstead frame. Gilmor, almost immediately upon arrival, was placed in "ruffles" (handcuffs) and later placed in shackles. All the while Harry had to endure his imprisonment in silence and solitude. His guards were not permitted to communicate with him, and he was granted no visitors, much to the dismay of his lady friends who pleaded with Sheridan to afford them a short visit with the "gallant Gilmor." Concerning his treatment during those three days in Winchester, Gilmor concludes, "I shall not soon forget those two days and three nights, nor shall I soon forget or forgive this inhuman treatment."[29]

On the third day of his captivity, Young told Gilmor that he was to be sent to another prison, and through intuition Gilmor expected to be sent to Fort Warren in Boston, Massachusetts. Even though Gilmor was not aware of it, a little over five hours after his arrival at Winchester, Sheridan sent a short message to Major General Henry W. Halleck, Chief of Staff, requesting permission to send Gilmor to either Fort Lafayette or far northward, to Fort Warren, Boston. Sheridan also added that Gilmor "is an energetic, shrewd, and unscrupulous scoundrel and a dangerous man. He must be closely watched, or he will escape."[30] Halleck granted Sheridan's wish, and in addition he stated that a special guard shall be implemented to escort Gilmor from Winchester to

Fort Warren.[31] This concern, especially as expressed by Sheridan and Halleck, bears testimony to the terror Gilmor struck into the hearts of Union soldiers and the "thorn in the side" that he was to Federal officers.

Arriving at Harper's Ferry, an angry crowd was on hand to meet Major Young and his captive partisan ranger. Young led Gilmor through the crowd by waving his fully cocked revolver, and, when the crowd began to threaten Gilmor with violence, Young, totally calm and collected, turned to Gilmor and whispered, "In case of an attack, take one of my pistols and shoot right and left." The two seemed to have attained a mutual respect for one another. As Gilmor stated in his postwar memoirs, even though Major Young maintained a close eye on him, "from first to last, [Young] was as kind to me as it was possible for him to be." Suddenly, a tall, almost intoxicated artillery lieutenant appeared from the crowd and screamed, "I say, Gilmor, where is the watch some of your damned thieves stole from me on the Philadelphia train?" in reference to the infamous train robbery of February 1864. For his efforts, the disgruntled artilleryman received the barrel of Young's pistol across his blaring mouth, which knocked him off the train platform. The man, dazed and bleeding profusely from the mouth, embarrassingly disappeared into the enraged crowd.[32]

Gilmor and Major Young then traveled to Baltimore, where nine miles outside of town they were warmly greeted by Lieutenant Colonel Woolley, the Provost Marshal of Baltimore. Lieutenant Colonel Woolley took great care in protecting the captive partisan as he passed through his native city. Gilmor was by 1865 a person of considerable fame and notoriety, especially among the numerous Southern sympathizers of the region. However, there were some in Baltimore who espoused Union convictions, and undoubtedly, the provost marshal realized that they might wish to inflict harm upon their fellow Marylander. After leaving the

Baltimore depot, he visited Woolley's crowded, bustling office, but not before a friend approached Gilmor and while jubilantly shaking his hand clandestinely slipped him a package of bank notes. He also had a reunion with an old friend, Mr. W.G. Woodside, who was ironically the paymaster of the Baltimore and Ohio Railroad. Gilmor spent the night in Lieutenant Colonel Woolley's office and was treated to a "capital breakfast." On the morning of February 9, the provost marshal accompanied Major Young and Colonel Gilmor "to the Philadelphia Depot, [where he] saw them off safe and sound on their way to Fort Warren."[33] Thus, Harry Gilmor's role in the War Between the States came to a conclusion.

24. Postwar photograph of Gilmor. Before the onset of his illness after the war, the famous partisan began to gain weight. He could only fit into his old uniform by tying it with twine around his waist. (Courtesy of the Barry Pipino Collection)

25. Anthony Brady postwar photograph of Harry Gilmor. Gilmor's handsome features, that attracted so many Southern belles to his side during the war, remained prominent after the conflict. (Courtesy of the Barry Pipino Collection)

Head Quarters
1st Batn Cavalry M.N.G.
Oct 13th 1874

Special Orders }
No 10 }

I In accordance with General orders No 2 from Brigade Hd Qtrs, dated 12th Oct 74 this Battalion will assemble for parade, & review by the Governor & Commander in Chief, on Monday the 19th inst, at half past 2 o'clock P.M. on Broadway, right resting on Broadway Market facing East —

II It is expected by the Major Commanding that each Company will turn out its full strength, & with the men well mounted, arms and accoutrements in good condition.

Signed
Harry Gilmor
Major Comdg

Official
[illegible]
Adjutant

26. Special Order Number Ten, signed by Harry Gilmor, Commander of the First Battalion Cavalry, Maryland National Guard, to assemble for a parade in 1874. Gilmor's service with the First Battalion allowed the former irregular to return once again to the saddle. (Courtesy of the Craig Horn Collection)

27. Funeral Ribbon from Gilmor's funeral. Both former Rebels and Yankees attended Gilmor's funeral. (Courtesy of the Craig Horn Collection)

28. Mourning Ribbon. In response to Gilmor's death, Baltimore police stations lowered their flags to half-mast in respect for their former commissioner. (Courtesy of the Craig Horn Collection)

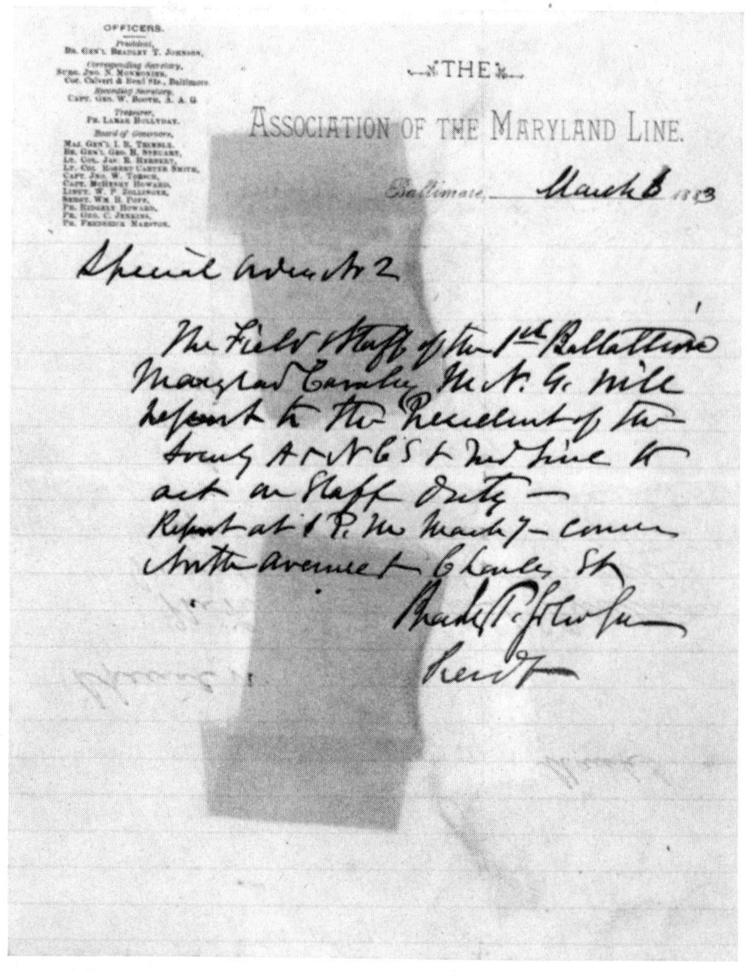

OFFICERS.

THE

ASSOCIATION OF THE MARYLAND LINE.

Baltimore, March 6 1883

Special Order No 2

The Field & Staff of the 1st Battalion Maryland Cavalry C.S.A. will report to the President of the Assoc. of Md Line to act on Staff Duty — Report at 1 P.M. March 7 — corner North avenue & Charles St

Bradley T. Johnson
Prest

29. Special Orders calling for Assembly for Gilmor's Funeral. Perhaps no group mourned more for Gilmor than his fellow Marylanders in the Association of the Maryland Line. (Courtesy of the Craig Horn Collection)

30. The Gilmor Monument on "Confederate Hill" in Loudon Park Cemetery, Baltimore, Maryland. Admirers of Gilmor still visit his monument in the Loudon Park Cemetery. (Courtesy of the Barry Pipino Collection)

9

"Maryland's Gallant Harry"

News of Gilmor's capture spread like wildfire among Union army officials and within elite circles in the North. After learning of Gilmor's capture, A.K. McClure, whose "Norland" residence was looted and fired by Confederate troops during the Chambersburg Raid of 1864, hurried a letter off to the War Department. McClure reminded the Secretary of War that Gilmor was one of "McCausland's officers in the sacking and burning of Chambersburg."[1] Less than three weeks later, the *New York Times* wrote a lengthy article describing how a "meritorious officer" (Lieutenant Colonel Whitaker) managed to bag the "ubiquitous Harry."[2]

Gilmor and his guards arrived at Boston during the early morning hours of February 10, 1865. The captive Marylander attracted the curious attention of not a few Bostonians, who wished to catch a glimpse of this elusive partisan as he was led off to confinement. Major Young, even though he granted Gilmor the opportunity to purchase some items in the Boston stores, still kept a close eye on his stealthy prisoner. However, once the Fort Warren prison gates closed behind Gilmor and his escorts, the colonel begrudgingly had to confess that "he had struck his last blow for the South."[3]

The Fort Warren authorities showed the partisan his cell. Gilmor gazed at his new home, a fifty foot long cell with a row of three tiered bunks situated along one of the walls. Each bunk contained a straw mattress, blanket, and kerosene lamp.

In the middle of the bland room sat a coal stove, which provided the cell's forty-six inhabitants with precious warmth during the frigid New England winter months. Every morning Gilmor and his comrades were given a pound of good wheat bread, and for dinner the Rebel captives ate "scant rations of meat." They were also served beans and hominy once a week and broth two times a week. They were never granted tea or coffee during their confinement. The stout Marylander, as to be expected, was dissatisfied with both the quality and quantity of his sustenance. He claimed that the food was underdone, which meant that he and his fellow prisoners had to reheat it on their cell's stove. Also, most of the time he went to bed hungry.[4]

As soon as Gilmor arrived at Fort Warren, he discovered several partisan irregulars, many of whom fought in his own Second Maryland. All were anxious to learn information concerning the welfare of the Southern armies, as well as the Cause for which they fought. Gilmor told the Confederates that General Lee had just been named the commander of all Confederate forces. Also, Gilmor and his fellow prisoners would soon discover that General Joseph E. Johnston was again placed at the helm of the battered Army of Tennessee. Indeed, General Johnston was charged with the unenviable task of reorganizing this small force and holding Union General Sherman's irresistible, destructive advance through the Deep South. As the Rebel prisoners contemplated these changes, their melancholy attitudes gave way to excitement; with the immortal Lee as the commander of all Southern forces, how could they lose? Some of the prisoners began to state that "We are all right now," convictions quickly confirmed by their comrades. Thus, as word trickled into the Boston prison that spring telling of Lee's surrender to Grant and Johnston's capitulation, Gilmor and his comrades were "totally unprepared." The Marylander and his haggard prison mates were praying for a miracle, but instead had to accept the angel of defeat, summoning the end of their Cause.[5]

The reaction of Gilmor and his prison comrades in the Federal stockade of Fort Warren to the changes in the command of the depleted Confederate armies was a microcosm of the overall Southern attitude during the last year of their fight for independence. Despite their personal losses, both in life and property, some Southerners attempted to maintain a positive mind set.[6] However, others were not so optimistic. They realized that a new reality and existence accompanied the Union hordes that were absorbing large tracts of their territory. Almost immediately after his arrival at Fort Warren, Gilmor received a letter from the Chief Quartermaster, Second Corps, that reflected a downcast sentiment.

> My dear fellow, I can sympathize with you fully, for I have a morbid consciousness that my day is past and gone. The grim hand of time is dealing harshly with your humble servant, and I can assure you that my appreciation of life is not now 'what *it used to was*' [sic]. If this d-d infernal war would only end there might be a few pleasures left for us in our own land, but there seems to be but a small chance of our soon enjoying the quiet of home again.

The writer concluded by stating that "the spirit of this army is first rate and if the enemy would only make our ground by fighting of it, we would like [lick] them to a certainty."[7] This was a conviction shared by most of the ragtag men in the Southern Army in 1865. However, the larger Union army was defeating "Johnny Reb" on the battlefield, and the "total war" being waged behind the Federal lines was destroying Dixie Land.

After Gilmor's capture and removal to far away

Massachusetts, his command steadily and quickly began to disintegrate. In the waning months of the war, Richard T. Gilmor, Harry's brother and First-Lieutenant of Company C, would command what was left of the Second Maryland. As with all partisan forces, Harry Gilmor's leadership and personality provided the cohesive substance that held his irregular force together. In every respect, Gilmor was the Second Maryland, and the Second Maryland was Gilmor. The same can be said of John Mosby, Jesse McNeill, and many other partisan units that harassed Union efforts during the four years of insurrection. Thus, with Gilmor gone, many of the men who formed the Second Maryland wandered into the camps of other less prominent, irregular chieftains. Undoubtedly, some who served in the Second could be found in those resolute bands that roamed the mountainous, rugged western Virginia terrain for weeks after the Confederacy officially laid down their arms.[8]

While some were drifting into obscure irregular commands in the waning months of the war, still other members of Gilmor's Second Maryland were being paroled by Union officials. C.M. Cox, a private in Company E, Second Maryland, was paroled at Appomattox Court House just one day after General Lee ordered his haggard but valiant soldiers of the Army of Northern Virginia to return to their towns and farms. On April 23, Captain John E. Sudler of Company E was paroled. More likely than not he would return to his residence in Kent County, Maryland. F.W. Burke, nineteen years of age, was a Second Lieutenant in Company D when he was paroled on May 8. Captain Henry D. Brewer of Company E, who probably preceded Sudler as captain of that company, took the oath of allegiance at Lynchburg, Virginia, later in the month. Brewer, a twenty-nine year old whose home was in Georgetown, District of Columbia, was an engineer. Physically exhausted after years in the saddle fighting "Billy Yank," and spiritually depleted after the Cause of Southern independence for which they fought came to a cessation, Gilmor's men returned to the postwar United States.[9]

On July 24, 1865, by action of President Andrew Johnson, Gilmor was paroled and released from captivity in the dark, New England confines of Fort Warren. The former partisan ranger "freely and voluntarily" took an oath to "support, protect, and defend the Constitution and Government of the United States against all enemies, whether domestic or foreign..."[10] Indeed, it was an inauspicious conclusion to his service to the Confederacy, a self-proclaimed nation now thoroughly crushed and relegated to the annals of history. Gilmor would leave Boston and enter a different social and political order in his native Maryland, a world at once uncertain and unwelcome to some former officers who wore the Confederate gray. Not unlike many of these Southern patriots, Gilmor hesitated before returning to his home state, where sentiment concerning "the late unpleasantness" was still strong and divisive.[11]

Gilmor made his way to Europe after his release. Like many of the previous Gilmor men who traveled in western Europe during more happier times, the defeated partisan found himself readily welcomed in the literary and military circles of the affluent. In one instance, he was privileged to stand with the Duke of Cambridge's staff during an elaborate military review. Sensing that the social climate around Baltimore was still too hostile for his return, he went south to Louisiana, where he made an attempt at planting. As the political officials of the United States attempted to administer and "reconstruct" the defeated South, Louisiana, like a magnet, attracted several former Confederate officers. Such a congregation of men who once openly fought against Union authority led to much alarm and consternation among United States administrators, particularly men like General Philip Sheridan, who administered Federal policies in the bayou state. At any rate, planting in the humid and arid summer months in Louisiana reminded Gilmor of his days of farming at Glen Ellen and his attempts at homesteading in Wisconsin and Nebraska.[12]

During this time period, Gilmor fell in love with Mentoria Nixon Strong. Miss Strong's father, Jasper Strong, boasted his own military record, serving as an officer in the United States Army from 1819 to 1823. Also, he later became an established planter in Florida after his service to the young republic. By all accounts, during the war many Southern belles wished to capture Gilmor's heart, just as many Yankee officers desired to capture the elusive partisan. Word that Gilmor's Second Maryland would shortly arrive at their quaint Shenandoah village would make not a few of the pretty women inhabitants swoon in anticipation of the arrival of their knight. Now, after the war, one would captivate him, only one would share his undivided affection. Gilmor shortly afterwards married the twenty-two year old Mentoria. Fate would prove to make this a union plagued by sickness and untimely death. In 1867, tiny Elizabeth, the couple's first child, died. It would be the first of many blows.[13]

Immediately after the war, Gilmor began to collaborate with Colonel Francis Henney Smith, of Virginia, to organize the former partisan's memoirs and war experiences into a form suitable for publication. While Gilmor was imprisoned at Fort McHenry after his first capture outside of Baltimore in September, 1862, he began to prepare a diary of his experiences and observations during the first two years of the conflict. Smith prepared the Marylander's writings for publication, and, after extensive discussions with Gilmor, also pieced together a draft of the ranger's role in the latter three years of the conflict. In 1866, their efforts came to a successful culmination as Harper and Brothers of New York published the writings under the title, *Four Years in the Saddle*, by Colonel Harry Gilmor.[14] Gilmor's *Four Years* would be called into question by many contemporary war veterans and by several modern Civil War scholars, but still it remains, due to its early publication in 1866, one of the freshest first hand recollections by any veteran of the American Civil War.[15]

Wanting to return to his beloved Baltimore, Gilmor penned a letter to General Ulysses S. Grant, beseeching personal protection while he was in Maryland. If Grant did reply, his letter or telegram is lost to history. Nonetheless, in 1867 Gilmor and his young wife did indeed return to Baltimore. Two years later the Gilmors produced another child, Alice.[16] During the late 1860s the emotional antipathy propagated by the war slowly began to lessen, allowing Gilmor greater access to the social limelight and business circles in Baltimore. The birth of their daughter indicated that the veteran was more willing to again firmly implant roots in Baltimore County.

The early 1870s appeared promising to the former Confederate, who was becoming ever more established in his native Baltimore. During this period his marriage with Mentoria produced a son, Harry Hunt. Still displaying a penchant for business, "in 1871 [Gilmor served as] a clerk and in 1873 the state weigher."[17] However, on May 6, 1873, the governor of Maryland granted Gilmor his first postwar commission. Maryland, as a border state, never seceeded from the Union, and was thus permitted to raise state militia and National Guard units. Its "unReconstructed" neighbors to the south were not afforded the same priviledge. Gilmor's commission read:

> ...that reposing especial trust and confidence in your fidelity, courage, good conduct, and attachment to the state of Maryland and the United States, you are appointed Major of the First Battalion Cavalry, Second Brigade, of the Maryland National Guard.

Gilmor's First Maryland was composed of both former Rebels and Yankees and the Baltimorean optimistically concluded that he was "very anxious to make a fine battalion of it."[18] Phrases such as "good conduct" and "attachment to Maryland and the United States" bespoke of the growing trust that authorities had placed in the former partisan ranger. Unlike many who fought under the Southern banner, Gilmor was slowly reconciling himself with the same authorities that he once rallied against.

However, not everybody welcomed Gilmor with open arms, and there still existed antipathy among Baltimoreans who remained loyal to the Union side during the war. A little over a month after receiving his commission, Gilmor wrote a letter to a Union official inquiring as to the whereabouts of a saber that fell into Federal hands during the war. Apparently, a group of "blue blood" Baltimorean belles purchased a magnificent, $125 saber from Messrs. Schuyler, Hartley and Graham, renowned arms dealers from New York City. They intended the expensive trophy to be sent to their native hero, but, much to their chagrin, the weapon fell into Federal hands before it arrived at its intended destination. The Union officer whom Gilmor queried did indeed know where the saber could be located and wished to return it to his former adversary, "but, [upon] conferring with Union people of Baltimore, [he] concluded not to; they thought any ostentatious display of the sword would help keep the wound open."[19]

Gilmor's failure to convince the Union officer to return the saber was indeed a setback. However, by the middle part of the decade another major appointment, coupled with a national economic panic and labor unrest in Baltimore, once again propelled Gilmor into the public eye. In 1874, the Marylander was appointed police commissioner of Baltimore, serving in this capacity with James R. Herbert, the city's other commissioner. It was Herbert who commanded the First Maryland Infantry Battalion during the Confederate assualt on Culp's Hill, July 2, 1863, in the Battle of Gettysburg.[20] Little did the veteran realize it at the time, but he was going to once again take to the saddle and lead one last charge into history.

Just as the nation's wounds were beginning to heal after four years of civil war, an economic depression rocked the country during the mid-1870s. After the sudden economic downswing in 1873, major railroad owners in the east, still panicked by the earlier shock, cut the wages of their laborers. In the summer of 1877 they again issued wage reductions, this time forcing workers to settle for a ten percent reduction. The wage decrease sparked unrest among hundreds of railroad workers along the Baltimore and Ohio Line. Finally, railroad employees in Martinsburg, West Virginia, walked off their jobs. Soon these disgruntled workers, themselves lacking direction and organization, were joined by sympathetic mobs, fuelling their destructive power and exacerbating a violent situation. The violence spread to Baltimore, Pittsburgh, and as far west as Chicago and San Francisco.[21]

As in other large cities during that turbulent month of July, 1877, Baltimore railroad workers, upon receiving notice of the wage reduction, left their jobs. The workers were joined by individuals who either sympathized with their cause or were recalcitrants out for mischief. Mobs began to fill Baltimore's streets, destroying railroad property and generally beating back any form of resistance on the part of local authority. Mayor Ferdinand C. Latrobe, after consulting with Commissioners Gilmor and Herbert, requested that Maryland Governor John Lee Carroll hold the state militia regiments in Baltimore. These regiments had been sent in earlier to quell the violence. With the prevailing panic and disorder in Baltimore, Governor Carroll acquiesced, and one of the regiments that was to have been sent to Cumberland was ordered to remain behind to restore order. The forces of authority in Baltimore appeared unable to check the ferocity of the mob, now numbering an estimated fifteen thousand. Some within the higher echelons of the Maryland government even feared that all of Baltimore may be set ablaze by the unruly masses. In desperation, Governor Carroll turned to President Rutherford B. Hayes to "protect [Maryland] against domestic violence" by sending national forces into the state. Soon, troops and artillery at Fort McHenry were ordered into Baltimore, along with marines from Washington and troops from as far away as New York.[22]

In one instance, Commissioner Gilmor along with two police marshals and a group of armed men were forced to hold back a mob that was threatening to fire the entire Baltimore and Ohio Railroad Depot situated on Camden Street. They were successful, and in the early morning hours of Saturday, July 21, the mob surrounding Camden Station slowly began to trickle away. The violence also began to subside, despite the large number of people still clogging Baltimore's streets. In an attempt to reduce the chance of further riots, Commissioners Gilmor and Herbert, along with Governor Carroll, signed the following proclamation, which was immediately circulated throughout the city:

> In the present excited state of the public mind it is important that no opportunity should be afforded for any disorder. All peaceable citizens are therefore expected to abstain from gathering in crowds, and to pursue their usual occupations, in order that the constituted authorities may maintain the peace of the city without difficulty or confusion.[23]

Gilmor, emotionally attached to his beloved Baltimore, was attempting to save the Maryland city from further damage.

The more unruly elements within the city did not heed

the police order and during the evening the crowd resumed rioting. Gilmor and a large police force were able to disperse a mob that again congregated along Camden Street before the throng could devastate the entire block. Gilmor, in a cavalry charge reminiscent of his attacks on Federals during the war, led his police force in an "advance upon the mob, [that proceeded only] under a heavy fire of pistol-shots and a storm of missiles." Once again the Marylander was firmly in the saddle, leading his men into harm's way. Gilmor ordered his men to charge the throng several times, until the disorganized mob eventually was dispersed in several different directions. Some would claim that "this cool and determined action of the police dispersed the crowd around the depot and suppressed the railroad riot in Baltimore." Gilmor's role in combating the riot would later be described as "contributing much towards protecting life and property during the labor-riots in 1877." Eventually, the reinforcements Governor Carroll requested earlier entered the beleaguered city, sealing the fate of the mob's anarchy.[24]

The strike ended on July 23, having lasted about a week, and order finally returned to Baltimore. The violent upheaval required responses from the Baltimore Police, Maryland National Guard units, two thousand United States soldiers, and some six hundred marines. Eventually, as a result of police action, militia units, public sympathy that began to turn against them, and their own inherent lack of organization, the railroad strikes throughout the nation failed. Slowly, throughout America, the railroaders returned to work.[25]

After the death of Robert Gilmor, the former partisan's father, in 1874, it was feared that his beautiful one-hundred acre estate, Glen Ellen, would fall into disrepair. Furthermore, with a wife and child, coupled with his constant forays into the prestigious, affluent Baltimore circles, the veteran could use an income in addition to that received by his police commission, which was terminated in 1878. In October of that year, Mentoria Strong Gilmor signed a contract with Robert E. Francis, agreeing to lease Glen Ellen to him for a one year period in return for $250. For his part, Francis was to insure that "the fences and water gaps [sic] [were] to be kept in a good and substantial order and the land cultivated and manure spread to the best advantage." In addition, fifty dollars would be set aside so that Francis could lay a fence on the estate according to specifications set by Mentoria. In return, Francis would receive any profits arising from his farming efforts at Glen Ellen, as well as use of "two buildings known as the 'White Cottage' and 'the Quarter.'" The lease would start in March 1879 and run for a one year period.[26]

In 1875, the Gilmor union bore another child, this time Elsie Graham. Mentoria became pregnant again, and by late 1879 the Gilmors were anxiously awaiting the birth of yet another addition to the Gilmor household. In December, their wait was over, Mentoria gave birth to twin males. One child was named Arthur, while the other, Jasper, took his name from Mentoria's prestigious father, Jasper Strong. Mentoria died following the birth of the twins; she was only thirty-four years of age. Sadly, the twins passed into eternity a short time later.[27] The deaths of his beloved Mentoria and their infant sons would be a tremendous blow to Gilmor, and it was a sad precursor to his own physical deterioration.

In 1880 the Gilmor family was rocked with another death. This time, Gilmor's mother, Ellen Ward, passed away. Sometime in the decades before the war, her husband, Robert, chose to name his estate after her. She survived her husband by six years.[28]

During the early 1880s, Gilmor continued his close personal association with his cousin, Hoffman. The two former Confederates, both of whom were nabbed together in Moorefield, West Virginia, by General Sheridan's scouts, confided in each other concerning social and business affairs. It was sometime during this period that Gilmor went into insurance, serving as an agent and broker, with an office situated in the Maryland Building, on the corner of P.O. Ave. and Second Street. Also, on July 19, 1881, Gilmor, Milo W. Locke, and Walter S. Wilkinson, all of Baltimore, agreed to form a partnership under the title Gilmor and Locke. The firm was to handle the signing of contracts for the pavement of streets and other road surfaces in Baltimore and the surrounding area. Furthermore, Gilmor and Locke would be responsible "for the execution of such contract[s] by the purchase of material, employment of labor," and other related matters. Quickly, advertisements appeared in the Baltimore newspapers, announcing that Gilmor and Locke were "sole licensees of the Maryland Pavement Company of Baltimore City for laying 'compressed asphalt blocks.'" The advertisement further boasted that their "pavement is smooth and practically noiseless, durable and economical, and for stables, cellars ... is unequaled, being rat-proof, cleanly, and sanitary." Gilmor and Locke's office was conveniently located in the same building as the veteran's insurance office.[29]

In early 1881, the partisan, now forty-three, began to complain about acute pain emanating beneath his left eye. Gilmor never did fully recover from the wounds he received in the left shoulder and jaw during the fighting around Bunker Hill, Virginia, in September 1864. That wound put the Marylander out of action for five months, and even after the war caused discomfort. Soon the pain became very severe, and Gilmor sought medical attention from a Dr. G. Halsted Boyland, a Frenchman who was married to the former partisan ranger's sister, Ellen. Boyland diagnosed Gilmor as having neuralgia, a painful condition in which peripheral nerves become damaged or irritated. Perhaps the injury to his jaw inflicted near Bunker Hill sparked the irritation to his facial nerves. Except for a slight, temporary improvement in his condition, Gilmor's health would gradually deteriorate.[30]

Gilmor's neuralgia might have been caused by facial

cancer that in turn originated as a result of a freak accident during a minor dental operation. Approximately three years prior to his death, a doctor accidentally fractured Gilmor's jaw while attempting to extract a tooth; obviously, his jaw was still in a weakened state due to the old war injury.[31] The fracture was said to spark facial cancer, which would spread. Indeed, facial cancer would be listed by many newspapers as the ultimate cause of the Confederate's death. At any rate, the old war wound that he received in Virginia in the closing stages of the Southern defense of the Shenandoah would figure prominently in his untimely death.[32]

At this point Gilmor's condition did not prevent him from continuing his active membership in The Society of the Army and Navy of the State of Maryland. Like thousands of other veterans representing both sides of the Civil War, Gilmor joined a postwar society. Organizations such as these hosted annual meetings where members listened to flamboyant speakers, discussed war stories, rekindled old friendships, and where perhaps many "unreconstructed Rebels" still openly discussed fomenting another rebellion. At Winchester in 1879, Gilmor and a host of other Confederate veterans were placed in charge of "the military and civic procession" during the unveiling of a monument to "The Unknown and Unrecorded Dead." Then, on January 19, 1882, Gilmor was elected a Vice-President of The Society of the Army and Navy of the State of Maryland at their annual meeting in Baltimore.[33] Gilmor's presence in the organization was obviously welcome by not only those members who served under his command during the war, but by Maryland veterans throughout the state. Gilmor, during the war actually personified that dogged spirit and tenacious fighting style that was embodied by their Cause. When their fellow Marylander fell ill, it was these veterans who rallied around their gallant, but ailing, commander.

In July, 1882, while Gilmor was still battling his failing health, he received a letter penned from General Henry A.

Barnum, Chairman of the Head-Quarters Memorial Committee, Grand Army of the Republic, New York City. The Union officer wished to draw Gilmor's attention to a section of his *Four Years in the Saddle* in which the Marylander claimed to have personally seized the colors of the 149th New York on the first day of fighting at Gettysburg. General Barnum, proud commander of the 149th New York Regiment of Volunteers, stated that his regiment never lost a flag, but instead, captured five regimental colors belonging to the South. The New Yorker further explained to Gilmor that veterans of his regiment were going to deposit their Gettysburg battleflag in the County Clerks building in Syracuse, New York. Barnum also reminded his former adversary of a recent discussion that the two had, in which he told the Marylander that the 149th New York did not arrive at Gettysburg until evening on the first day. The Union General concluded by requesting that Gilmor write a formal correction that would "be attached to its [the flag's] torn and riddled fold," as it lay in public viewing.[34] It is not known if Gilmor responded to Barnum's letter, which was written in a manner that did not portend malaise, but was explanatory and succinct. At any rate, this would not be the last time that veterans, general readers, as well as later Civil War scholars would take issue with Gilmor's *Four Years*.

By early autumn of 1882, Gilmor's facial pain increased, and in a few months he would suffer from paralysis; it was more than obvious to friends, family members, and business associates that the veteran's life was slowly slipping away. Around this time period, Gilmor, in a sealed letter, granted his old war comrade and loyal cousin, Hoffman, power of attorney. However, business and legal interests were not the center of Gilmor's concerns. His children, the only surviving elements of his marriage to Mentoria, was a deep concern to the Marylander, especially their future welfare after his death. On January 23, 1883, Gilmor dictated a letter that was sent off to Hoffman in which he expressed a deep interest in his children's education. A friend of the Gilmor family, a Miss Seal, earlier stated that the Gilmor children should go south and reside with her. Gilmor, in this letter to Hoffman, strongly objected on the grounds that he felt that there were no suitable schools near her and that furthermore, Alice, the oldest child, would have to travel far in order to visit her siblings. The former partisan ranger stated that it was "[his] desire that they should finish their education at a Ms. Carey's... provided the means are at hand to [further] instruction." The concerned father also recommended the Patapsco Institute for "little Harry," who was quickly approaching school age. The dying Gilmor concluded by repeating his conviction that "[he] is totally opposed to their going South under any circumstance."[35]

Gilmor's friends in The Society of the Army and Navy of the State of Maryland were quick to remember their ailing comrade. At a meeting on February 2, 1883, a Mr. Lamar Hollyday offered a tribute to the Maryland veteran:

> Like Marion and Sumpter as a partizan [sic] leader he illustrated the force and value of audacity and enterprise, and like Light Horse Harry Lee, the favorite subordinate of Washington, Harry Gilmor won the love, respect, and unbounded confidence of Stonewall Jackson.[36]

Word quickly made its way to Gilmor concerning the February 2 meeting, especially of the kind words said in his favor. In a return letter to a friend who told the dying Gilmor about the sentimental meeting, the former partisan wrote that "it [the letter] gave me more pleasure than I can express..." Gilmor also stated that he often thought of his old comrades, and though he was briefly optimistic, he honestly replied that "I can only trust now in God's infinite mercy, and when the summons comes I am prepared to go."[37]

Later that month, on February 22, The Society of the Army and Navy of the State of Maryland had their annual reunion in Baltimore at the Carrollton Hotel. There, during the proceedings, General Bradley T. Johnson, President of the Association of the Maryland Line, announced to the audience that their Maryland comrade was ill and therefore could not attend. Then, with his glass raised, the proud Marylander proposed a toast to the former ranger.[38] A little less than two decades earlier the two prominent Marylanders played a critical role in General Jubal Early's Washington Raid; Gilmor now lay dying in the same city that, if afforded more men, he may have captured during "Old Jube's" Washington Raid. Shortly after Johnson was finished with his kind toast to Gilmor, a poem by Miss Zitella Cocke was read to the audience. All listened in silence as the speaker read each line of Cocke's tribute to their fellow Marylander, which was entitled "Maryland's Gallant Harry."

Proudly disdaining the foeman's might,
Nobly resolving to help the right,
Boldly encount ' ring the thickest fight,
Rode Maryland's gallant Harry.
Rode on - no matter if shell and shot
Fell like the hailstones - no matter what
Voice called him back, his true word was not
To waver - never to tarry!
O'er mountain and moor, through brake and fen,
Through bayonets where honor led, when
One sword flashed to the glitter of ten,
Went Maryland's gallant Harry.
Down on the enemy's ranks he bore,
Sabres behind him, sabres before,
Into the fierce artillery's roar,

Brave Pelham's corse to carry.
When Alabama shall her jewels claim
To set them in bright, undying fame,
Tenderly her youthful hero's name
With Gilmor shall she marry
In wedded lustre, for ne'er again
Shall braver than Pelham fall on plain -
Nor bolder ride than bold Ashby's man
Proud Maryland's gallant Harry![39]

The poet, being a native from Alabama, centered her piece around Gilmor's role in removing Major John Pelham's body from the field of battle at Kelly's Ford in March 1863. Despite Gilmor's efforts, the young artillerist later would succumb to death.

In addition to the toasts, poems, and other warm speeches given in Gilmor's honor at veteran societies, the ailing Marylander also received a number of letters expressing sympathy with his failing physical condition. On February 22, a Winfield Deters penned a short letter to Gilmor, stating his condolences and warm wishes for a recovery, but realistically concluding, "or, if you are summoned 'over the river to rest under the shade of the trees,'" he ardently wishes that the veteran will join the glorious others who have preceded him. Five days later President Bradley T. Johnson of the Maryland Line wrote to his former subordinate, commending Gilmor for his bravery during his illness and sending his sympathy on behalf of the Maryland Line. Johnson concluded by stating "we all send our love [and] our warmest sympathy and best wishes for you and your dear children."[40]

During the same month a New Yorker by the name of H. R. Duval wrote Hoffman Gilmor a letter while the latter was at the Maryland Club. As Hoffman removed the folded letter from the carefully sealed, stainless white envelope, he noticed a check for one hundred dollars. Hoffman's eyes quickly scanned the letter and noted that the benevolent Duval wrote the check, a sum that the wealthy Northerner labeled "a moderate amount," for the care of his sick cousin. Duval, irrefutably aware of Harry Gilmor's headstrong pride, admonished Hoffman not to tell the veteran of the gift. Duval also wrote that he was going to meet with officials of the Northern Central Railroad and attempt to encourage them to officially recognize Gilmor for his role in helping to suppress the Great Baltimore Railroad Strike of 1877. This acknowledgment, heretofore not forthcoming, at this moment could have served to lift Gilmor's spirits. However, as with the one-hundred dollar check, the New Yorker told Hoffman not to tell Gilmor of his discussions with the Northern Central, for fear the plan would "fall through." Duval finished by stating that he received word from Dr. Boyland that the Marylander's condition is improving. Little did Duval or Hoffman know, but Gilmor would be dead within two weeks.[41]

Sometime in late February, Generals Jubal Early and Bradley T. Johnson visited the ailing Gilmor, who was then residing at 35 Denmead Street. By this time Gilmor was paralyzed and almost totally blind. The cancer that originated in his fractured jaw now began to dissolve Gilmor's optic nerves. The visit served well for all their spirits. Early had aged considerably. "Old Jubilee," as he was affectionately called by his men, sported a long, flowing white beard that caressed Gilmor's shoulder as the men in the room spoke while standing around their sick comrade's bed.[42] Early had that pugnacious spirit and a penchant for fowl language, tobacco chewing, and coarseness of manners that made him the marked antithesis of the Robert E. Lee model of the Southern general and the idealistic mold of the Southern gentleman. Gilmor, as a partisan ranger, in this very mode of warfare, violated the Victorian "gentlemen qualities" of warfare. Their shared abrasive demeanor, inconsequential attitude toward contemporary folkways, and moreover, their headstrong spirit that inwardly propelled both of them, served as forces of mutual attraction, despite Early's unflattering view of cavalry. Undoubtedly the three reminisced about their raid into Maryland and the firing of Chambersburg in 1864. Johnson and Early visited Gilmor for less than an hour, for the Marylander, who used to spend most of the day on horseback rambling through the Shenandoah countryside, could muster just enough energy to stay awake long enough to carry on a conversation.

Shortly after eight o'clock on the evening of March 4, death mercifully sapped the last remaining foothold of life from Gilmor's body.[43] News of the partisan's demise quickly spread throughout Baltimore. Baltimore police stations lowered their flags at half-mast in respect to their former police commissioner, who just one decade prior helped to quelch the riots that caused such alarm and destruction in their beloved city. In the meantime, the Gilmor family, as well as The Society of the Army and Navy of the State of Maryland and Association of the Maryland Line, began to prepare for the former Confederate's funeral. Two days after his cousin passed into eternity, Hoffman received a letter from the Headquarters of the Grand Army of the Republic, announcing that they too wished to attend Gilmor's funeral.[44] Death could not diminish the mutual respect that the former enemies had for one another, neither on the field of battle during the "late unpleasantness" nor in the postwar years.

The funeral took place at Gilmor's church, the North Avenue Presbyterian Church, and he was buried next to his wife, Mentoria, in Loudon Park. A distinguished marker highlights their place of rest. In addition to family members, fellow comrades-in-arms, and former Yankee antagonists who attended the funeral services, countless men from other prominent organizations undoubtedly made their appearance in order to pay their last regards to a fellow Baltimorean. Gilmor was a member of "the Mizpah Association, the Knights of Pythias, the Masonic fraternity in Virginia, the Corn and Flour Exchange and the St. Andrew's Society."[45]

After his death, a fund, supported by private donations, was established in order to support Gilmor's children. In the summer of 1883, the late Marylander's only surviving son, Harry Hunt, was accepted into the McDonogh School; even in the dark months of illness before his death, Gilmor expressed concern about his children's welfare, particularly education. In a move to perhaps raise money for Gilmor's orphans as well as other expenses, Hoffman suggested to his cousin's publisher, Harper and Brothers, to publish a new edition of *Four Years in the Saddle.* However, they replied that they had 478 copies of Gilmor's work in stock, and that they would sell these copies at a low price. The letter, frank but not an impolite rejection, stated that at the time of his death, the former partisan ranger was $175.00 in debt to the publishing house, and concluded that they wished to sell the remaining copies of *Four Years* and thus end the contract. However, in a bizarre change of heart, Harper and Brothers in a letter to Hoffman two weeks later stated that they would furnish the remaining copies of *Four Years* at prices set at .22 cents for the unbound copies and .36 cents for each bound copy. Then, the publisher wrote that they would go ahead and print additional copies.[46]

A short time after Gilmor's death, a family member sent George W. Earhart, of the Northwestern Police Station, the former partisan's spurs. Earhart, a friend of the late Gilmor, was to receive a high quality pair of spurs, made of "Mexican workmanship, of heavy polished brass, with large steel rowels." More importantly, those spurs were worn by Gilmor as he and his Second Maryland roamed the dusty trails of the Shenandoah Valley.[47]

Harry Hunt, Gilmor's only surviving son, Engineer and Clubman from Baltimore, committed suicide at the Fort Pitt Hotel in Pittsburgh, Pennsylvania, on August 16, 1912. He was only forty-three years of age. His body was laid to rest beside his father's in Loudon Park.[48] Alice Gilmor, Harry's oldest surviving offspring, inhereted his belongings, but would later give the lion's share of her inheritance away, due to the high cost of storage. Alice, according to one source, was a maverick in the Gilmor family. She opposed having a monument dedicated to her father and would spend many an hour in the circles of Northerners.[49] Alice Brainard Gilmor died in Canada on July 27, 1943. Like her siblings, she would not marry.[50]

A poetic epitaph entitled "Our Gallant Harry" is boldly engraved upon the proud monument that marks Gilmor's final resting place in Loudon Park Cemetery. The first three lines read that the Baltimorean was "Dauntless in Battle; Splendid in Success; Constant in Defeat."[51] Indeed, these three lines serve to outline Gilmor's role in the War Between the States.

Gilmor was both dauntless and splendid in success. The Northern press labeled the Marylander "notorious," and one of his major nemeses in the Shenandoah Valley, General Sheridan, termed the partisan "a shrewd, unscrupulous scoundrel." References such as these highlight the fear and frustration that the Second Maryland Cavalry Battalion struck into the hearts of its Union adversaries. With reckless abandon, Gilmor's "Band" would ride hard upon a Federal encampment or supply train, spark chaos, confusion, and death, then, just as quickly disappear into the lush countryside. In essence, a dauntless spirit was a necessity for a partisan command. Without courage and a certain amount of recklessness a guerrilla unit would be of no value.

Gilmor was also "Constant in Defeat." Even though the Union's industrial and numerical superiority was taking a severe toll upon the South during the last two years of the war, Gilmor at no time admitted to defeat prior to his capture. However, he does note the impact of attrition upon Southern units and the devastating results of total war upon the

Shenandoah Valley, the Confederacy's breadbasket. Gilmor fought on, despite the growing odds against him. His resilience and tenacity was mirrored by others who dawned torn and bloody ragtag Southern uniforms.

From another perspective, Gilmor can also be evaluated in some instances as too hardheaded and reckless, perhaps even clumsy. In October of 1863 he left his troopers under the command of subordinates while he visited lady friends on a wealthy estate. This move revealed a shocking lack of forethought, and it ultimately resulted in large numbers of his command being captured by the Yankees. Also, a seeming lack of discipline over the Second Maryland led to the embarrassing Baltimore and Ohio Train Robbery and the Hyman Affair of 1864. Beneath his handsome features was a robust spirit of independence which pleaded for the appropriate moment to break lose; in such a case the first characteristics jettisoned were coolness and rationality. Before the war, Gilmor turned from the riches of Glen Ellen in order to attempt homesteading on the frontier. Also, his adventurous spirit coupled with events in Baltimore in April of 1861 to draw him like a magnet to Virginia. Adventurous, aggressive, and reckless were the allies and the enemies of Gilmor's persona.

Beyond his personality and fighting spirit, Gilmor's career can shed enormous light onto the impact that irregulars had upon Northern strategy and tactics. Furthermore, a study of Gilmor's *Four Years* provides a window through which the student of military history can better comprehend total war. Gilmor's career transverses both phases of the struggle. From 1861 to 1863 Gilmor fought in the "gentleman's war," and in 1864, as leader of a partisan unit, was a combatant in the all new, frightful "total war." Gilmor would leave a much greater mark upon history during the second phase of the conflict. Indeed, Gilmor's anecdotes and personality are key, special ingredients in the making of novels; however, his story was all so very real, and as such, affords the student of history a glimpse into the past.

Notes

Preface

[1]See Daniel C. Toomey's introduction to *Four Years in the Saddle* (the reprinted version by Butternut and Blue), page xix; citing James I. Robertson, Jr., "The War in Words," *Civil War Times Illustrated* XVI, No. 2 (May 1977): 48, and McHenry Howard, *Recollections of a Maryland Confederate Soldier and Staff Officer under Johnson, Jackson and Lee* (Dayton, Ohio: Morningside edition, 1975), foreword 1-2,19.

Chapter 1

[1] *The National Cyclopaedia of American Biography*, vol. 11, (New York: James T. White and Company, 1909), 401.

[2] Ibid., 401; Jerome R. Garitee, *The Republic's Private Navy* (Middletown, Connecticut: Wesleyan University Press, 1977), 15.

[3] *The National Cyclopaedia*, vol. 23, 401-2; Robert I. Vexler, ed. and comp., *Baltimore: A Chronological and Documentary History* (Dobbs Ferry, New York: Oceana Publications, Inc., 1975), 23; Francis F. Beirne, *The Amiable Baltimoreans*, (Hatboro, Pennsylvania: Tradition Press, 1968), 378; Thomas J. Scharf, *History of Maryland*, vol. 2, (n.p., 1879; reprint, Hatboro, Pennsylvania: Tradition Press, 1967), 575-79.

[4] Scharf, *History of Maryland*, vol. 2, 615-18; Matthew Page Andrews, *History of Maryland*: Province and State (Hatboro, Pennsylvania: Tradition Press, 1965), 420; Garitee, *Republic's Navy*, 55.

[5] *The National Cyclopaedia*, vol. 11, 401-2; Beirne, *Amiable Baltimoreans*, 378.

[6] John B. Boles, *Maryland Heritage. Five Baltimore Institutions Celebrate the American Bicentennial* (Baltimore: n.p., 1976), 93.

[7] "Gilmor Family Tree," (photocopy) Gilmor Family Papers, Baltimore County Historical Society (hereafter denoted as BCHS), The original Gilmor Family Tree is in the Maryland Historical Society holdings; History of Long Green, Maryland (manuscript), by Henrietta Schmidt Astin, 1948, (photocopy of page two) taken from the files of the BCHS; *The National Cyclopaedia*, vol. 11, 402.

[8] Allen Johnson and Dumas Malone, eds., *Dictionary of American Biography*, vol. 7, (New York: Charles Scribner's Sons, 1931), 309; *The National Cyclopaedia*, vol. 23, 372; "Col. Gilmor Dying. His Death

Momentarily Expected — A Sketch of His Career," *Baltimore Sun*, 1 March 1883, taken from Gilmor Family Papers, BCHS; Richard L. Armstrong, *7th Virginia Cavalry* (Lynchburg: H.E. Howard, Inc., 1992), 153.

[9] "Col. Gilmor Dying. His Death Momentarily Expected — A Sketch of His Career," *Baltimore Sun*, 1 March 1883, taken from Gilmor Family Papers, BCHS; Johnson, ed., *American Biography*, vol. 7, 309.

[10] Harry Wright Newman, *Maryland and the Confederacy* (Annapolis: By the author, 1976), 31; Emory M. Thomas, *The Confederate Nation: 1861-1865* (New York: Harper and Row, Publishers, 1979), 89; Gen. Clement A. Evans, ed., *Confederate Military History* (Secaucus, New Jersey: The Blue and Grey Press, n.d.), vol. 2, Maryland and West Virginia, 26. This volume is composed of two parts. One section details West Virginia, while the other, written by Brig.-Gen. Bradley T. Johnson, outlines Maryland's contribution to the Confederacy. All subsequent references will be to the section on Maryland (hereafter cited Johnson, *Maryland*, vol. 2, designated page numbers.) Chris Bishop, Ian Drury, and Tony Gibbons, *1400 Days: The Civil War Day by Day* (New York: Gallery Books, 1990), 25; Sherry H. Olson, *Baltimore: The Building of An American City* (Baltimore: John Hopkins University Press, 1980), 144.

[11] John S. Bowman, ed., *The Civil War Almanac* (New York: World Almanac Publicatins, 1983), 52; U.S. War Department, *The War of the Rebellion: A Compilation of the Official Records of the Union and Confederate Armies*, 128 Vols. (Washington: Government Printing Office, 1880-1901), Series 1, Vol. 2, 7 (hereafter cited as *War of the Rebellion*); Patricia L. Faust, ed., *Historical Times Illustrated Encyclopedia of the Civil War* (New York: Harper and Row, Publishers, 1986), 37; Mark Mayo Boatner III, *The Civil War Dictionary* (New York: David McKay Company, Inc., 1959; reprint, 1988), 42 (page references are to reprint edition).

[12] Edward Ayrault Robinson, "Some Recollections of April 19, 1861," *Maryland Historical Magazine* 27 (December 1932): 275-76; Erick F. Davis, "The Baltimore County Horse Guard," *History Trails* 10 (Winter 1975-76): 5. According to Robinson, Gilmor was "orderly sergeant of Company A, Fifth Regular Maryland Guard" (Recollections, 275). However, as Davis highlights in "Horse Guard," in late January Gilmor was elected corporal of a company labeled the Baltimore County Horse Guard. Also, "on February 23, 1861, the company ...was attached to the First Regiment of Cavalry, Maryland Militia" (Horse Guard, 5).

[13] Robinson, "Recollections," 275-76.

[14] Johnson, *Maryland*, vol. 2, 11,22-23; Newman, *Maryland*, 36; Davis, "Horse Guard," 5.

[15] *The National Cyclopaedia*, vol. 23, 372; Johnson, ed., *American Biography*, vol. 7, 309; Davis, "Horse Guard," 5.

[16] Davis, "Horse Guard," 5-6.

[17] Newman, *Maryland*, 36; Johnson, *Maryland*, vol. 2, 25; Thomas J.

Scharf, *History of Baltimore City and County*, part 1, (Philadelphia: Louis H. Everts, 1881; reprint, Baltimore: Regional Publishing Company, 1971), 130 (page references are to reprint edition); Scharf, *Baltimore City*, part 2, 790; Davis, "Horse Guard," 6-7.

[18] Bowman, *Civil War Almanac*, 53.

[19] Robinson, "Recollections," 277,279.

[20] Scharf, *Baltimore City*, part 1, 131; One day prior to Butler's occupation of Federal Hill, "the order prohibiting the display of flags was rescinded," Ibid, 131; Davis, "Horse Guard," 7.

[21] Scharf, *Baltimore City*, part 1, 132-33; Johnson, ed., *American Biography*, vol. 7, 309; *The National Cyclopaedia*, vol. 23, 373; *The National Cyclopaedia*, vol. 11, 401.

[22] Harry Gilmor, *Four Years in the Saddle* (New York: Harper and Brothers, Publishers, 1866; reprint, Baltimore: Butternut and Blue, n.d.), 13.

[23] Johnson, ed., *American Biography*, vol. 7, 309; Gilmor, *Four Years*, 13. Gilmor was joined by five brothers in Virginia, two of which, Arthur and Howard, died in Confederate service during the war. Please see Virgil Carrington Jones, *Gray Ghosts and Rebel Raiders* (New York: Holt, Rinehart and Winston, 1956), 46,377.

[24] Mrs. D. Giraud Wright, "Maryland and the South," *Southern Historical Society Papers* 31 (1903): 212.

Chapter 2

[1] Gilmor, *Four Years*, 13; Mary Ann Jackson, *Memoirs of Stonewall Jackson* (Dayton, Ohio: Morningside Bookshop, 1976), 216; Description of Ashby is taken from the latter source.

[2] Stewart Sifakis, *Who Was Who in the Confederacy,* vol. 2, (New York/ Oxford: Facts on File, 1988), 9, 106-7; Lee Wallace, Jr., *A Guide to Virginia Military Organizations, 1861-1865*, 2d. ed., (n.p., H.E. Howard Inc., 1986), ?; Daniel D. Hartzler, *Arms Makers of Maryland* (York, Pennsylvania: George Shumway Publishers, 1977), 105; *War of the Rebellion*, Series 1, Vol. 5, Part 1, 919.

[3] Gilmor, *Four Years*, 14-15.

[4] Ibid., 18; Armstrong, *7th Virginia Cavalry*, 153; "Obituary - Col. Harry Gilmor," *New York Times*, 5 March 1883, 5; R. D. Steuart, "Rare Confederate Relics," *Confederate Veteran Magazine*, 16 November 1909, 562.

[5] Gilmor, *Four Years*, 15,17; Armstrong, *7th Virginia Cavalry*, 152,236; Davis, "Horse Guard," 5; G.B. Philpot, "A Maryland Boy in the Confederate Army," *Confederate Veteran Magazine*, 24 July 1916, 312.

[6] Gilmor, *Four Years*, 18-21; *War of the Rebellion*, Series 1, Volume 5, 247-48; For a description of Harper's Ferry and the surrounding area, see

Shelby Foote, *The Civil War: Fort Sumter to Perryville*, vol. 1, (New York: Vintage Books, 1986), 667.

[7] Gilmor, *Four Years*, 22; *War of the Rebellion*, Series 1, Vol. 5, 248.

[8] Gilmor, *Four Years*, 22-24; *War of the Rebellion*, Series 1, Vol. 5, 248; Please note that, according to Turner Ashby's report concerning the skirmish at Bolivar Heights, he stated that "the detachment from the large gun [after the axle-tree snapped] was transferred to the rifled piece." However, Gilmor, in his memoirs, claims that he and five volunteers "worked the rifled gun," with himself in command of its operations.

[9] *War of the Rebellion*, Series 1, Vol. 5, 247.

[10] Ibid., Series 1, Vol. 5, 242,898-99.

[11] Gilmor, *Four Years*, 18,24; *War of the Rebellion*, Series 1, Vol. 5, 858-59; *War of the Rebellion*, Series 1, Vol. 5, 390.

[12] Gilmor, *Four Years*, 25; Lieutenant Colonel Ashby became Colonel of the Seventh Virginia in late October 1861, please see Sifakis, *Who Was Who Confederacy*, vol. 2, 9; *War of the Rebellion*, Series 1, Vol. 5, 390.

[13] Gilmor, *Four Years*, 25-26; For further discussion concerning the importance that Civil War soldiers placed upon the display of courage, please see Gerald L. Lindermann's *Embattled Courage* (New York: The Free Press, 1987).

[14] George F. R. Henderson, *Stonewall Jackson and the American Civil War* (Gloucester, Massachusetts: Peter Smith, 1968), 141-42; His original plan called for a march into western Virginia, where his force would be augmented by the recruitment of approximately twenty-thousand mountain men. This force would march upon Pittsburgh, destroy the arsenal located there, then march eastward, where they would join a much larger Confederate force at Harrisburg. This force would then assualt Philadelphia. The plan, due to its extremely ambitious nature, was rejected by the Confederate Congress. Please see Henderson, *Stonewall Jackson*, 141 and Burke Davis, *They Called Him Stonewall* (New York and Chicago: Holt, Rinehart and Winston, Inc., 1954), 161.

[15] Henderson, *Stonewall Jackson*, 142,144.

[16] *War of the Rebellion*, Series 1, Vol. 2, 954; Millard K. Bushong, *General Turner Ashby and Stonewall's Valley Campaign* (Waynesboro, Virginia: The McClung Companies, 1992), 36; Gilmor, *Four Years*, 26.

[17] Davis, *Stonewall*, 160; Gilmor, *Four Years*, 26; *War of the Rebellion*, Series 1, Vol. 5, 390; Armstrong, *7th Virginia Cavalry*, 18.

[18] *War of the Rebellion*, Series 1, Vol. 5, 390; John Esten Cooke, *Stonewall Jackson and the Old Stonewall Brigade*, editor Richard Barksdale Harwell (Charlottesville: University of Virginia Press, 1954), 17; Henry Kyd Douglas, *I Rode With Stonewall* (n.p.: The University of North Carolina Press, 1940; reprint, n.p.: Fawcett Publications, Inc., 1961), 30-32; Davis, *Stonewall*, 160-61.

[19] Gilmor, *Four Years*, 26-27; *War of the Rebellion*, Series 1, Vol. 5,

391; Even though the sequence of events in Gilmor's memoirs and Jackson's official accounts may not coincide perfectly, the evidence presented in both sources concerning the fighting around Bath, such as the mention of Lt. Lontz, offers irrefutable proof that Gilmor was indeed present.

[20] Armstrong, *7th Virginia Cavalry*, 18; Gilmor, *Four Years*, 27; *War of the Rebellion*, Series 1, Vol. 5, 392.

[21] Gilmor, *Four Years*, 27-28.

[22] Ibid., 28; Philpot, "Maryland Boy," 313.

[23] Philpot, "Maryland Boy," 313.

[24] Gilmor, *Four Years*, 28.

[25] Ibid., 28; *War of the Rebellion*, Series 1, Vol. 5, 392.

[26] *War of the Rebellion*, Series 1, Vol. 5, 393.

[27] Ibid., 393-94; Jackson, *Stonewall Memoirs*, 223,227-29.

[28] William W. Goldsborough, *The Maryland Line in the Confederate Army*, 2d. ed., (New York and London: Kennikat Press, 1972), 242.

Chapter 3

[1] James I. Robertson, Jr., "Stonewall Jackson: Molding the Man and Making A General," *Blue and Gray Magazine*, 9 June 1992, 22-24.

[2] Albert Castel, "The Guerrilla War: 1861-1865," *Civil War Times Illustrated Special Issue* (October 1974): 7; *War of the Rebellion*, Series 1, Vol. 12, Part 3, 196.

[3] *War of the Rebellion*, Series 1, Vol. 12·Part 1, 496.

[4] Ibid., Series 1, Vol. 12, Part 3, 169.

[5] Gilmor, *Four Years*, 30,32; Twelfth Virginia Cavalry, Compiled Service Records of Confederate Soldiers, Record Group 109, M324, Roll 117, National Archives, Washington, D.C. (hereafter cited as Twelfth Virginia Cavalry Records, with all references to Roll 117); Daniel D. Hartzler, *Marylanders in the Confederacy* (Westminster, Maryland: Family Line Publications, 1986; repr. 1990), 36; Armstrong, *7th Virginia Cavalry*, 93; Goldsborough, *Maryland Line*, 242. According to Hartzler, in *Marylanders*, Gilmor's company "was sent to the 12th Virginia Cavalry where they became Company F on April 10, 1862," instead of the June date cited in the narrative (page 36). As a captain in the Seventh Virginia Cavalry, Gilmor was paid $163.33 for services rendered from March 26 to May 1, 1862. Please see Seventh Virginia Ashby's Cavalry, Compiled Service Records of Confederate Soldiers, Record Group 109, M324, Roll 75, National Archives, Washington, D.C. (hereafter cited as Seventh Virginia Records, with all references to Roll 75).

[6] Gilmor, *Four Years*, 32.

[7] Ibid., 32-33.

[8] Shawn C. Harris, "Stonewall in the Valley," *America's Civil War*, 5

January 1993, 36-37; Bowman, *Civil War Almanac*, 90-91; Bishop and Drury, *1400 Days*, 72-74; Robertson, Jr., "Stonewall," 22-24; *War of the Rebellion*, Series 1, Vol. 12, Part 1, 470.

[9] *War of the Rebellion*, Series 1, Vol. 12, Part 1, 470; Sanford C. Kellogg, *Shenandoah Valley and Virginia* (New York and Washington: The Neale Publishing Company, 1903), 53; Armstrong, *7th Virginia Cavalry*, 28.

[10] Kellogg, *Shenandoah and Virginia*, 53; In an official report, General John C. Fremont lists the combined force under Jackson as fourteen thousand, instead of the nine thousand cited by Kellogg. Please see *War of the Rebellion*, Series 1, Vol. 2, Part 1, 9.

[11] *War of the Rebellion*, Series 1, Vol. 12, Part 1, 9,472; Gilmor, *Four Years*, 36; Armstrong, *7th Virginia Cavalry*, 29.

[12] "Winfield commanded the regiment during this time, both Colonel Ashby and Major Funsten being absent sick [sic], see Armstrong, *7th Virginia Cavalry*, 28, Gilmor, *Four Years*, 37.

[13] Gilmor, *Four Years*, 38.

[14] *War of the Rebellion*, Series 1, Vol. 12, Part 1, 473; Gilmor, *Four Years*, 37-38.

[15] *War of the Rebellion*, Series 1, Vol. 12, Part 1, 8-10,473; *War of the Rebellion*, Series 1, Vol. 12, Part 3, 892.

[16] Armstrong, *7th Virginia Cavalry*, 30; Gilmor, *Four Years*, 39; Robert G. Tanner, *Stonewall in the Valley: Thomas J. "Stonewall" Jackson's Shenandoah Valley Campaign, Spring 1862* (Garden City, New York: Doubleday and Company, Inc., 1976), 256.

[17] Kellogg, *Shenandoah and Virginia*, 54-57,59,61; Robertson, "Stonewall Jackson," 24.

[18] *War of the Rebellion*, Series 1, Vol. 12, Part 1, 11-12; By moving eastward toward the Shenandoah Valley via the Wardensville Road, General Fremont also felt that he could gather supplies for his forces, see the aforementioned citation; Gilmor, *Four Years*, 40; Douglas, *Stonewall*, 75-76; Goldsborough, *Maryland Line*, 242; Foote, *The Civil War*, vol. 1, 453-54; Harris, "Stonewall," 40; Kellogg, *Shenandoah and Virginia*, 62; Robertson, "Stonewall," 24-26.

[19] Bowman, *Civil War Almanac*, 312.

[20] Robertson, "Stonewall Jackson," 26; *War of the Rebellion*, Series 1, Vol. 12, Part 3, 910.

[21] Edward Longacre, "Boots and Saddles: The Eastern Theater," *Civil War Times Illustrated*, 31 March/April 1992, 35; Bushong, *Turner Ashby*, 51,53.

[22] Armstrong, *7th Virginia Cavalry*, 37-38,93; Gilmor, *Four Years*, 42.

[23] Armstrong, *7th Virginia Cavalry*, 130,246; Gilmor, *Four Years*, 42.

[24] Gilmor, *Four Years*, 44.

[25] Ibid., 44; "Cavalry, South and North," *New York Times*, 20 November 1863, 4.

[26] Jerry Korn and others, eds., *Pursuit to Appomattox: The Last Battles* (Alexandria: Time-Life Books, 1987), 21.

[27] Gilmor, *Four Years*, 45-48,50-52.

[28] Ibid., 53-54; Bowman, *Civil War Almanac*, 109; Bishop and Drury, *1400 Days*, 93; Douglas, *Stonewall*, 128-29; Sifakis, *Who Was Who Confederacy*, vol. 2, 308.

[29] Bowman, *Civil War Almanac*, 112.

[30] Twelfth Virginia Cavalry Records; Gilmor, *Four Years*, 56-57; *The National Cyclopaedia*, vol. 23, 372; Johnson, ed., *American Biography*, vol. 7, 309.

[31] Twelfth Virginia Cavalry Records; Gilmor, *Four Years*, 57.

[32] Gilmor, *Four Years*, 58; George Baylor, *Bull Run to Bull Run* (Richmond: B. F. Johnson Publishing Co., 1900), 92,100,102.

[33] Baylor, *Bull Run*, 95; Gilmor, *Four Years*, 59.

[34] Twelfth Virginia Cavalry Records.

[35] Gilmor, *Four Years*, 59-60; James M. McPherson, *Battle Cry of Freedom* (New York: Ballantine Books, 1988), 566.

[36] Gilmor, *Four Years*, 59-61.

Chapter 4

[1] Gilmor, *Four Years*, 63-64; Bishop and Drury, *1400 Days*, 125; Burke Davis, *Jeb Stuart , The Last Cavalier* (New York: Rinehart and Company, Inc., 1957; reprint, Avenel, New Jersey: Wings Books, 1992), 269; Time-Life Books, *Brother Against Brother* (New York: Prentice Hall Press, 1990), 209,211.

[2] Time-Life Books, *Brother*, 209; Bishop and Drury, *1400 Days*, 124-25.

[3] Gilmor, *Four Years*, 65-66; Davis, *Stuart*, 270; Bowman, *Civil War Almanac*, 135-36.

[4] Gilmor, *Four Years*, 66-67.

[5] Ibid., 68-70.

[6] Ibid., 70-71.

[7] Ibid., 71-72; Time-Life Books, *Brothers*, 210; Davis, *Stuart*, 273.

[8] Gilmor, *Four Years*, 73-74; Sifakis, *Who Was Who Confederacy*, vol. 2, 220-21; Virgil Carrington Jones, in his monumental *Gray Ghosts and Rebel Raiders*, claims that Gilmor hastened Pelham's death by "dropping him, wounded, over the neck of a horse where accelerated bleeding speeded his death." (Page 178) However, such a contention must be taken in light of Jones's overall unfavorable opinion of Gilmor, who he claims was an "extrovert" and a "pistol shooting egotist." (See pages 106 and 114)

[9] Bishop and Drury, *1400 Days*, 125; Bowman, *Civil War Almanac*, 135-36; Time-Life Books, *Brothers*, 210; The last citation in this paragraph is

taken from two lines in a poem by James R. Randall entitled "The Gallant Pelham," *Southern Historical Society Papers* 30 (1902): 338-39.

[10] Gilmor, *Four Years*, 74-76; *War of the Rebellion*, Series 1, Vol. 25, Part 1, 63; Ibid., Series 1, Vol. 25, Part 1, 58; Twelfth Virginia Cavalry Records.

[11] Gilmor, *Four Years*, 76-77; Kevin Conley Ruffner, "'More Trouble than a Brigade:' Harry Gilmor's 2d Maryland Cavalry in the Shenandoah Valley," *Maryland Historical Magazine* 89 (Winter 1994): 392,406-7; Jeffry D. Wert, *Mosby's Rangers* (New York: Simon and Schuster, 1991), 70-71; Hartzler, *Marylanders*, 34; *War of the Rebellion*, Series 1, Vol. 36, Part 2, 959.

[12] Twelfth Virginia Cavalry Records; Ruffner, "'More Trouble than a Brigade,'" 392-94; According to Hartzler, in *Marylanders*, "the recruitment [of Gilmor's battalion] was very rapid, for within a month five new Maryland companies were ordered up the [Shenandoah] Valley." Please see page 34.

[13] Ruffner, "'More Trouble than a Brigade,'" 394-95.

[14] Hartzler, *Marylanders*, 34; Second Maryland Battalion Cavalry, Compiled Service Records of Confederate Soldiers, Record Group 109, M321, Roll 7, National Archives, Washington, D.C. (hereafter cited as Second Maryland Cavalry Records, with appropriate Roll number designated).

[15] Ruffner, "'More Trouble than a Brigade,'" 393-94.

[16] Gilmor, *Four Years*, 77; Second Maryland Cavalry Records, Roll 7; Second Maryland Cavalry Records, Roll 8; Wert, *Mosby's Rangers*, 71; The archival material cited lists William W. McKaig as a First Lieutenant in Company A. However, these sources are making reference to events in March 1864. By this time Company B, in which McKaig was originally elected First Lieutenant, was renamed Company A. Please see Second Maryland Cavalry Records, Roll 7 and Roll 8.

[17] Ruffner, "'More Trouble than a Brigade,'" 393.

[18] Ian Hogg, *Robert E. Lee* (Greenwich, CT: Brompton Books Corporation, 1990; repr, Stamford, CT: Longmeadow Press, 1992), 46-47; William C. Davis, *The Battlefields of the Civil War* (New York: Smithmark Publishers Inc., 1991), 155-57; McPherson, *Battle Cry of Freedom*, 647-48,650-51; Bowman, *Civil War Almanac*, 150-51.

[19] David K. Snider and William R. Brooksher, "Errant Rider's Misbegotten Errand," *Military History*, 5 (June 1989), 42; Gilmor, *Four Years*, 77-78; John Bakeless, *Spies of the Confederacy* (Philadelphia and New York: J.B. Lippincott Company, 1970), 170-71.

[20] Gilmor, *Four Years*, 78.

[21] William W. Goldsborough, *The Maryland Line in the Confederate States Army* (Baltimore: Kelly, Piet, 1869), 217 (Please differentiate between this edition and the second edition of Goldsborough's *The Maryland Line in the Confederate Army*, for the latter contains numerous editions and contextual modifications.); Gilmor, *Four Years*, 78-79.

[22] Goldsborough, *The Maryland Line*, 1st edition, 215; Gilmor, *Four Years*, 80-81.

[23] Gilmor, *Four Years*, 80-82; Goldsborough, *The Maryland Line*, 1st Edition, 215-16; Goldsborough takes issue with Gilmor's interpretation of events that occurred outside of Newtown. He claims that Captain Raisin tried to prevent his men from charging into the ambush. In support of his conviction, he states that he and Raisin's unit set a similar trap for the Federals only a week prior to the events described above. Thus, Raisin would have been familiar with the situation and would not have allowed himself to fall into such a trap. Moreover, Goldsborough contends "that if an order to charge was given, it was given by Harry himself," because a participant after the action declared "may I be darned ef I'm goin' to foller that thar feller with the sprang new yaller clothes any more [sic]." Recall, that Goldsborough claims Harry was wearing yellow on that fateful day. (Please see Goldsborough, 216-17)

[24] Bishop and Drury, *1400 Days*, 137-38; Bowman, *Civil War Almanac*, 153; Gilmor, *Four Years*, 84-86; Gilmor, in *Four Years in the Saddle*, stated that "having no command of my own, I went into action with Major William W. Goldsborough, who had charge of the skirmish-line" (page 84). However, in a letter written some nine months after Early's assault on Milroy's position in Winchester, Gilmor claims that Company F, Twelfth Virginia Cavalry, was with him. Please see Second Maryland Cavalry Records, Roll 7.

[25] Gilmor, *Four Years*, 87; John Bakeless, "Catching Harry Gilmor," *Civil War Times Illustrated* 10 (April 1971): 35; Bakeless, *Spies*, 314-15.

[26] Bakeless, *Spies*, 315-16; Gilmor, *Four Years*, 87-88.

[27] McPherson, *Battle Cry of Freedom*, 648; Sifakis, *Who Was Who Confederacy*, vol. 2, 89; Gilmor, *Four Years*, 89-90.

[28] Bowman, *Civil War Almanac*, 153; Bishop and Drury, *1400 Days*, 138; Gilmor, *Four Years*, 91-92.

[29] Bishop and Drury, *1400 Days*, 138; Bowman, *Civil War Almanac*, 153; Goldsborough, *Maryland Line*, 177; *War of the Rebellion*, Series 1, Vol. 27, Part 2, 290; Armstrong, *7th Virginia Cavalry*, 133; Gilmor, *Four Years*, 92-94.

[30] Goldsborough, *Maryland Line*, 177; Randolph H. McKim, *A Soldier's Recollections* (New York: Longman's, Green, and Co., 1911), 162-63. Maryland historian Daniel Carroll Toomey offers an explanation for the proper name of the First Maryland Infantry Battalion. According to Toomey, the First Maryland Battalion was formed from officers and men from the First Maryland Infantry Regiment plus new recruits from Maryland. The First Maryland Regiment was mustered out of Confederate service on August 17, 1862, "as its term of enlistment was determined to be for one year only." The men of the First Maryland Regiment were unable to form another complete regiment, however, they did have enough to form a battalion. "The First Maryland Battalion was mustered into Confederate service in October

of 1862." In 1864 the Maryland Battalion would be labeled the Second Maryland Infantry Battalion. As Toomey further explains, "in post-war writings it is almost exclusively referred to as the Second Battalion from its inception. Please see Daniel Carroll Toomey, *Marylanders at Gettysburg* (Baltimore: Toomey Press, 1994), 7.

[31] McKim, *Recollections*, 163-64; Goldsborough, *Maryland Line*, 177; Gilmor, *Four Years*, 94.

[32] McKim, *Recollections*, 164-65; Gilmor, *Four Years*, 94; Goldsborough, *Maryland Line*, 177.

[33] Goldsborough, *Maryland Line*, 177-78.

[34] McPherson, *Battle Cry of Freedom*, 649-50; McKim, *Recollections*, 162.

[35] McKim, *Recollections*, 165.

[36] Ibid., 165-66; Goldsborough, *Maryland Line*, 178; Gilmor, *Four Years*, 94-96.

[37] Armstrong, *7th Virginia Cavalry*, 243; Johnson, *Maryland*, vol. 2, 139; Gilmor, *Four Years*, 96; Foote, *The Civil War*, vol. 2, 476-77.

[38] Toomey, *Marylanders at Gettysburg*, 5.

[39] Gilmor, *Four Years*, 97-98; Charles C. Osborne, *Jubal: The Life and Times of General Jubal A. Early, C.S.A.* (Chapel Hill: Algonquin Books of Chapel Hill, 1992), 4.

[40] Toomey, *Marylanders at Gettysburg*, 5-6; Ruffner, "'More Trouble than a Brigade,'" 393. According to Gilmor, in *Four Years in the Saddle*, General Ewell appointed him Provost Marshal of Gettysburg on July 2, 1863 (page 98).

[41] Gilmor, *Four Years*, 98-100.

[42] Bowman, *Civil War Almanac*, 160; Bishop and Drury, *1400 Days*, 139-41; McPherson, *Battle Cry of Freedom*, 663.

[43] Gilmor, *Four Years*, 100-2; Bowman, *Civil War Almanac*, 162; Bishop and Drury, *1400 Days*, 142.

[44] Gilmor, *Four Years*, 102-4.

[45] Ibid., 104-6. According to Gilmor, during this time period he "had but one company of mounted men, although two or three others were being formed." Please see Gilmor, *Four Years*, 104.

[46] Fritz Haselberger, "2nd Maryland Cavalry Battalion C.S.A.: Roster and Losses Arranged by Date-Name-Place-Type" (Maryland Historical Society Library, 1992), 1; Second Maryland Cavalry Records, Roll 7.

[47] Ruffner, "'More Trouble than a Brigade,'" 406.

[48] "Letter from 'Ella' to Major Harry Gilmor," August 29, 1863, Harry Gilmor Papers, MS 1287, Manuscripts Division, Maryland Historical Society Library (hereafter denoted as MHSL). For additional letters from female admirers to Gilmor, please see Lizzie Welch to Harry Gilmor, October 27, 1862, December 10, 1862 and Miss C. Kearney to Harry Gilmor, April 12, 15, 19, 29, 1863. Miss Kearney received a substantial loan of $120 from

Gilmor. All of these letters can be found in Harry Gilmor Papers, MS 1287, Manuscripts Division, MHSL.

[49] James E. Taylor, *The James E. Taylor Sketchbook* (Cleveland: Western Reserve Historical Society, 1989), 224; *War of the Rebellion*, Series 1, Vol. 29, Part 1, 210; Gilmor, *Four Years*, 107-8.

[50] Taylor, *Taylor Sketchbook*, 225,227; *War of the Rebellion*, Series 1, Vol. 29, Part 1, 210.

[51] Taylor, *Taylor Sketchbook*, 226-27; "West Virginia Battle Ground," *Confederate Veteran Magazine*, 34 September 1926, 340; *War of the Rebellion*, Series 1, Vol. 29, Part 1, 210; The official record account (by Col. George D. Wells, Thirty-fourth Massachusetts Infantry) is a marked antithesis to Gilmor and Taylor's ("Taylor appears to have summarized Gilmor's account of the incident") version of events at the Morrow's residence. It concludes that "[Summers] instantly charged them [Gilmor's men], and as he did so received a volley from a squad which had dismounted and were concealed behind a stone fence skirting the road. Captain Summers fell at the first fire." Thus, if Colonel Wells's report is correct, Gilmor did not kill Summers, and, furthermore, James Taylor's depiction of the event is a sad misrepresentation. Please see his *Sketchbook* page 225-27.

[52] Gilmor, *Four Years*, 109-11; *War of the Rebellion*, Series 1, Vol. 29, Part 1, 211.

[53] "Letter from Major D.H. Wood Quartermaster to Captain B.W. Edwards Storekeeper (From Invoices and Orders, 1863-65)," October 14, 1863, Harry Gilmor Papers, MS 1287, Manuscripts Division, MHSL; Frank Moore, ed., *The Rebellion Record* vol. 7, (New York: Arno Press A New York Times Company, 1977), 565; Gilmor, *Four Years*, 111.

[54] Moore, ed., *Rebellion Record*, vol. 7, 565; Gilmor, *Four Years*, 111-12; Goldsborough, *Maryland Line*, 246; Johnson, *Maryland*, vol. 2, 141.

[55] Gilmor, *Four Years*, 111-12; Haselberger, "2nd Maryland Cavalry Battalion," 3; Ruffner, "'More Trouble than a Brigade,'" 396. Gilmor, in *Four Years* in the Saddle, referred to Blackford as a "Captain," even though he no longer held a command.

[56] Moore, ed., *Rebellion Record*, vol. 7, 63,565-66; Gilmor, *Four Years*, 112.

[57] Second Maryland Cavalry Records, Roll 7.

[58] Gilmor, *Four Years*, 113; Carter F. Berkeley, "Imboden's Dash Into Charlestown," *Confederate Veteran Magazine*, 25 April 1917, 149; "Imboden's Dash Into Charlestown," *Southern Historical Society Papers* 31 (1903): 11; *War of the Rebellion*, Series 1, Vol. 29, Part 1, 490.

[59] Gilmor, *Four Years*, 113; Berkeley, "Imboden's Dash," 149; "Imboden's Dash," 14; *War of the Rebellion*, Series 1, Vol. 29, Part 1, 490-91.

[60] Gilmor, *Four Years*, 114; Goldsborough, *Maryland Line*, 246; Johnson, *Maryland*, vol. 2, 141.

[61] Gilmor, *Four Years*, 115-16; Berkeley, "Imboden's Dash," 150; "Imboden's Dash," 15.

[62] Laura Virginia Hale, *Four Valiant Years in the Lower Shenandoah Valley (1861-1865)* (Strasburg, VA: Shenandoah Publishing House, Inc., 1968), 306; *War of the Rebellion*, Series 1, Vol. 29, Part 1, 491; Carter, "Imboden's Dash," 149-50; "Imboden's Dash," 16.

[63] *War of the Rebellion*, Series 1, Vol. 29, Part 1, 491,411; The figure of 360 Union men captured at Charles Town is cited from Ruffner's "'More Trouble than a Brigade,'" 397.

[64] Thomas, *Confederate Nation*, 249; Linderman, *Embattled Courage*, 196,198.

[65] Castel, "Guerrilla War," 7-9; Wert, *Mosby's Rangers*, 71.

[66] Wert, *Mosby's Rangers*, 71.

[67] Linderman, *Embattled Courage*, 198; Linderman's study offers a tremendous examination of the changing nature of the American Civil War in 1863 and 1864.

Chapter 5

[1] "The Rebels Attack and Capture Charlestown, Va.," *Philadelphia Inquirer*, 20 October 1863, 1; Gilmor, *Four Years*, 115,117; Goldsborough, *Maryland Line*, 246; Johnson, *Maryland*, vol. 2, 141.

[2] Hale, *Four Valiant Years*, 312; Gilmor, *Four Years*, 117-19.

[3] Gilmor, *Four Years*, 119-22; Goldsborough, *Maryland Line*, 247.

[4] Gilmor, *Four Years*, 121,124-25.

[5] Ibid., 124-25; Hale, *Four Valiant Years*, 316-17.

[6] Gilmor, *Four Years*, 126-28.

[7] Ibid., 130-35; Hale, *Four Valiant Years*, 313.

[8] Jones, *Gray Ghosts*, 210-11; Sifakis, *Who Was Who in the Confederacy*, vol. 2, 167; Gen. Jubal A. Early, *Narrative of the War Between the States*, with an Introduction by Gary Gallagher (Philadelphia: n.p., 1912; reprint, New York: Da Capo Press, 1989), 332-33.

[9] Second Maryland Cavalry Records, Roll 7; Gilmor, *Four Years*, 135-38; Goldsborough, *Maryland Line*, 247.

[10] Gilmor, *Four Years*, 138-39; Early, *Narrative*, 333; *War of the Rebellion*, Series 1, Vol. 33, 8.

[11] *War of the Rebellion*, Series 1, Vol. 33, 1111; Jones, *Gray Ghosts*, 214; Osborne, *Jubal*, 224; Ralph Haas, *Dear Esther: The Civil War Letters of Private Aungier Dobbs*, ed. Philip Ensley (Apollo, Pennsylvania: Closson Press, 1991), 197.

[12] Jones, *Gray Ghosts*, 214-15; Gilmor, *Four Years*, 140; Osborne, *Jubal*, 226.

[13] Gilmor, *Four Years*, 141.

[14] Ibid., 143-44; Taylor, *Taylor Sketchbook*, 206.

[15] Gilmor, *Four Years*, 144; Taylor, *Taylor Sketchbook*, 144; *War of the Rebellion*, Series 1, Vol. 33, 154; "Bold Exploit of a Guerrilla Band," *New York Times*, 14 February 1864, 1; Jones, *Gray Ghosts*, 216.

[16] Gilmor, *Four Years*, 144-45; Taylor, *Taylor Sketchbook*, 206-7.

[17] Gilmor, *Four Years*, 145; "Bold Exploit," *New York Times*, 14 February 1864, 1.

[18] "Bold Exploit," *New York Times*, 14 February 1864, 1; Jones, *Gray Ghosts*, 216-17; citing the *Baltimore American*.

[19] *War of the Rebellion*, Series 1, Vol. 33, 152-53.

[20] William C. Davis, *The Battle of New Market* (Garden City, New York: Doubleday and Company, Inc., 1975), 49; Jones, *Gray Ghosts*, 217.

[21] *War of the Rebellion*, Series 1, Vol. 33, 223.

[22] Bowman, *Civil War Almanac*, 183.

[23] Jones, *Gray Ghosts*, 213-14; Osborne, *Jubal*, 224.

[24] Jones, *Gray Ghosts*, 214; Osborne, *Jubal*, 224.

[25] Wert, *Mosby's Rangers*, 139-40.

[26] Ibid., 140.

[27] "Letter from [?] Meem to Major Gilmor," March 1864, Harry Gilmor Papers, MS 1287, Manuscripts Division, MHSL (letter from a friend at the Mount Airy estate); "Letter from George Treaver to Maj. Harry Gilmer [sic]," March 7, 1864, Harry Gilmor Papers, MS 1287, Manuscripts Division, MHSL.

[28] "Brig. Genl. J. D. Imboden releases Gilmor from arrest, revokes Sp. Orders No. 45," March 21, 1864, Harry Gilmor Papers, MS 1287, Manuscripts Division, MHSL; Gilmor, Four Years, 146; "Letter from George Treaver to Major Gilmor," April 20, 1864, Harry Gilmor Papers, MS 1287, Manuscripts Division, MHSL.

[29] Jones, *Gray Ghosts*, 217-18; *War of the Rebellion*, Series 1, Vol. 33, 1252-53; Davis, *New Market*, 49; "Maj. Gen. Breckinridge issues Special Orders No. 1," May 10, 1864, Harry Gilmor Papers, MS 1287, Manuscripts Division, MHSL.

[30] "Letter from J. Louis Smith to Major H. W. Gilmer [sic]," May, 1864, Harry Gilmor Papers, MS 1287, Manuscripts Division, MHSL; *War of the Rebellion*, Series 1, Vol. 33, 1253; Series 1, Vol. 36, Part 2, 959; Series 1, Vol. 40, Part 2, 650; Hartzler, *Marylanders*, 34,39-40.

[31] Gilmor, *Four Years*, 147-48; *War of the Rebellion*, Series 1, Vol. 36, Part 2, 959; Series 1, Vol. 40, Part 2, 650; "Letter from J. Louis Smith to Brigd. Genl. Imboden," May 7, 1864, Harry Gilmor Papers, MS 1287, Manuscripts Division, MHSL. At this point in time, perhaps the fifty men located at Staunton had yet to arrive in the lower Valley, for Gilmor writes that "one half my command was at Staunton, and only the best mounted were in the Valley, eighty-five men in all." Please see Gilmor, *Four Years*, 148.

[32] "Order of Maj. Genl. Elzey, Headquarters Maryland Line," May 10, 1864, Harry Gilmor Papers, MS 1287, Manuscripts Division, MHSL; Hartzler, *Marylanders*, 34; "Letter from eleven Maryland men who wish to join Gilmor's command," September 3, 1864, Harry Gilmor Papers, MS 1287, Manuscripts Division, MHSL.

[33] "Letter from Eva Lee to Major Harry Gilmor," April 9,13, 1864, Harry Gilmor Papers, MS 1287, Manuscripts Division, MHSL.

[34] Time-Life Books, *Brother*, 384-85; Bowman, *Civil War Almanac*, 378; Foote, *The Civil War*, vol. 3, 18; Jones, *Gray Ghosts*, 238-39; Burgess Meredith, narrater, *Bloody Shenandoah*, produced by Lou Reda Productions, 50 min., Easton, Pennsylvania, n.d., videocassette; "Walking military disaster who bawled out orders in German when rattled" is cited from the latter source.

[35] Time-Life Books, *Brother*, 384-85; Jones, *Gray Ghosts*, 238-39.

[36] Gilmor, *Four Years*, 148-51; *War of the Rebellion*, Series 1, Vol. 37, Part 1, 731.

[37] Jones, *Gray Ghosts*, 239.

[38] Gilmor, *Four Years*, 152-55.

[39] Ibid., 155-56; Brig.-Gen. John D. Imboden, "The Battle of New Market, Virginia, May 15th, 1864," vol. 4, *Battles and Leaders of the Civil War* (New York and London: Thomas Yoseloff, 1956), 481.

[40] Gilmor, *Four Years*, 156; Maj.-Gen. Franz Sigel, "Sigel in the Shenandoah Valley in 1864," vol. 4, *Battles and Leaders*, 488.

[41] Jones, *Gray Ghosts*, 239-40.

[42] Bowman, *Civil War Almanac*, 202; Jones, *Gray Ghosts*, 240; Bishop and Drury, *1400 Days*, 185; Time-Life Books, *Brother*, 385.

[43] Time-Life Books, *Brother*, 385; Jones, *Gray Ghosts*, 243; McPherson, *Battle Cry of Freedom*, 737.

[44] Bishop and Drury, *1400 Days*, 186; Bowman, *Civil War Almanac*, 204-5; Jones, *Gray Ghosts*, 246.

[45] Gilmor, *Four Years*, 162-63,166; *War of the Rebellion*, Series 1, Vol. 37, Part 1, 161.

[46] Gilmor, *Four Years*, 166-67.

[47] McPherson, *Battle Cry of Freedom*, 737; Bishop and Drury, *1400 Days*, 188; Foote, *The Civil War*, vol. 3, 302; Sifakis, *Who Was Who Confederacy*, vol. 2, 156; *War of the Rebellion*, Series 1, Vol. 37, Part 1, 96.

[48] *War of the Rebellion*, Series 1, Vol. 37, Part 1, 96-97; McPherson, *Battle Cry of Freedom*, 738; Foote, *The Civil War*, vol. 3, 310.

[49] Early, *Narrative*, 373.

[50] Gilmor, *Four Years*, 171-73.

[51] *War of the Rebellion*, Series 1, Vol. 37, Part 1, 99.

[52] Osborne, *Jubal*, 258.

[53] Ibid., 258; McPherson, *Battle Cry of Freedom*, 739; *War of the Rebellion*, Series 1, Vol. 37, Part 1, 100; Gilmor, *Four Years*, 173-74; Time-Life Books, *Brother*, 387.

[54] Gilmor, *Four Years*, 174.

[55] Osborne, *Jubal*, 259; Early, *Narrative*, 376; Gilmor, *Four Years*, 175.

[56] Gilmor, *Four Years*, 178,181; Early, *Narrative*, 378-79.

[57] McPherson, *Battle Cry of Freedom*, 739.

[58] Gilmor, *Four Years*, 167,183.

[59] Linderman, *Embattled Courage*, 180.

Chapter 6

[1] Bishop and Drury, *1400 Days*, 189; Bowman, *Civil War Almanac*, 210-11.

[2] Early, *Narrative*, 380; Osborne, *Jubal*, 261-62; Foote, *The Civil War*, vol. 3, 446; Clifford Dowdey and Louis H. Manarin, eds., *The Wartime Papers of R. E. Lee* (Boston and Toronto: Little, Brown and Company, 1961), 807; Burgess Meredith, narrater, *Bloody Shenandoah*, produced by Lou Reda Productions, 50 min., Easton, Pennsylvania, n.d., videocassette; Jack Hanrahan, narrater, *The Civil War*, produced by Dan Dalton Productions, 90 min., n.p., 1991, videocassette. The question invariably arises if Early wished to just "threaten" Washington or actually capture the Federal capital when he invaded Maryland that summer of 1864, and it is still debated among Civil War scholars.

[3] Foote, *The Civil War*, vol. 3, 446-47; Osborne, *Jubal*, 263-65.

[4] Osborne, *Jubal*, 263,265; Gilmor, *Four Years*, 184; Walt Albro, "The Forgotten Battle for the Capital," *Civil War Times*, 31 (February 1993), 41; Foote, *The Civil War*, vol. 3, 448.

[5] Gilmor, *Four Years*, 184-85; Foote, *The Civil War*, vol. 3, 447.

[6] Early, *Narrative*, 383; Foote, *The Civil War*, vol. 3, 447; Gilmor, *Four Years*, 184-87; *War of the Rebellion*, Series 1, Vol. 37, Part 2, 591.

[7] *War of the Rebellion*, Series 1, Vol. 37, Part 2, 591; Bishop and Drury, *1400 Days*, 192.

[8] Early, *Narrative*, 384; Bowman, *Civil War Almanac*, 213-14; Osborne, *Jubal*, 266.

[9] Osborne, *Jubal*, 268; *War of the Rebellion*, Series 1, Vol. 37, Part 1, 349; Bowman, *Civil War Almanac*, 214; Foote, *The Civil War*, vol. 3, 448-49.

[10] Early, *Narrative*, 385.

[11] Magnus S. Thompson, "Plan to Release Our Men at Point Lookout," *Confederate Veteran Magazine*, 20 February 1912, 69; Dowdey and Manarin, *Lee's Papers*, 807-8; Douglas Southall Freeman, *Lee's Lieutenants* vol. 3, (New York: Charles Scribner's Sons, 1944), 564.

[12] Geoffrey W. Fielding, ed., "Gilmor's Field Report of His Raid in Baltimore County," *Maryland Historical Magazine*, 47 (1952): 235; The original document detailing Gilmor's activities around Baltimore can be

found in the Maryland Historical Society, under "Letter from Harry Gilmor to Captain G.W. Booth," July 28, 1864, Harry Gilmor Papers, MS 1287, Manuscripts Division, MHSL.

[13] Osborne, *Jubal*, 267.

[14] Gilmor, *Four Years*, 187. Although Gilmor stated that he was given command of the First Maryland Cavalry Battalion, he also writes that it was "commanded by [his] old friend and companion, Warner Welsh." Welsh was captain of only Company D, First Maryland, not the entire battalion as Gilmor suggests. Thus, perhaps Gilmor was placed in charge of only Company D of the First Maryland. (Please see Johnson, *Maryland*, vol. 2, 139 and Armstrong, *7th Virginia Cavalry*, 243); Bradley T. Johnson, "My Ride Around Baltimore in Eighteen Hundred and Sixty-Four," *Southern Historical Society Papers* 30 (1902): 217; Early, *Narrative*, 385-86.

[15] Gilmor, *Four Years*, 188; Johnson, *Maryland*, vol. 2, 141; Goldsborough, *Maryland Line*, 247.

[16] Gilmor, *Four Years*, 189-90; Johnson, *Maryland*, vol. 2, 141; Goldsborough, *Maryland Line*, 248.

[17] "The Rebel Raid," *New York Times*, 8 July 1864, 1.

[18] Early, *Narrative*, 387; Osborne, *Jubal*, 279,282.

[19] Johnson, "My Ride Around Baltimore," 217-18. Since the Washington Railroad runs directly between Baltimore and Washington, Johnson must have been referring to this road instead of the Baltimore and Ohio Railroad, which runs due west of Baltimore.

[20] Ibid., 218; Thompson, "Point Lookout," 69.

[21] Johnson, *Maryland*, vol. 2, 126; Gilmor, *Four Years*, 190; Robert E. Michel, *Colonel Harry Gilmor's Raid Around Baltimore* (Baltimore: Erbe Publishers, 1976), 5.

[22] Michel, *Gilmor's Raid*, 5; Gilmor, *Four Years*, 191; Johnson, *Maryland*, vol. 2, 126; Johnson, "My Ride Around Baltimore," 218-19.

[23] Bowman, *Civil War Almanac*, 214. Such levies were placed upon Hagerstown and Frederick ostensibly as retaliation for Hunter's destruction in the Shenandoah earlier that summer. However, these payments served a greater purpose in filling the empty coffers of the Confederacy's Treasury. Furthermore, such activities were indicative of the new total war, as towns were threatened with the torch unless their citizens meant the Rebel demands.

[24] Osborne, *Jubal*, 275-76,280; E.B. Long, *The Civil War Day by Day An Almanac 1861-1865* (Garden City, New York: Doubleday and Company, Inc., 1971), 535-36; Roy P. Basler, ed., *The Collected Works of Abraham Lincoln* vol. 7, (New Brunswick, New Jersey: Rutgers University Press, 1953), 437-38.

[25] Michel, *Gilmor's Raid*, 6-7, citing the *Baltimore Sun*, July 11, 1864. General Henry Halleck, the Union Army's Chief of Staff, was slow to respond to the crisis before Washington. When Grant wanted to send a whole corps from the Army of the Potomac to Washington during Early's first few days

in Maryland, "Halleck responded that an entire corps would be superfluous," and he convinced Grant to send only "2,500 dismounted cavalrymen (many of them convalescents) and one division from the Sixth Corp." But by July 10, as Early camped near Rockville, Halleck requested the entire Sixth Corps as well as "the Union Nineteenth Corps, newly arrived in Virginia from Louisiana." (See Osborne, *Jubal*, 269,281).

[26] Fielding, ed., "Gilmor's Field Report," 237; Michel, *Gilmor's Raid*, 7; Johnson, *Maryland*, vol. 2, 139-40.

[27] Johnson, "My Ride Around Baltimore," 219.

[28] Fielding, ed., "Gilmor's Field Report," 235; Johnson, *Maryland*, vol. 2, 126-27.

[29] Michel, *Gilmor's Raid*, 7-9,11; Gilmor, *Four Years*, 192; Osborne, *Jubal*, 287.

[30] Michel, *Gilmor's Raid*, 12; Gilmor, *Four Years*, 192-93; Neale A. Brooks, *A History of Baltimore County* (Towson, Maryland: Friends of the Towson Library, Inc., 1979), 248.

[31] Gilmor, *Four Years*, 193-94; Fielding, ed., "Gilmor's Field Report," 235; Goldsborough, *Maryland Line*, 247; Brooks, *Baltimore County*, 248-50; Michel, *Gilmor's Raid*, 15; Haselberger, "2nd Maryland Cavalry Battalion," 11.

[32] Gilmor, *Four Years*, 194; Fielding, ed., "Gilmor's Field Report," 237; "Gunpowder Bridge Probably not Burnt - Further Respecting the Capture of the Trains - Rebels Expected to Retreat Under Cover of Night," *New York Times*, 12 July 1864, 1.

[33] Gilmor, *Four Years*, 194.

[34] "The Capture of the Trains on the Philadelphia Railroad," *Baltimore Sun*, 15 July 1864, 1.

[35] Fielding, ed., "Gilmor's Field Report," 237-38; "Gunpowder Bridge Probably not Burnt," *New York Times*, 12 July 1864, 1; Gilmor, *Four Years*, 194-96.

[36] Brooks, *Baltimore County*, 250.

[37] Fielding, ed., "Gilmor's Field Report," 238; "The Excitement in Baltimore - The Burning of Gunpowder Bridge - Destruction of Gov. Bradford's House - An Act of Retaliation...," *New York Times*, 12 July 1864, 1; Michel, *Gilmor's Raid*, 18-20, citing the *Baltimore Sun*, July 12, 1864. Michel's narrative of Gilmor's activities in eastern Maryland cites numerous dispatches and newspaper articles that refer to the Maryland cavalier.

[38] Johnson, *Maryland*, vol. 2, 127; Michel, *Gilmor's Raid*, 13-15.

[39] Early, *Narrative*, 389.

[40] Albro, "Forgotten Battle," 60; Early, *Narrative*, 389,392; Johnson, *Maryland*, vol. 2, 127; Johnson, "My Ride Around Baltimore," 220.

[41] Early, *Narrative*, 391,394; Bowman, *Civil War Almanac*, 214-15; Time-Life Books, *Brother*, 387-88.

[42] Osborne, *Jubal*, 289; Johnson, *Maryland*, vol. 2, 128; Thompson,

"Point Lookout," 69; Early, *Narrative*, 394-95; Gen. J. A. Early, "The Advance on Washington in 1864," *Southern Historical Society Papers* 9 (1881): 309.

[43] Gilmor, *Four Years*, 197-99; Michel, *Gilmor's Raid*, 21-23, citing the *Baltimore County Advocate*, July 16, 1864.

[44] Michel, *Gilmor's Raid*, 20-21; Johnson, *Maryland*, vol. 2, 141; Goldsborough, *Maryland Line*, 247; Gilmor, *Four Years*, 198-200; Brooks, *Baltimore County*, 250.

[45] Fielding, ed., "Gilmor's Field Report," 238-39; Johnson, *Maryland*, vol. 2, 141; Goldsborough, *Maryland Line*, 246,248; Gilmor, *Four Years*, 198,201-3.

[46] Michel, *Gilmor's Raid*, 25-26; Fielding, ed., "Gilmor's Field Report," 239-40; Gilmor, *Four Years*, 204; Millard Kessler Bushong, *Old Jube* (Boyce, Virginia: Carr Publishing Company, Inc., 1955), 201; Goldsborough, *Maryland Line*, 241. Whereas many Civil War historians, both past and present, have considered Gilmor a braggart or an egotist, his apparent lack of concern for military rank seems to contradict such notions.

[47] Douglas, *Stonewall*, 284.

[48] Jefferson Davis, *The Rise and Fall of the Confederate Government* vol. 2, (New York and London: Sagamore Press, Inc., 1958), 530.

Chapter 7

[1] Osborne, *Jubal*, 4,302; Early, *Narrative*, 401; Davis, *Confederate Government*, 531.

[2] Charles T. Alexander, "McCausland's Raid and the Burning of Chambersburg" (Masters Thesis, University of Maryland, 1988), 11; Ted Alexander and others, *Southern Revenge! Civil War History of Chambersburg, Pennsylvania* (Shippensburg: White Mane Publishing Company, Inc. and Greater Chambersburg Chamber of Commerce, 1989), 100; Early, *Narrative*, 401; Gen. John McCausland, "The Burning of Chambersburg, Penn.," *Southern Historical Society Papers* 31 (1903): 267.

[3] Gilmor, *Four Years*, 172.

[4] Bushong, *Old Jube*, 222.

[5] Ted Alexander, "McCausland's Raid and the Burning of Chambersburg," *Blue and Gray Magazine* 11 (August 1994): 13. Ted (Charles) Alexander, in this article, affords the reader a very interesting narrative of the burning of Chambersburg. Alexander uses Gilmor's *Four Years* in parts of his narrative; Osborne, *Jubal*, 302; Fielder C. Slingluff, "The Burning of Chambersburg," *Southern Historical Society Papers* 37 (1909): 156.

[6] Alexander, "McCausland's Raid and the Burning of Chambersburg" (Masters Thesis), 14-16; McCausland, "Chambersburg," 267-69; Alexander

and others, *Southern Revenge!*, 104; Early, *Narrative*, 401.

[7] Gilmor, *Four Years*, 205; J. Scott Moore, "Unwritten History," *Southern Historical Society Papers* 26 (1898): 317; Jacob Hoke, *The Great Invasion of 1863* (New York and London: Thomas Yoseloff, 1959), 581.

[8] Gilmor, *Four Years*, 205-6; Early, *Narrative*, 402; *War of the Rebellion*, Series 1, Vol. 37, Part 1, 332; Alexander, "McCausland's Raid and the Burning of Chambersburg" (Masters Thesis), 25; Alexander and others, *Southern Revenge!*, 114; Goldsborough, *Maryland Line*, 247.

[9] McCausland, "Chambersburg," 269; Early, *Narrative*, 402; Moore, "Chambersburg," 317.

[10] McCausland, "Chambersburg," 269; Gilmor, *Four Years*, 206.

[11] Hoke, *Great Invasion*, 581.

[12] *War of the Rebellion*, Series 1, Vol. 37, Part 1, 331; Daniel Carroll Toomey, *The Patapsco Guards Independent Company of Maryland Volunteer Infantry* (Baltimore: Toomey Press, 1993), 14; Hoke, *The Great Invasion*, 581.

[13] Gilmor, *Four Years*, 206-8; Alexander, "McCausland's Raid," 16; Goldsborough, *Maryland Line*, 248; Haselberger, "2nd Maryland Cavalry Battalion," 12.

[14] *War of the Rebellion*, Series 1, Vol. 37, Part 1, 332,337,355; McCausland, "Chambersburg," 269; Osborne, *Jubal*, 303; Gilmor, *Four Years*, 208-9.

[15] During the Gettysburg Campaign of 1863 Jubal Early had Thaddeus Stevens's Caledonia ironworks destroyed. A foreman at the plant asked Early if he would have taken Stevens South for imprisonment upon capture. Early replied "No, sir, I would hang him on the spot and divide his bones and send them to the several [Southern] States as curiosities." Please see Fawn M. Brodie, *Thaddeus Stevens* (New York: W.W. Norton and Company, Inc., 1959), 180.

[16] Alexander, "McCausland's Raid and the Burning of Chambersburg" (Masters Thesis), 38; Alexander and others, *Southern Revenge!*, 118; Gilmor, *Four Years*, 209; *War of the Rebellion*, Series 1, Vol. 37, Part 1, 333.

[17] Gilmor, *Four Years*, 209-10.

[18] Osborne, *Jubal*, 304-5.

[19] Carl Sandburg, *Abraham Lincoln : The War Years* vol. 3, (New York: Harcourt, Brace, and Company, 1939), 149.

[20] Slingluff, "Chambersburg," 158; Moore, ed., *Rebellion Record*, vol. 11, 541.

[21] Moore, ed., *Rebellion Record*, vol. 11, 540.

[22] Ibid., 540.

[23] *War of the Rebellion*, Series 1, Vol. 43, Part 1, 7-8; Moore, ed., *Rebellion Record*, vol. 11, 540.

[24] Moore, ed., *Rebellion Record*, vol. 11, 541.

[25] Gilmor, *Four Years*, 210-11.

[26] Ibid., 212-213.

[27] Liva Baker, "The Burning of Chambersburg," *Civil War Chronicles*, 3 (Summer 1993), 46.

[28] J. Scott Moore, "Unwritten History," 320; Osborne, *Jubal*, 306-7.

[29] "Pennsylvanians To Arms! To Arms," *Post-Pittsburgh*, 1 August 1864, 1; Leland D. Baldwin, *Pittsburgh The Story of a City 1750-1865* (Pittsburgh: University of Pittsburgh Press, 1937; n.p., 1970), 317-18.

[30] "Philadelphia, July 30," *Post-Pittsburgh*, 1 August 1864, 1.

[31] "Rebel Occupation and Burning of Chambersburg - Interesting Details," and "Harry Gilmor Supposed to be Killed," *Philadelphia Inquirer*, 1 August 1864, 8.

[32] "The Rebel Raid," *New York Times*, 2 August 1864, 1.

[33] Pennsylvania Governor, *Address*, "To the Assembly Concerning Measures for the Defense of the State and Union," Pennsylvania Archives (9 August 1864) vol. 8, 595-99; *War of the Rebellion*, Series 1, Vol. 43, Part 1, 751-53; Hoke, *The Great Invasion*, 581.

[34] Gilmor, *Four Years*, 213; Robert R. Zell, "The Raid into Pennsylvania - The First Armored Train," *Confederate Veteran Magazine*, 28 July 1920, 260. The friction between McCausland and Johnson is demonstrated by the latter's official report dated August 10, 1864 (Please see *War of the Rebellion*, Series 1, Vol. 43, Part 1, 4-8.

[35] Gilmor, *Four Years*, 215; Early, *Narrative*, 404-5.

[36] Gilmor, *Four Years*, 215-16; Zell, "Pennsylvania Raid," 260; Newman, *Maryland*, 334.

[37] Gilmor, *Four Years*, 216-17; *War of the Rebellion*, Series 1, Vol. 37, Part 1, 188-89; Zell, "Pennsylvania Raid," 260-1.

[38] Gilmor, *Four Years*, 218; *War of the Rebellion*, Series 1, Vol. 37, Part 1, 189.

[39] Gilmor, *Four Years*, 218-20; Johnson, *Maryland*, vol. 2, 142; Zell, "Pennsylvania Raid," 261; Goldsborough, *Maryland Line*, 290. Ironically, McElwee was firing upon a fellow Marylander's command, for the iron-clad car was commanded by Captain Petrie, of the Second Regiment Potomac Home Brigade, Maryland Volunteer Infantry. (Please see *War of the Rebellion*, Series 1, Vol. 37, Part 1, 189)

[40] Gilmor, *Four Years*, 220-21; Goldsborough, *Maryland Line*, 248; Johnson, *Maryland*, vol. 2, 141; *War of the Rebellion*, Series 1, Vol. 37, Part 1, 189.

[41] *War of the Rebellion*, Series 1, Vol. 37, Part 1, 189.

[42] Alexander, "McCausland's Raid and the Burning of Chambersburg" (Masters Thesis), 61-63,65; Zell, "Pennsylvania Raid," 261; Gilmor, *Four Years*, 221.

[43] Slingluff, "Chambersburg," 160; Osborne, *Jubal*, 307; *War of the Rebellion*, Series 1, Vol. 43, Part 1, 5.

[44] Osborne, *Jubal*, 307; Gilmor, *Four Years*, 222-23; Baker,

"Chambersburg," 46.

[45] Osborne, *Jubal*, 307-8; *War of the Rebellion*, Series 1, Vol. 43, Part 1, 495; Early, *Narrative*, 405.

[46] Gilmor, *Four Years*, 225; Johnson, *Maryland*, vol. 2, 141; Second Maryland Cavalry Records, Roll 7.

[47] Gilmor, *Four Years*, 225; Haselberger, "2nd Maryland Cavalry Battalion," 4,12-13.

[48] Early, *Narrative*, 405.

[49] Osborne, *Jubal*, 309.

[50] Fletcher Pratt, *Ordeal By Fire* (London: Butler and Tanner Ltd., 1950), 354.

[51] Bowman, *Civil War Almanac*, 218; Thomas A. Lewis, *The Shenandoah in Flames* (Alexandria: Time-Life Books, 1987), 103.

[52] Lewis, *Shenandoah*, 101.

[53] Ibid., 101,104; Osborne, *Jubal*, 319; Gilmor, *Four Years*, 226.

[54] Early, *Narrative*, 407-8; Gilmor, *Four Years*, 226-28.

[55] Gilmor, *Four Years*, 227-29; Goldsborough, *Maryland Line*, 244.

[56] Gilmor, *Four Years*, 229-30; Goldsborough, *Maryland Line*, 244. There exists no official account of either Gilmor's capture of the infantrymen at the stone fence or his exploit with the sixty troopers of the First New Jersey Cavalry. In regards to his capture of the twenty-five infantrymen, he states that "General Lomax bears testimony to the truth of this statement. - Baltimore, November 24, 1865." Please see Gilmor, *Four Years*, 229.

[57] Lewis, *Shenandoah*, 105; Gilmor, *Four Years*, 229-30,237.

[58] Osborne, *Jubal*, 326; Early, *Narrative*, 409; Gilmor, *Four Years*, 230-37.

[59] Early, *Narrative*, 409; Gilmor, *Four Years*, 237; Lewis, *Shenandoah*, 105-6.

[60] Lewis, *Shenandoah*, 106; Osborne, *Jubal*, 326-27; Douglas, *Stonewall*, 294-95.

[61] Gilmor, *Four Years*, 239-43; Haselberger, "2nd Maryland Cavalry Battalion," 14-15; *War of the Rebellion*, Series 1, Vol. 43, Part 1, 571. John D. Clarke must have replaced Captain James L. Clark of Company F after the latter was captured in the Moorefield Valley raid.

[62] Gilmor, *Four Years*, 244.

[63] Ibid., 244-46.

[64] Ibid., 246-49.

[65] Ibid., 249-50.

[66] Ibid., 249-51.

[67] Ibid., 249-53; Goldsborough, *The Maryland Line*, 1st edition, 257; Johnson, *Maryland*, vol. 2, 139,141. The reader is reminded to differentiate between this version of *The Maryland Line*, published in 1869, and the second edition, published in 1972.

[68] Gilmor, *Four Years*, 253-54; Gilmor writes that it was alleged that

General Lomax ordered "J—'s" brigade to help the embattled Marylanders, but the men of this brigade were uncooperative. Gilmor was told by an unidentified informant that Lomax scolded the hesitant brigade by saying "Are you not ashamed to see a handful of Marylanders cut to pieces fighting for your state...while you refuse to assist them" (Gilmor, *Four Years*, 254). The unidentified brigade obviously begins with a "J," and Lomax's alleged comment, "fighting for your state," seems to suggest that Bradley Johnson's brigade was uncooperative with Lomax.

[69] Ibid., 254-56; Armstrong, *7th Virginia Cavalry*, 243; *War of the Rebellion*, Series 1, Vol. 43, Part 1, 572; Goldsborough, in the 1st edition of *The Maryland Line* (1869), takes issue with Gilmor's description of the action at Bunker Hill on September 3, 1864, in particular, the major's rather unflattering narrative concerning the behavior of the First Maryland Battalion. According to Goldsborough, Gilmor ordered a charge, which was obeyed by the First, and then he was wounded by a Union bullet. Goldsborough claims that "this was the last order to charge given that day, and most faithfully was it obeyed, even by twenty against a thousand." (Please see Goldsborough, *The Maryland Line*, 1st edition, 258)

[70] "Letter from James F. Cook to Major H. Gilmor," September 8, 1864, Harry Gilmor Papers, MS 1287, Manuscripts Division, MHSL.

[71] Gilmor, *Four Years*, 256-57; "Letter from Delia to Harry Gilmor," September 7, 1864, Harry Gilmor Papers, MS 1287, Manuscripts Division, MHSL.

[72] Gilmor, *Four Years*, 257; Goldsborough, *The Maryland Line*, 1st edition, 258-59.

[73] Bowman, *Civil War Almanac*, 224; Gilmor, *Four Years*, 257-63; Taylor, *Taylor Sketchbook*, 370-71.

[74] Gilmor, *Four Years*, 261-68,271-74.

[75] Ibid., 264-65; Moore, ed., *Rebellion Record*, vol. 11, 731.

Chapter 8

[1]Goldsborough, *Maryland Line*, 241-42; Edward J. Stackpole, *Sheridan in the Shenandoah* (Harrisburg: The Stackpole Company, 1992), 175,368; Col. John Mosby, "Retaliation. The Execution of Seven Prisoners," *Southern Historical Society Papers* 27 (1899): 314; Philip Sheridan, *Personal Memoirs of P.H. Sheridan*, vol. 2, (New York: Charles L. Webster and Company, 1888), 99; Also, please read Jeffry Wert's *Mosby's Rangers* for evidence of the difficulties partisans caused Union officials.

[2]Stackpole, *Sheridan in Shenandoah*, 175; H.P. Moyer, comp., *History of the 17th Regiment Pennsylvania Volunteer Cavalry* (Lebanon, Pennsylvania: Sowers Printing Company, 1911), "How Sergeant J.E. McCabe Became One of General Sheridan's Scouts," by Joseph E. McCabe,

219-22; Taylor, *Taylor Sketchbook*, 589.

[3]Bakeless, *Spies*, 315; Taylor, *Taylor Sketchbook*, 589.

[4]Stackpole, *Sheridan in Shenandoah*, 175; Moyer, comp., *History of the 17th Regiment Pennsylvania Volunteer Cavalry*, "The Capture of Major Harry W. Gilmor and Captain George W. Stump of Guerrilla Fame," by George D. Mullihan, 224-25; Taylor, *Taylor Sketchbook*, 589.

[5]Gilmor, *Four Years*, 249-56,276; Mullihan, "Capture of Gilmor," 223; *War of the Rebellion*, Series 1, Vol. 51, Part 2, 1060-61; *War of the Rebellion*, Series 1, Vol. 46, Part 2, 278; Sheridan, *Personal Memoirs*, vol. 2, 105.

[6]"Letter from Ellen Gilmor to Harry Gilmor," January 1865, *Harry Gilmor Papers*, MS 1287, Manuscripts Division, MHSL.

[7]Gilmor, *Four Years*, 277.

[8]*War of the Rebellion*, Series 1, Vol. 46, Part 2, 285.

[9]Gilmor, *Four Years*, 277.

[10]Sheridan, *Personal Memoirs*, vol. 2, 105; William Beymer, *On Hazardous Service* (New York: 1912), 28.

[11]Sheridan, *Personal Memoirs*, vol. 2, 105-6; *War of the Rebellion*, Series 1, Vol. 46, Part 1, 455-57; Taylor, *Taylor Sketchbook*, 589; Newman, *Maryland*, 320.

[12]*War of the Rebellion*, Series 1, Vol. 46, Part 1, 455-57.

[13]Ibid., Series 1, Vol. 46, Part 1, 455-57; Sheridan, in his *Personal Memoirs*, implies that Young had no difficulty in discovering Gilmor's location (vol. 2, page 106).

[14] J. W. Duffey, "The Blue and the Gray in Reunion," *Confederate Veteran Magazine*, 37 January 1929, 6.

[15]Gilmor, *Four Years*, 277.

[16]*War of the Rebellion*, Series 1, Vol. 46, Part 1, 455-57.

[17]Ibid., 455-57.

[18]Ibid., 455-57; Mullihan, "Capture of Gilmor," 226; Bakeless, "Catching Gilmor," 38.

[19]*War of the Rebellion*, Series 1, Vol. 46, Part 1, 455-57; Mullihan, "Capture of Gilmor," 226.

[20]*War of the Rebellion*, Series 1, Vol. 46, Part 1, 455-57; Mullihan, "Capture of Gilmor," 226; Gilmor, *Four Years*, 277-78; Sheridan, *Personal Memoirs*, vol. 2, 106-7.

[21]Gilmor, *Four Years*, 278-79; Mullihan, "Capture of Gilmor," 226; H.B. Smith, *Between the Lines , Secret Service Stories* (New York: J.J. Little and Ives Co., 1911), 233.

[22]Gilmor, *Four Years*, 278-79; *War of the Rebellion*, Series 1, Vol. 46, Part 1, 455-57.

[23]Gilmor, *Four Years*, 279; *War of the Rebellion*, Series 1, Vol. 46, Part 1, 455-57.

[24]Gilmor, *Four Years*, 280-81; *War of the Rebellion*, Series 1, Vol. 46, Part 1, 455-57.

[25]*War of the Rebellion*, Series 1, Vol. 46, Part 1, 457.

[26]Ibid., 457.

[27]Ibid., 457.

[28]Bakeless, "Catching Gilmor," 40; Richard P. Weinert, "The South had Mosby; The Union: Maj. Henry Young," *Civil War Times Illustrated*, 3 (April 1964), 40.

[29]Gilmor, *Four Years*, 284.

[30]*War of the Rebellion*, Series 1, Vol. 46, Part 2, 442.

[31]Newman, *Maryland*, 320.

[32]Gilmor, *Four Years*, 284-85; *War of the Rebellion*, Series 1, Vol. 33, 152-54.

[33]Gilmor, *Four Years*, 285-86; Smith, *Between Lines*, 233; Second Maryland Cavalry Records, Roll 7.

Chapter 9

[1] Moore, ed., *Rebellion Record*, vol. 11, 541-42; Second Maryland Cavalry Records, Roll 7.

[2] "The Capture of Harry Gilmore [sic]," *New York Times*, 26 February 1865, 1.

[3] Gilmor, *Four Years*, 286-87; Second Maryland Cavalry Records, Roll 7.

[4] Gilmor, *Four Years*, 288-90.

[5] Ibid., 288-89,291; Thomas, *Confederate Nation*, 281-82,289,304.

[6] Thomas, *Confederate Nation*, 289.

[7] "Letter from Chf. Quarter-master 2nd Corps to Gilmor," February 9, 1865, Harry Gilmor Papers, MS 1287, Manuscripts Division, MHSL.

[8] Ruffner, "'More Trouble than a Brigade,'" 406; Johnson, *Maryland*, vol. 2, 141; Jones, *Gray Ghosts*, 368-69; Marshall Moore Brice, *Conquest of a Valley* (Charlottesville: University Press of Virginia, 1965), 156.

[9] Haselberger, "2nd Maryland Cavalry Battalion," 18; Second Maryland Cavalry Records, Roll 7; Second Maryland Cavalry Records, Roll 8.

[10] Gilmor, *Four Years*, 291; Second Maryland Cavalry Records, Roll 7.

[11] John C. Breckinridge was also not able to return to his native state of Kentucky, also a border state. Please see William C. Davis's *Breckinridge: Statesman, Soldier, and Symbol* (Baton Rouge and London: Louisiana State University Press, 1974).

[12] Brooks, *Baltimore County*, 252; "Col. Gilmor Dying. His Death Momentarily Expected — A Sketch of His Career," *Baltimore Sun*, 1 March 1883, taken from Gilmor Family Papers, BCHS; "Obituary - Col. Harry Gilmor," *New York Times*, 5 March 1883, 5; Johnson, ed., *American Biography*, vol. 7, 309; *The National Cyclopaedia*, vol. 23, 372; Robert J. Trout, *They Followed the Plume* (Mechanicsburg, Pennsylvania: Stackpole

Books, 1993), 140.

[13] Johnson, ed., *American Biography*, vol. 7, 309; *The National Cyclopaedia*, vol. 23, 373; Trout, *Plume*, 144; "Gilmor Family Tree," (photocopy) Gilmor Family Papers, BCHS.

[14] This information was taken from Daniel C. Toomey's introduction to *Four Years in the Saddle*, the reprinted version by Butternut and Blue. Please see pages xviii-xix.

[15] As Daniel C. Toomey writes in his modern introduction to *Four Years in the Saddle*, "[Gilmor's] association with a ghost writer [Colonel Smith] has contributed significantly to the book's deprecation by modern historians such as James I. Robertson, Jr." The book would also be derided due to factual errors as well as Gilmor's unabashed ego, which all too often enters into his narrative and tends to make the Marylander appear as a one man army.

[16] Brooks, *Baltimore County*, 252; "Obituary - Col. Harry Gilmor," *New York Times*, 5 March 1883, 5; "Colonel Harry Gilmor," *Richmond Dispatch*, 6 March 1883, 3; "Letter from Ellen Gilmor Buchanan to a Mr. Foster," November 18, 1959, Harry Gilmor Papers (ca. 1865-1883), MS 1288, Manuscripts Division, MHSL; "Gilmor Family Tree," (photocopy) Gilmor Family Papers, BCHS.

[17] "Gilmor Family Tree," (photocopy) Gilmor Family Papers, BCHS; Trout, *Plume*, 144.

[18] "Gilmor's Commission," May 6, 1873, Harry Gilmor Papers (ca. 1865-1883), MS 1288, Manuscripts Division, MHSL; Smith, *Between Lines*, 235.

[19] Smith, *Between Lines*, 227,234-35.

[20] Trout, *Plume*, 144; *The National Cyclopaedia*, vol. 23, 372; Scharf, *History of Maryland*, vol. 3, 739; Johnson, ed., *American Biography*, vol. 7, 309; "Obituary - Col. Harry Gilmor," *New York Times*, 5 March 1883, 5; "Colonel Harry Gilmor," *Richmond Dispatch*, 6 March 1883, 3; Toomey, *Marylanders at Gettysburg*, 19-20.

[21] George Brown Tindall, *America: A Narrative History*, vol. 2, (New York and London: W. W. Norton and Company, 1984), 799-800; Scharf, *Baltimore City*, part 2, 791.

[22] Scharf, *Baltimore City*, part 2, 791; Scharf, *Maryland History*, vol. 3, 735-38 (page references are to reprint edition).

[23] Scharf, *Maryland History*, vol. 3, 736,738-39.

[24] Ibid., 739-40; "Colonel Harry Gilmor," *Richmond Dispatch*, 6 March 1883, 3.

[25] Scharf, *Maryland History*, vol. 3, 738-41; Tindall, *America*, vol. 2, 800.

[26] *The National Cyclopaedia*, vol. 11, 402; Brooks, *Baltimore County*, 252; "Glen Ellen Lease," October 23, 1878, Harry Gilmor Papers (ca. 1865-1883), MS 1288, Manuscripts Division, MHSL.

[27] "Letter from Ellen Gilmor Buchanan to Mr. Foster," November 18,

1959, Harry Gilmor Papers (ca. 1865-1883), MS 1288, Manuscripts Division, MHSL; "Gilmor Family Tree," (photocopy) Gilmor Family Papers, BCHS.

[28] *The National Cyclopaedia*, vol. 11, 402.

[29] Trout, *Plume*, 144; A manuscript letter with the letterhead "Gilmor, Insurance Agent and Broker," n.d., confirms that Gilmor was in the insurance business. Please see Harry Gilmor Papers (ca. 1865-1883), MS 1288, Manuscripts Division, MHSL; "Gilmor and Locke's Contract," July 19, 1881, Harry Gilmor Papers (ca. 1865-1883), MS 1288, Manuscripts Division, MHSL.

[30] Trout, *Plume*, 144; "Col. Harry Gilmor," *Chicago Tribune*, 5 March 1883, 7; "Colonel Harry Gilmor," *Richmond Dispatch*, 6 March 1883, 3; *The National Cyclopaedia*, vol. 11, 402.

[31] "Col. Harry Gilmor," *Chicago Tribune*, 5 March 1883, 7.

[32] Ibid., 7; "Col. Harry Gilmor," *New York Times*, 5 March 1883, 5; "Colonel Harry Gilmor," *Richmond Dispatch*, 6 March 1883, 3.

[33] "Editorial Paragraphs," *Southern Historical Society Papers* 7 (1879): 349-52; "Editorial Paragraphs," *Southern Historical Society Papers* 9 (1881): 574.

[34] "Letter from General Henry A. Barnum to Col. Harry Gilmor," July 14, 1882, Harry Gilmor Papers (ca. 1865-1883), MS 1288, Manuscripts Division, MHSL; For Gilmor's account of the episode, please see *Four Years*, pages 95-97.

[35] Trout, *Plume*, 144; "Sealed letter granting Hoffman [Gilmor] power of attorney," n.d., Harry Gilmor Papers (ca. 1865-1883), MS 1288, Manuscripts Division, MHSL; "Letter from Harry Gilmor to Hoffman Gilmor," January 23, 1883, Harry Gilmor Papers (ca. 1865-1883), MS 1288, Manuscripts Division, MHSL.

[36] "Tribute by Mr. Lamar Hollyday," February 2, 1883, Harry Gilmor Papers (ca. 1865-1883), MS 1288, Manuscripts Division, MHSL.

[37] "Col. Gilmor Dying. His Death Momentarily Expected — A Sketch of His Career," *Baltimore Sun*, 1 March 1883, taken from Gilmor Family Papers, BCHS.

[38] "Annual Re-Union of the Society of the Army and Navy of the Confederate States in the State of Maryland," February 22, 1883, Harry Gilmor Papers (ca. 1865-1883), MS 1288, Manuscripts Division, MHSL.

[39] "Undated and Unidentified Newspaper clipping entitled, 'A Confederate Reunion,'" Harry Gilmor Papers (ca. 1865-1883), MS 1288, Manuscripts Division, MHSL. This clipping was probably from the *Baltimore Sun*, February 23, 1883.

[40] "Letter from Winfield Deters to Harry Gilmor," February 22, 1883 and "Letter from Bradley T. Johnson to Col. Harry Gilmor," February 27, 1883. Both letters can be located in the Harry Gilmor Papers (ca. 1865-1883), MS 1288, Manuscripts Division, MHSL.

[41] "Letter from H. R. Duval to Hoffman Gilmor," February 21, 1883,

and "Letter from an unknown source [probably H. R. Duval] to Hoffman Gilmor," February 26, 1883. Both letters can be found in the Harry Gilmor Papers (ca. 1865-1883), MS 1288, Manuscripts Division, MHSL.

[42] Trout, *Plume*, 144; "Col. Harry Gilmor," *Chicago Tribune*, 5 March 1883, 7; "An unknown and undated newspaper clipping detailing Generals Johnson and Early's visit to Gilmor," Harry Gilmor Papers (ca. 1865-1883), MS 1288, Manuscripts Division, MHSL.

[43] "Col. Harry Gilmor," *Chicago Tribune*, 5 March 1883, 7; "Col. Harry Gilmor," *New York Times*, 5 March 1883, 5; "Colonel Harry Gilmor," *Richmond Dispatch*, 6 March 1883, 3; "Col. Gilmor's Death. Ending a Terrible Disease with Tranquil Courage to the Last," *Baltimore Sun*, 5 March 1883, taken from Gilmor Family Papers, BCHS.

[44] "Col. Gilmor's Death. Ending a Terrible Disease with Tranquil Courage to the Last," *Baltimore Sun*, 5 March 1883, taken from Gilmor Family Papers, BCHS; "Letter from the Headquarters of the Grand Army of the Republic to Hoffman Gilmor," March 6, 1883, Harry Gilmor Papers (ca. 1865-1883), MS 1288, Manuscripts Division, MHSL.

[45] "Col. Gilmor's Death. Ending a Terrible Disease with Tranquil Courage to the Last," *Baltimore Sun*, 5 March 1883, taken from Gilmor Family Papers, BCHS; Trout, *Plume*, 144-45; "Col. Gilmor Dying. His Death Momentarily Expected — A Sketch of His Career," *Baltimore Sun*, 1 March 1883, taken from Gilmor Family Papers, BCHS.

[46] Information concerning a donation fund for Gilmor's children can purportedly be found in March 6 and 8 (1883) issues of the *Baltimore Sun*; "Letter from the Office of Trustees of McDonogh Educational Fund and Institute to Harry Gilmor," June 14, 1883, Harry Gilmor Papers (ca. 1865-1883), MS 1288, Manuscripts Division, MHSL; "Letter from Harry Gilmor to Hoffman Gilmor," January 23, 1883, Harry Gilmor Papers (ca. 1865-1883), MS 1288, Manuscripts Division, MHSL; "Letter from Harper and Brothers to Hoffman Gilmor," April 19, 1883, Harry Gilmor Papers (ca. 1865-1883); MS 1288, Manuscripts Division, MHSL; "Letter from Harper and Brothers to Hoffman Gilmor," May 2, 1883, Harry Gilmor Papers (ca. 1865-1883), MS 1288, Manuscripts Division, MHSL.

[47] "Unknown and Undated Newspaper Clipping" (probably the *Baltimore Sun*), Harry Gilmor Papers (ca. 1865-1883), MS 1288, Manuscripts Division, MHSL.

[48] *Baltimore Sun*, 16 August 1912; "Gilmor Family Tree," (photocopy) Gilmor Family Papers, BCHS.

[49] "Letter from Ellen Gilmor Buchanan to Mr. Foster," November 18, 1959, Harry Gilmor Papers (ca. 1865-1883), MS 1288, Manuscripts Division, MHSL.

[50] "Gilmor Family Tree," (photocopy) Gilmor Family Papers, BCHS.

[51] Trout, *Plume*, 144-45.

Works Cited

Unpublished Sources

Baltimore County Historical Society:
Gilmor Family Papers
Maryland Historical Society:
Harry Gilmor Papers, MS. 1287
Harry Gilmor Papers, MS. 1288
Washington, D.C. National Archives. Compiled Service Records of Confederate Soldiers. Record Group 109. Second Maryland Battalion Cavalry, M321, Rolls 7-8.
Washington D.C. National Archives. Compiled Service Records of Confederate Soldiers. Record Group 109. Seventh Virginia Ashby's Cavalry, M324, Roll 75.
Washington D.C. National Archives. Compiled Service Records of Confederate Soldiers. Record Group 109. Twelfth Virginia Cavalry, M324, Roll 117.

Published Sources

Government Documents

Pennsylvania Governor. Address. "To the Assembly Concerning Measures for the Defense of the State and Union." *Pennsylvania Archives* (9 August 1864) Vol. 8.
U.S. War Department. *The War of the Rebellion: A Compilation of the Official Records of the Union and Confederate Armies*. 128 Vols. Washington, D.C.: Government Printing Office, 1880-1901.

Primary Books

Basler, Roy P., ed. *The Collected Works of Abraham Lincoln*. Vol. 7, New Brunswick, New Jersey: Rutgers University Press, 1953.
Baylor, George. *Bull Run to Bull Run*. Richmond: B.F. Johnson Publishing Co., 1900.
Beymer, William. *On Hazardous Service*. New York: 1912.
Cooke, John Esten. *Stonewall Jackson and the Old Stonewall Brigade*. Edited by Richard Barksdale Harwell. Charlottesville: University

of Virginia Press, 1954.

Davis, Jefferson. *The Rise and Fall of the Confederate Government*. Vol. 2. New York and London: Sagamore Press, Inc., 1958.

Douglas, Henry Kyd. *I Rode With Stonewall*. n.p.: The University of North Carolina Press, 1940; reprint, n.p.: Fawcett Publications, Inc., 1961.

Dowdey, Clifford, and Louis H. Manarin. *The Wartime Papers of R.E. Lee*. Boston and Toronto: Little, Brown and Company, 1961.

Early, Jubal A., Gen. *Narrative of the War Between the States*. With an Introduction by Gary Gallagher. Philadelphia: n.p., 1912; reprint, New York: Da Capo Press, 1989.

Evans, Clement A., Gen., ed. *Confederate Military History*. Vol. 2, *Maryland and West Virginia*, "Maryland" by Brig.-Gen. Bradley T. Johnson. Secaucus, New Jersey: The Blue and Grey Press, n.d.

Gilmor, Harry, Col. *Four Years in the Saddle*. New York: Harper and Brothers, Publishers, 1866; reprint, Baltimore: Butternut and Blue, n.d.

Goldsborough, William W. *The Maryland Line in the Confederate States Army*. Baltimore: Kelly, Piet, 1869.

____. *The Maryland Line in the Confederate Army*. 2d. ed. New York and London: Kennikat Press, 1972.

Haas, Ralph. *Dear Esther: The Civil War Letters of Private Aungier Dobbs*. Edited by Philip Ensley. Apollo, Pennsylvania: Closson Press, 1991.

Jackson, Mary Ann. *Memoirs of Stonewall Jackson*. Dayton, Ohio: Morningside Bookshop, 1976.

McKim, Randolph H. *A Soldier's Recollections*. New York: Longmans, Green, and Co., 1911.

Moyer, H.P., comp. *History of the 17th Regiment Pennsylvania Volunteer Cavalry*. "How Sergeant J.E. McCabe Became One of General Sheridan's Scouts," by Joseph E. McCabe. Lebanon, Pennsylvania: Sowers Printing Company, 1911.

____. *History of the 17th Regiment Pennsylvania Volunteer Cavalry*. "The Capture of Major Harry W. Gilmor and Captain George W. Stump of Guerrilla Fame," by George D. Mullihan. Lebanon, Pennsylvania: Sowers Printing Company, 1911.

Sheridan, Philip H. *Personal Memoirs of P.H. Sheridan*. Vol. 2, New York: Charles L. Webster and Company, 1888.

Smith, H.B. *Between the Lines Secret Service Stories*. New York: J.J. Little and Ives Co., 1911.

Taylor, James E. *The James E. Taylor Sketchbook*. Cleveland: Western Reserve Historical Society, 1989.

Primary Articles

Berkeley, Carter, F. "Imboden's Dash Into Charlestown." *Confederate Veteran Magazine*, 25 (April 1917), 149-51.

Duffy, J.W., Rev. "The Blue and the Gray in Reunion." *Confederate Veteran Magazine*, 37 (1929), 6-7.

Early, Jubal. "The Advance on Washington in 1864." *Southern Historical Society Papers* 9 (1881): 297-312.

"Editorial Paragraphs." *Southern Historical Society Papers* 9 (1881): 574.

Imboden, John D., Brig.-Gen. "The Battle of New Market, Virginia, May 15th, 1864." *Battles and Leaders of the Civil War*. 4 Vols. New York and London: Thomas Yoseloff, 1956. 4:480-86.

"Imboden's Dash Into Charlestown." *Southern Historical Society Papers* 31 (1903): 11-19.

Johnson, Bradley T. "My Ride Around Baltimore in Eighteen Hundred and Sixty-Four." *Southern Historical Society Papers* 30 (1902): 215-25.

McCausland, John. "The Burning of Chambersburg, Penn." *Southern Historical Society Papers* 31 (1903): 266-70.

Moore, Frank, ed. *The Rebellion Record*. New York: Arno Press A New York Times Company, 1977.

Moore, J. Scott. "Unwritten History." *Southern Historical Society Papers* 26 (1898): 315-22.

Mosby, John Col. "Retaliation. The Execution of Seven Prisoners." *Southern Historical Society Papers* 27 (1899): 314.

Philpot, G.B. "A Maryland Boy in the Confederate Army." *Confederate Veteran Magazine*, 24 (July 1916), 312-15.

Randall, James R. "The Gallant Pelham." *Southern Historical Society Papers* 30 (1902): 338-39.

Robinson, Edward Ayrault. "Some Recollections of April 19, 1861." *Maryland Historical Magazine*, 27 (December 1932), 274-79.

Sigel, Franz, Maj.-Gen. "Sigel in the Shenandoah Valley in 1864." *Battles and Leaders of the Civil War*. 4 Vols. New York and London: Thomas Yoseloff, 1956. 4:487-91.

Slingluff, Fielder. "The Burning of Chambersburg." *Southern Historical Society Papers* 37 (1909): 152-63.

Steuart, R.D. "Rare Confederate Relics." *Confederate Veteran Magazine*, 16 (November 1909), 562.

Thompson, Magnus S. "Plan to Release Our Men at Point Lookout." *Confederate Veteran Magazine*, 20 (February 1912), 69-70.

Wright, D. Giraud. "Maryland and the South." *Southern Historical*

Society Papers 31 (1903): 209-14.

Zell, Robert R. "The Raid into Pennsylvania - the First Armored Train." *Confederate Veteran Magazine*, 28 (July 1920), 260-61.

Newspapers Cited

Baltimore American
Baltimore Sun
Chicago Tribune
New York Times
Philadelphia Inquirer
Post-Pittsburgh
Richmond Dispatch

Secondary Books

Alexander, Ted, Virginia Stake, Jim Neitzel, and William P. Conrad. *Southern Revenge! Civil War History of Chambersburg, Pennsylvania.* Shippensburg: White Mane Publishing Company, Inc. and Greater Chambersburg Chamber of Commerce, 1989.

Andrews, Matthew Page. *History of Maryland Province and State.* Hatboro, Pennsylvania: Tradition Press, 1965.

Armstrong, Richard L. *7th Virginia Cavalry.* Lynchburg: H.E. Howard, Inc., 1992.

Bakeless, John. *Spies of the Confederacy.* Philadelphia and New York: J.B. Lippincott Company, 1970.

Baldwin, Leland D. *Pittsburgh The Story of a City 1750-1865.* Pittsburgh: University of Pittsburgh Press, 1937; third reprint, 1947.

Beirne, Francis F. *The Amiable Baltimoreans.* Hatboro, Pennsylvania: Tradition Press, 1968.

Bishop, Chris, Ian Drury, and Tony Gibbons. *1400 Days The Civil War Day by Day.* New York: Gallery Books, 1990.

Boatner III, Mark Mayo. *The Civil War Dictionary.* New York: David McKay Company, Inc., 1959; reprint, 1988.

Boles, John B. *Maryland Heritage. Five Baltimore Institutions Celebrate the American Bicentennial.* Baltimore: n.p., 1976.

Bowman, John S., ed. *The Civil War Almanac.* New York: World Almanac Publications, 1983.

Brice, Marshall Moore. *Conquest of a Valley.* Charlottesville: University Press of Virginia, 1965.

Brodie, Fawn M. *Thaddeus Stevens.* New York: W.W. Norton and Company, Inc., 1966.

Brooks, Neale A. *A History of Baltimore County.* Towson, Maryland: Friends of the Towson Library, Inc., 1979.

Bushong, Millard Kessler. *Old Jube*. Boyce, Virginia: Carr Publishing Company, Inc., 1955.

______. *General Turner Ashby and Stonewall's Valley Campaign*. Waynesboro, Virginia: The McClung Companies, 1992.

Davis, Burke. *They Called Him Stonewall*. New York and Chicago: Holt, Rinehart and Winston, Inc., 1954.

____. *Jeb Stuart The Last Cavalier*. New York and Toronto: Rinehart and Company, Inc., 1957.

Davis, William C. *Breckinridge: Statesman, Soldier, Symbol*. Baton Rouge and London: Louisiana State University Press, 1974.

____. *The Battle of New Market*. Garden City, New York: Doubleday and Company, Inc., 1975.

___. *The Battlefields of the Civil War*. New York: Smithmark Publishers Inc., 1991.

Faust, Patricia L., ed. *Historical Times Illustrated Encyclopedia of the Civil War*. New York: Harper and Row, Publishers, 1986.

Foote, Shelby. *Fort Sumter to Perryville*. Vol. 1, *The Civil War*. New York: Vintage Books, 1986.

_____. *Fredericksburg to Meridian*. Vol. 2, *The Civil War*. New York: Vintage Books, 1986.

_____. *Red River to Appomattox*. Vol. 3, *The Civil War*. New York: Vintage Books, 1986.

Freeman, Douglas Southall. *Lee's Lieutenants*. Vol. 3, New York: Charles Scribner's Sons, 1944.

Garitee, Jerome R. *The Republic's Private Navy*. Middletown, Connecticut: Wesleyan University Press, 1977.

Hale, Laura Virginia. *Four Valiant Years in the Lower Shenandoah Valley (1861-1865)*. Strasburg, VA: Shenandoah Publishing House, Inc., 1968.

Hartzler, Daniel D. *Arms Makers of Maryland*. York, Pennsylvania: George Shumway Publishers, 1977.

___. *Marylanders in the Confederacy*. Westminster, Maryland: Family Line Publications, 1986; repr. 1990.

Haselberger, Fritz. *2nd Maryland Cavalry Battalion, C.S.A.: Roster and Losses Arranged by: Date-Name-Place-Type*. Maryland Historical Society Library, 1992.

Henderson, George F.R. *Stonewall Jackson and the American Civil War*. Gloucester, Mass: Peter Smith, 1968.

Hogg, Ian. *Robert E. Lee*. Greenwich, CT: Brompton Books Corporation, 1990; reprint, Stamford, CT: Longmeadow Press, 1992.

Hoke, Jacob. *The Great Invasion of 1863*. New York and London: Thomas Yoseloff, 1959.

Johnson, Allen, and Dumas Malone. *Dictionary of American Biography*. Vol. 7, New York: Charles Scribner's Sons, 1931.

Jones, Virgil Carrington. *Gray Ghosts and Rebel Raiders*. New York: Holt, Rinehart and Winston, 1956.

Kellogg, Sanford C. *Shenandoah Valley and Virginia*. New York and Washington: The Neale Publishing Company, 1903.

Korn, Jerry and others, eds. *Pursuit to Appomattox: The Last Battles*. Alexandria: Time-Life Books, 1987.

Lewis, Thomas A. *The Shenandoah in Flames*. Alexandria: Time-Life Books, 1987.

Linderman, Gerald L. *Embattled Courage*. New York: The Free Press, 1987.

Long, E.B. *The Civil War Day by Day An Almanac 1861-1865*. Garden City, New York: Doubleday and Company, Inc., 1971.

McPherson, James M. *Battle Cry of Freedom*. New York: Ballantine Books, 1988.

Michel, Robert E. *Colonel Harry Gilmor's Raid Around Baltimore*. Baltimore: Erbe Publishers, 1976.

Newman, Harry Wright. *Maryland and the Confederacy*. Annapolis: By the author, 1976.

Olson, Sherry H. *Baltimore The Building of An American City*. Baltimore and London: John Hopkins University Press, 1980.

Osborne, Charles C. *Jubal: The Life and Times of General Jubal A. Early, C.S.A.* Chapel Hill: Algonquin Books of Chapel Hill, 1992.

Pratt, Fletcher. *Ordeal By Fire*. London: Butler and Tanner Ltd., 1950.

Sandburg, Carl. *Abraham Lincoln The War Years*. Vol. 3, New York: Harcourt, Brace, and Company, 1939.

Scharf, J. Thomas. *History of Maryland*. Vol. 3, n.p., 1879; reprint, Hatboro, Pennsylvania: Tradition Press, 1967.

____. *History of Baltimore City and County*. Part I, Philadelphia: Louis H. Everts, 1881; reprint, Baltimore: Regional Publishing Company, 1971.

____. *History of Baltimore City and County*. Part II, Philadelphia: Louis H. Everts, 1881; reprint, Baltimore: Regional Publishing Company, 1971.

Sifakis, Stewart. *Who Was Who in the Confederacy*. Vol. 2, New York and Oxford: Facts on File, 1988.

Stackpole, Edward J. *Sheridan in the Shenandoah*. Harrisburg: The Stackpole Company, 1992.

Tanner, Robert G. *Stonewall in the Valley: Thomas J. "Stonewall" Jackson's Shenandoah Valley Campaign, Spring 1862*. Garden City, New York: Doubleday and Company, Inc., 1976.

The National Cyclopaedia of American Biography. Vol. 11, New York: James T. White and Company, 1909.

____. Vol. 23, New York: James T. White and Company, 1933.

Thomas, Emory M. *The Confederate Nation: 1861-1865*. New York: Harper and Row, Publishers, 1979.

Time-Life Books. *Brother Against Brother*. New York: Prentice Hall Press, 1990.

Tindall, George Brown. *America: A Narrative History*. Vol. 2, New York and London: W.W. Norton and Company, 1984.

Toomey, Daniel C. *The Patapsco Guards Independent Company of Maryland Volunteer Infantry*. Baltimore: Toomey Press, 1993.

____. *Marylanders at Gettysburg*. Baltimore: Toomey Press, 1994.

Trout, Robert J. *They Followed the Plume*. Mechanicsburg, Pennsylvania: Stackpole Books, 1993.

Vexler, Robert I, ed. and comp. *Baltimore: A Chronological and Documentary History*. Dobbs Ferry, New York: Oceana Publications, Inc., 1975.

Wallace, Lee Jr. *A Guide To Virginia Military Organizations, 1861-1865*. 2d. ed.?: H.E. Howard Inc., 1986.

Wert, Jeffry D. *Mosby's Rangers*. New York: Simon and Schuster, 1991.

Thesis

Alexander, Charles T. "McCausland's Raid and the Burning of Chambersburg." Masters Thesis, University of Maryland, 1988.

Secondary Articles

Albro, Walt. "The Forgotten Battle for the Capital." *Civil War Times Illustrated*, 31 (February 1993), 40-43,56-61.

Alexander, Ted. "McCausland's Raid and the Burning of Chambersburg." *Blue and Gray Magazine*, (August 1994), 10-18,46-61.

Bakeless, John. "Catching Harry Gilmor." *Civil War Times Illustrated*, 10 (April 1971), 35-40.

Baker, Liva. "The Burning of Chambersburg." *Civil War Chronicles*, 3 (Summer 1993), 41-46.

Castel, Albert. "The Guerrilla War: 1861-1865." *Civil War Times Illustrated*, Special Issue (October 1974): 4-50.

Davis, Erick F. "The Baltimore County Horse Guard." *History Trails* 10 (Winter 1975-1976): 5-8.

Fielding, Geoffrey, ed. "Gilmor's Field Report of His Raid in Baltimore County." *Maryland Historical Magazine*, 47 (1952), 234-40.

Harris, Shawn C. "Stonewall in the Valley." *America's Civil War*, 5 (January 1993), 34-40.

Longacre, Edward. "Boots and Saddles: The Eastern Theater." *Civil War Times Illustrated*, 31 March/April 1992, 35-40.

Robertson, James I., Jr. "Stonewall Jackson Molding the Man and Making A General." *Blue and Gray Magazine*, 9 (June 1992), 8-26, 52-55.

Ruffner, Kevin Conley. "'More Trouble than a Brigade:' Harry Gilmor's 2d Maryland Cavalry in the Shenandoah Valley." *Maryland Historical Magazine*, 89 (Winter 1994), 389-411.

Snider, David K., and William R. Brooksher. "Errant Rider's Misbegotten Errand." *Military History*, 5 (June 1989), 42-49.

Weinert, Richard P. "The South had Mosby; The Union: Maj. Henry Young." *Civil War Times Illustrated*, 3 (April 1964), 38-42.

"West Virginia Battle Ground." *Confederate Veteran Magazine*, 34 (September 1926), 340-41.

Videocassettes

Hanrahan, Jack, narrater. *The Civil War*. Produced by Dan Dalton Productions. 90 min. n.p., 1991. Videocassette.

Meredith, Burgess, narrater. *Bloody Shenandoah*. Produced by Lou Reda Productions. 50 min. Easton, Pennsylvania, n.d. Videocassette.

Index

Other titles available from the Publisher:

Four Years in the Saddle by Colonel Harry Gilmor

The Great Invasion of 1863 or General Lee in Pennsylvania by Jacob Hoke

The Baltimore and Ohio in the Civil War by Festus Summers

"Bayonet! Forward": My Civil War Reminiscences by General Joshua Lawrence Chamberlain

Soul of the Lion: A Biography of General Joshua Lawrence Chamberlain by Willard Wallace

The Attack and Defense of Little Round Top, Gettysburg, July 2, 1863 by Oliver W. Norton

High Tide at Gettysburg: The Campaign in Pennsylvania by Glenn Tucker

The Killer Angels: A Novel About the Four Days of Gettysburg by Michael Shaara

Confederate Monuments at Gettysburg: The Gettysburg Battle Monuments by David Martin

Sickles the Incredible: A Biography of General Daniel Edgar Sickles by W. A. Swanberg

Lee: A Biography by Clifford Dowdey

The Heart of a Soldier: Intimate Wartime Letters from General George E. Pickett, C.S.A. to His Wife by La Salle Corbell Pickett

Above and Beyond: A History of the Medal of Honor from the Civil War to Vietnam edited by Gordon Hardy

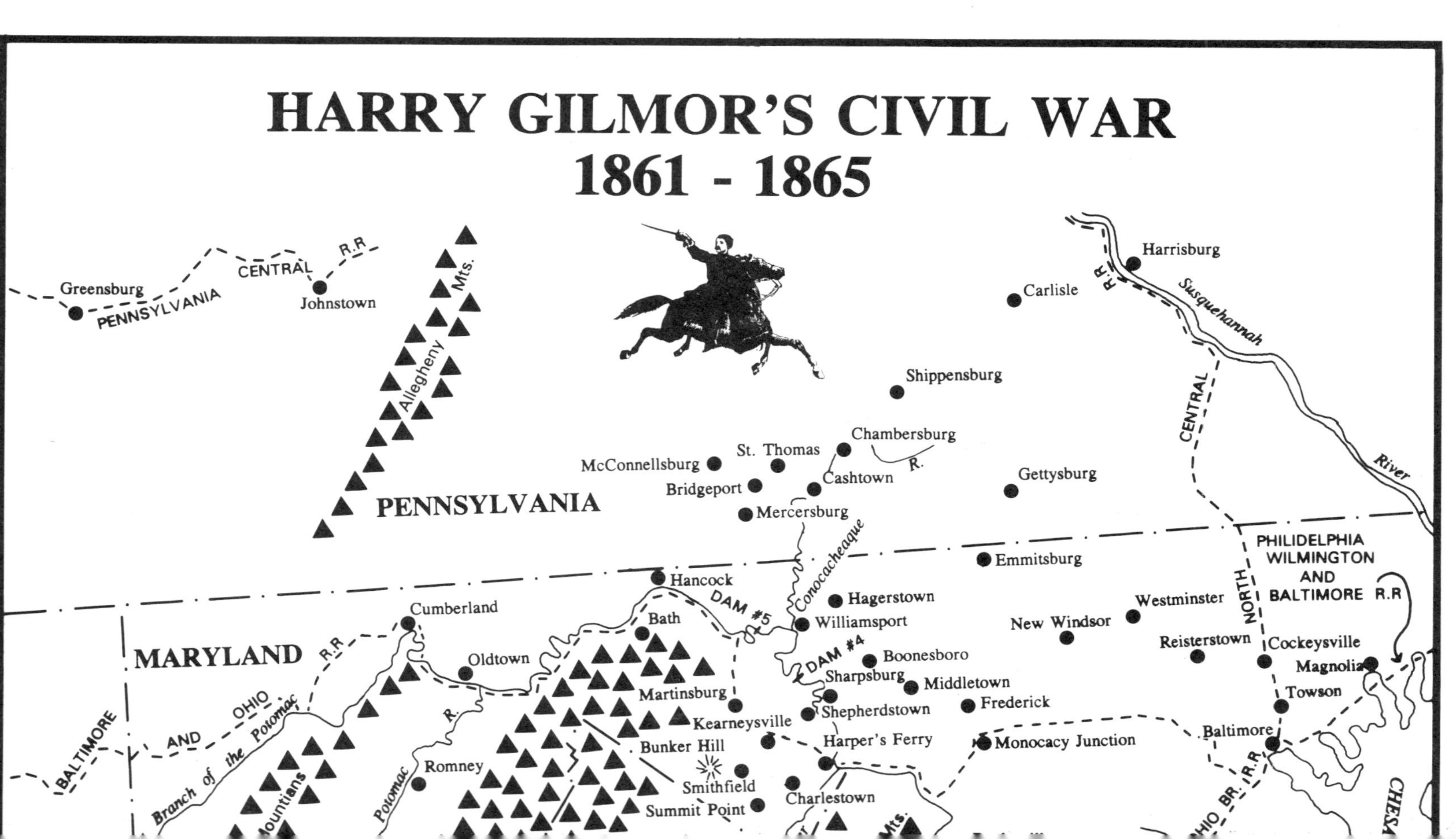
HARRY GILMOR'S CIVIL WAR
1861 - 1865
Greensburg
PENNSYLVANIA
CENTRAL
R.R
Johnstown
Allegheny
Mts.
PENNSYLVANIA
McConnellsburg
St. Thomas
Chambersburg
R.
Bridgeport
Cashtown
Mercersburg
Shippensburg
Carlisle
Harrisburg
R.R
Susquehannah
CENTRAL
River
Gettysburg
Emmitsburg
PHILIDELPHIA
WILMINGTON
AND
BALTIMORE R.R
NORTH
Westminster
New Windsor
Reisterstown
Cockeysville
Magnolia
Towson
Baltimore
Hancock
DAM #5
Conocacheaque
Hagerstown
Williamsport
DAM #4
Boonesboro
Sharpsburg
Middletown
Frederick
Shepherdstown
Harper's Ferry
Monocacy Junction
Cumberland
MARYLAND
R.R
Bath
Oldtown
Martinsburg
Kearneysville
Bunker Hill
Smithfield
Summit Point
Charlestown
Romney
Potomac
R.
BALTIMORE
AND
OHIO
Branch of the Potomac
Mountians
Mts.
OHIO BR. R.R
CHESA